PRIMITIVE AND PIONEER SPORTS

By the Same Author

CAMPING AND EDUCATION

❖❖❖

Co-Author with E. D. Mitchell

THE THEORY OF PLAY

SOCIAL GAMES FOR RECREATION

ACTIVE GAMES AND CONTESTS

PRIMITIVE AND PIONEER SPORTS

For Recreation Today

By

BERNARD S. MASON

A · S · BARNES & COMPANY

NEW YORK · 1937

PRINTED IN THE UNITED STATES OF AMERICA

PREFACE

The eager questionings and pleading faces of countless hundreds of boys and girls created the resolve to produce this book. Fortifying this resolve were the equally eager questions of many leaders of youth—physical educators, playground leaders, camp directors, recreational administrators, club leaders, and teachers. To both of these groups this volume of primitive and pioneer sports is offered. But primarily it is offered to *youth*—offered to them directly through the medium of its printed pages and offered to their leaders in order that it may be relayed to them. But more —it is offered to all those with youthful spirits, regardless of age, to all who like the romantic way in recreational and physical activities, who love the colorful lives of those rugged riders of the plains and rovers of the woods who traveled the romantic way throughout the long years of yesterday.

If I read aright the longings of boys and girls, their skill-hungry hearts go out to the romantic lives of these robust outdoorsmen of yesterday—cowboys, lumberjacks, Indians, Bushmen, and pioneers—colorful folks all, who symbolize a glorious life of conquest and adventure. Youthful spirits seek ever new and changing experiences—*and always romantic and colorful experiences*. In the movies they live this romantic outdoor life in fancy—far better would it be if they could experience many of these activities in fact. Certain it is that in the presence of one who does them, the average boy and girl is overcome with longing.

Progressive physical educators and recreational leaders have long sought, as program material, the activities of these colorful and sturdy outdoor folk who carry so much of imaginative appeal. Yet the necessary information has not been available. I am happy to be able to bring some of these skills within the reach of those who seek them.

Here, then, is a collection of picturesque outdoor sports that should appeal strongly to physical directors and recreational leaders—sports very ancient, yet very new in their use in the recreational and physical educational circles. There is no mistaking the trend toward the colorful and imaginative in the present-day gymnasium and playground. The time-honored and somewhat stereotyped gym demonstration has given way to a pageant-like program built around some particular source of color. This book presents many such sources of color. The individualized type of activities is coming into its own, but such activities, to succeed to the fullest extent, must possess a strong imaginative appeal. Many activities fulfilling this requirement are within these pages. Corrective exercises that are bolstered up with glamour and intrigue, are in demand—the type of material in this book, therefore, should be of peculiar interest also to corrective specialists.

Camp directors and counselors should find these pages right down on the level of their interests. Camping emulates the practices of those who live the outdoor life successfully. The activities here recorded are drawn from such types of folk. Further, the leaders of all kinds of groups for boys and girls should welcome these activities for the glamour they will add to programs for imaginative youth.

And so this book is offered to all with youthful spirits. Those who acquire these skills will have developed hobbies that very probably will carry on throughout the future years of their lives.

This book is born of years of joyous participation from childhood on in the sports it describes. The recording of them has been a long task but a happy one, for work becomes play when one's heart and soul are wrapped up in his task. The undertaking has been made lighter by the enthusiastic coöperation of Kenneth Ozier in preparing so carefully the great bulk of the drawings. Harry Raschbacher, too, contributed valuable assistance in preparing part of the roping illustrations. My gratitude also goes to Arthur T. Condit who proof-read the entire manuscript carefully and painstakingly.

The sports within these covers have been an endless source of joy to me—they were life in childhood and hobby in adulthood, equally joyous in both periods. In learning them I knew the torment of hunger for knowledge. I record them here in order that the hunger of others may be relieved. And in so doing, I hope that I may make a little richer and fuller those leisure hours of adulthood when one is free to live, but more particularly, I hope to make a little brighter that enchanted world of dreams called childhood.

BERNARD S. MASON.

Cincinnati, Ohio.
February, 1937.

TABLE OF CONTENTS

PART I

THE BUSHMAN'S SECTION

Boomerangs

PART II

THE COWBOY'S SECTION

Ropes and Whips

Part III

THE WOODSMAN'S SECTION

Blowguns, Darts, Tomahawk Throwing, Log Rolling

Part I

THE BUSHMAN'S SECTION

Boomerangs

CHAPTER I

Boomerangs the World Around

There is mystery in the boomerang. Nothing more than a piece of wood, yet with uncanny accuracy it circles through the air and comes back to the thrower. Obviously enough the thrower holds no magnet that plays upon the sailing missile, has no magical·power that pulls it back to him—the secret rests entirely in the mechanical construction of the stick and the physical laws of ballistics. Yet, however completely these laws may be expounded and comprehended, there will always be something of magic in the uncanny ability of these flying sticks to find their way into the waiting hands of the thrower.

Doubtless this element of mystery has much to do with the universal appeal of the sailing boomerang. Certain it is that it holds a peculiar fascination to young and old of every clime. There is intrigue in the very appearance of the boomerang in the air, in the ease and grace with which it soars and sails, circles and double circles, and finally floats effortlessly back to its starting point. No bird ever soared the sky with more harmony of movement and easy elegance than does a good boomerang.

And then, too, coming as it does from the primitive, boomerang throwing carries with it that glamour that all things primitive have to the civilized mind.

Little wonder that the thrower takes so much pride in sailing these graceful sticks. The sheer beauty of the flight and the perfection and precision of the return are a never-ending joy—he throws until weary and obtains thereby excellent physical exercise and the self-expression that comes from good recreation. Almost equally as great is the appeal to the spectator: one glimpse of the floating missile and the onlooker is arrested—he remains to thrill and to enjoy æsthetic satisfaction.

3

Boomerang throwing has few equals as an individual sport. It offers as much of physical benefit as any throwing and catching activity. It grips and compels. It is one of those colorful activities that not only challenges the performer but has unique show value. It carries a romantic appeal—it does things to the imaginations of people. Being an unusual type of activity, it serves admirably as a hobby. I have never known a person to become familiar with the art of the boomerang and not be caught in the irresistible, sweeping tide of its appeal. The sport becomes a major interest and a constant source of pride.

But there is another aspect of this sport that plays a most conspicuous rôle in its appeal—*the making of the boomerang is as interesting as the throwing*. In fact the making and the throwing are inseparably related in the full enjoyment of the pastime. There is pleasure in throwing a boomerang that is purchased or obtained from some one else, but it is in no respect comparable to the joy and thrill that results in handling one which you yourself have made. All the time the boomerang is being whittled you are looking forward to throwing it—constantly in your mind is the question, "Will it come back?" And when the last chip has been removed, you hasten to hurl it—*and it works!* There is thrill and glowing satisfaction as can come from few other pastimes! Even the old-timer at the boomerang game never fails to experience it; he may have made a thousand boomerangs, yet each time he throws a new one and it works perfectly just as he planned that it should, he feels a surge of pride and satisfaction that is worth many times over the effort required for the making. It is a feeling of craftsmanship, of having been the cause! So great, in fact, is this joy that comes from seeing a newly-made boomerang work perfectly, that one is always tempted to put the stick away after throwing it enough to test it thoroughly, and then to make another designed to act in a different way.

And happily, the making is easy—nothing more forbidding than jackknife whittling, and not very difficult whittling at that. Most boomerangs are made from soft wood that is very easy to work. And when a boomerang is roughly whittled out, so anxious is the maker to see if it will function that he throws it before finishing it carefully. If it works, he is usually reluctant to touch it again with the knife and so it is left in a crude and rough state. But this crudeness enhances rather than detracts from its appearance. Since these are primitive instruments, a machine-like perfection in appearance unmakes the picture. All of this adds to the simplicity of the making.

PLACE IN THE EDUCATIONAL AND RECREATIONAL PROGRAM

The recreational value of boomerang making and throwing is clearly indicated in the foregoing paragraphs.

An ideal play activity serves two purposes: It is gripping and compelling at the moment—it appeals as play, and makes the typical contributions of play to growth—and secondly, it is an activity of the type that will carry on throughout life, that is, the learning of the skills necessary to play it is an education for leisure.

The use of boomerangs meets these requirements outstandingly. It is an individual rather than a team or group activity; experience indicates that the activities that can be enjoyed alone or with two or three others are the life-time type. Once one is familiar with the art of the boomerang, he will doubtless come back to it again and again throughout life—he is equipped with an enduring and lasting hobby. This being the case, the use of boomerangs has a place in any school or club that attempts to educate in leisure-time activities.

In any group or class of children, there will be some who for temperamental or physical reasons do not participate regularly in the usual team games. Boomerangs will hold a peculiar appeal to such types. In individual corrective work in physical education, this activity has much to recommend it. But its glamour is not confined to these special types of people—practically all boys, girls, and men will be challenged by the boomerang in any play and recreational program.

Viewed from the handicraft standpoint, boomerang making has a purpose, an objective unknown in the usual crafts—it has a reward beyond the satisfaction of good craftsmanship—that of throwing the boomerang when completed. This activity is therefore ideal for use in clubs, playgrounds, camps, and schools, both as a craft and as a sport. In schools the making of boomerangs is usable in manual-training and industrial-arts departments, and the throwing of boomerangs is delightful in the physical education department. Most boomerangs of the types we shall recommend work more effectually indoors where there are no air currents to interfere and consequently, the school gymnasium is an ideal place for their use.

The element of danger immediately comes to mind when boomerangs are mentioned, and this fear has often militated against the consideration of the activity in school manual-training departments. The element of danger has been greatly exaggerated, due in part to the fact that few are familiar with types of boomerangs other than the curved Australian type. This boomerang is heavy and does carry a considerable element of danger. Not so, however, with the come-back sticks which will be described in the chapters that follow. The use of the curved Australian boomerangs is not recommended for boys. There are other types which are light and much more efficient, operate in a small space, and are relatively safe. Given instruction equal to that afforded for other sports, the element of danger can be reduced to the point where it is no more important than in any of the usual activities of children.

TYPES OF BOOMERANGS

The art of the boomerang, both in respect to the methods of construction and the manner of throwing, is practically unknown as far as the general public is concerned. The secrets of the boomerang have been held in this country by a very few actors and circus performers, and even these can be counted on the fingers of one's hand. Many of the boomerangs described in the chapters which follow are entirely original in design.

To the average person, the word *boomerang* brings to mind the curved weapons used by the Australian primitives. In fact, Webster's dictionary defines the word as "a curved or angular club used, mainly by the natives of Australia, as a missile weapon. It can be thrown so that its flight will bring it back near to the place where it was thrown."

For the purpose of this book it is assumed that the name, *boomerang*, is applicable to any missile which when hurled will return to or near the place from which it was thrown. With this as a definition, there are many types of boomerangs in addition to the curved style used by the native Australian. In fact the curved Australian type (Figure 34, page 66) is the least efficient type as a come-back stick. There are of course excellent and perfect boomerangs of the curved type, but they are few in number and as a type they are not comparable in efficiency to the others that these chapters will describe. No boomerang is worth the name if one has to step to reach it as it returns.

In addition to the curved or Australian style, there are three main types, each with many variations: (1) *The Cross-stick Boomerang*, (2) *the Boomabird*, and (3) *the Tumblestick*.

The *Cross-stick Boomerang* consists of two or more sticks fastened together—Figure 4, page 19, shows the appearance of a boomerang of this type. The methods of construction and the many varieties are described in Chapter II.

The *Pin-wheel Boomerang*, which, in fact, is a variation of the Cross-stick, is made of three sticks as shown in Figure 18, page 37. It is the ·most popular and efficient of the boomerangs. Chapter III describes it in detail.

The *Boomabird* is a boomerang so constructed as to look like a bird. This novelty, shown in Figure 26, page 51, is unique both in appearance and performance—it does many fascinating and clever things in the air. The Boomabird and its variations are described in Chapter IV.

The *Tumblestick* is in many respects the most unusual type of boomerang. It is essentially a straight stick that will return to the thrower. Figure 31, page 59, shows it and the methods of making and throwing are presented in Chapter V.

There are many other styles of boomerangs described in the

following chapters but each is related to one of the four main types mentioned above.

THE BOOMERANG IN HISTORY

Although the art of the boomerang was common in many parts of Australia, it was a single tribe of Australian primitives living in New South Wales that applied the name *boomerang* to the come-back missiles they used in hunting, the other tribes using other names for these same weapons. The word *boomerang*, however, has become universally accepted in the English language. The Australian word *womera* is occasionally seen in print as synonymous with *boomerang*, but this is incorrect—womera refers to spear throwing.

It should not be assumed that boomerangs were the exclusive property of the primitive Australians. The ancient Egyptians are said to have made extensive use of a boomerang-like missile, and today there are certain sections of northwest Africa in which returning weapons resembling the Australian type are still used. Furthermore, the natives of South India use a boomerang-shaped weapon made of ivory and steel which can be made to return in the direction of the thrower. The Hopi (Mosquis) Indians of Arizona use a type of boomerang resembling the Australian for hunting, this being the only record of the use of boomerangs on the North American continent.

There are two types of boomerangs used by the Australian Bushmen—*the return boomerang* and the *non-return boomerang*. The names used in this classification are scarcely correct, however, in that both can be thrown so as to return toward the thrower, although they must be thrown in different ways. The return type, when held in a vertical position and thrown straight forward will circle to the left and return. If the non-return type were thrown in this way, it would go straight forward with great speed and accuracy in the direction of the target at which it was hurled, showing not the slightest inclination to turn either to the right or left. However, if one of these non-return boomerangs is held parallel to the ground and thrown, it will rise high in the air and then volplane down to the ground near the sender.

Much of myth has been said and written regarding the use of the boomerang by the Bushmen. For example, we hear the boomerang glorified as a weapon of warfare. Certain it is that the non-return boomerang would have been a valuable and efficient fighting weapon, for it is probably true that the Bushmen had no other weapon that could be hurled so accurately for so great a distance. However, these boomerangs were so difficult to make, the materials so hard to find, and there were so few really expert boomerang makers, that it is doubtful that they saw much service in battle. Spears and clubs did good enough service in the close fighting that primitives enjoy and were much easier to fashion. A fine boomerang was so highly prized for hunting that its owner would be reluctant to risk losing it in warfare—and lose it he probably would, sooner or later, for when hurled so as to go straight for the target, the boomerang would not return to the sender, either if it missed its mark or if it hit it. But in spite of all this, there is no doubt that boomerangs did fighting duty, although not to the extent that is popularly supposed.

Boomerangs were chiefly hunting weapons. Here again, there were limitations to their use contrary to the common conception. It is true that the non-return type was used in hunting the kangaroo, and there is no gainsaying that a three or four-foot boomerang would easily cripple an animal of that size. True it is, too, that it would zip toward its prey with amazing speed and accuracy. However, such use in hunting animals was incidental to its use in hunting *birds*. The method here was not to throw at a perched or standing bird so much as it was to hurl the boomerang into a flock of flying birds. When the non-return boomerang is thrown horizontally it rises high into the air, and if sent into a flock of flying birds, its arms, whirling about viciously as they do, would have an excellent chance of bringing meat into the lodge. Curiously enough, birds are attracted to flying boomerangs, rather than being frightened away from them. The appearance

of the boomerang in the air resembles a flying bird so much as
to serve as a sort of decoy.

While the smaller and lighter boomerangs of the return type
were also frequently used in hunting birds, they found their
greatest use as playthings in sport. If such a boomerang were
thrown at an animal or bird and missed its mark, it would circle
back toward the sender. However, if it hit the object, it would
not return, but rather drop to the ground.

While boomerangs have been used elsewhere in the world, it
was certainly on the Australian continent that they found their
greatest development. The flat country that is the home of the
Bushmen is ideal for the manipulation of these curved sticks and
the little brown men of that region who were so adept in their
use relied heavily on them for meat. The Bushmen made up-
wards of twenty different styles of curved boomerangs, ranging
from ten inches from tip to tip, up to four-and-one-half feet in
length.

The large non-return type of boomerang is of little interest in
recreation. In appeal it gives way rather completely to the smaller
models of the return type. A boomerang that circles around to
the left and comes back to you is always more interesting than
one that merely sails up and then skids down again.

The difference in construction of these two types of boomerangs is described in Chapter V.

CHAPTER II

Making Cross-Stick Boomerangs

The Cross-stick Boomerangs are the pinnacle of boomerang perfection. They are the most accurate of all the boomerangs and consequently are the most satisfying. So accurate is a good Cross-stick Boomerang that an expert can stand upon a stage, even in a small theater or hall, and throw it out over the heads of the audience without fear that it will hit a wall or dive surreptitiously onto the head of an unsuspecting spectator. So accurate is it in fact that one can often "call his shots," that is, throw the boomerang and immediately hold out his hand indicating the exact spot to which it will return. The symmetrical, balanced construction of these boomerangs causes them to cut a more perfect circle in the air and return with more precision than any other type. A good Cross-stick or Pin-wheel can be depended upon to act in precisely the same way each time it is thrown.

The Cross-stick Boomerangs are usually made of light, soft wood, and this, together with their accuracy and dependability, recommends them as relatively harmless, delightful playthings. They can be used with safety in any gymnasium or large hall, following the directions given in Chapter VII, "How to Throw Boomerangs."

Moreover, the Cross-sticks are the easiest type of boomerang to make. The process is so simple that any one, after reading the instructions in this chapter, should be able to fashion one in a few minutes that will work with the utmost perfection if properly thrown. Certainly the beginner at the sport should be introduced to the simple Cross-stick before he makes the acquaintance of the other styles. In fact, practically all of the essentials in the art of the come-back missile are presented in this chapter on the Cross-sticks—this is the basic type. The unique models of boomerangs

11

described later are unusually fascinating novelties and very much worth while, but they are merely colorful variations based on the principles of the Cross-stick.

There are two main types of Cross-sticks: The first is the *Four-wing Cross-stick* made of two pieces of wood set at right angles to each other as in Figure 4, page 19. This is the simplest form of boomerang. The second is the *Pin-wheel* which is a six-wing boomerang made of three pieces of wood fastened together in the middle. It is illustrated in Figure 18, page 37. This is the Cross-stick at its best—the steadiest and most dependable of the boomerangs. The present chapter deals with the simple Four-wing Cross-stick and its variation, the two-wing type. The Pin-wheels are described in the next chapter.

The methods of throwing boomerangs are described in Chapter VIII. Since all boomerangs are manipulated according to the same principles, these instructions apply to the Cross-sticks in this chapter and to all other types.

MATERIALS REQUIRED

Few indeed are the materials required for making boomerangs—some wood of the suitable type and a few simple tools.

WOOD FOR BOOMERANGS

Of utmost importance is the wood that goes into a boomerang, yet happily, the proper woods are never scarce in any community. With one exception all types of boomerangs call for soft, light wood, the exception being the curved boomerangs of the Australian type which are made of heavy, hard wood as described in Chapter VI. Wood is the only material from which boomerangs can be made successfully, all efforts to construct them from metal having proved unsatisfactory to date.

The ideal woods are *basswood, tulip (whitewood)*, and select cuts of Number 1 *white pine. Spruce* and *cedar* are usable but less satisfactory. Basswood is the choice above all others; it is usually straight-grained, does not split and splinter as much as most soft woods, is strong for its weight, and very easy to whittle. Furthermore, as compared to many woods, it has the excellent quality of consistency in weight and texture.

There is no better wood than the right piece of white pine, but many pine boards contain so much pitch in the grain as to make them hard to whittle evenly with a jackknife. Moreover, the sticks cut from a board often vary too much in weight. Some lumber yards sell small boards prepared for cabinet work which they label as "select cuts of Number 1 pine." These strips usually come in thicknesses of one-eighth inch and one-fourth inch, these being the exact measurements needed for our purpose. The finest boomerang wood I have ever used has been found by sorting over such strips and selecting light-weight pieces free from pitch. Not all pine comes up to this standard.

Often as perfect a piece of wood as one could desire can be picked up from an old packing box. If it is soft, strong, and straight-grained, it should make a good boomerang. However, much better results will be obtained by securing from a lumber yard some strips of basswood, whitewood, or Number 1 pine in the proper thicknesses. The boomerangs in this chapter call for two thicknesses—one-eighth inch and one-fourth inch. Care should be taken to select clear, straight-grained pieces, free from knots.

Much of the joy of boomerang making will be lost if the wood is so coarse and stubborn that it does not whittle easily and smoothly.

Balsa wood immediately comes to one's mind in connection with boomerangs because of its use in making model airplanes. However, this wood is so light as to be entirely unsatisfactory and has no place whatever in boomerang making. A boomerang made of it is so very light that it cannot be thrown with enough force to carry it.

TOOLS REQUIRED

Boomerang making is essentially jackknife whittling. The only absolutely indispensable implement is a good, sharp, pocket-knife. In making boomerangs of ordinary size a three-fourths-inch gouge and a candle will be helpful, and in undertaking very large boomerangs, a wood rasp and a brace and bit will find use. In assembling the boomerangs an assortment of bolts and nuts will be needed, the sizes being stated in connection with the description of each boomerang.

A tube of liquid solder or quick-drying cement will be of assistance in repairing the broken wings of boomerangs and the sticks that split while being whittled.

If one is interested in finished and polished workmanship, a drawknife, plane, and some sandpaper will be useful. Such a quality of workmanship is always commendable in any line of effort, but the typical boomerang is left in a rather rough stage of finish—being a primitive type of instrument, it seems to possess more color and atmosphere if rather crude and irregular in appearance. Such a boomerang performs just as accurately as does a finely polished one. This is a matter of taste, however, and one can finish them to suit his fancy.

The matter of paint is discussed later in the chapter under the heading, "Decorating Boomerangs."

FOUR-WING BOOMERANGS

The four-wing boomerangs are made of two sticks crossed at right angles and bolted in the center, as illustrated in Figure 1. They are frequently referred to simply as Cross-sticks.

When thrown, a light-weight boomerang of this type will cut almost a perfect circle in the air. They move more swiftly than do the Pin-wheel (six-wing) Boomerangs which will be described in the next chapter, but are no less accurate. Large and heavy Cross-sticks frequently travel in a straight line for a long distance, then turn around rather abruptly to the left and return in almost a direct course. However, the characteristic course of flight of this type of boomerang is a circular one.

YOUR FIRST BOOMERANG

One's first attempt at boomerang making should be confined to small sticks. In making the little boomerang here described, we will become familiar with all of the essential techniques in boomerang construction, thus making it possible for us to attempt the larger ones with ease and assured success.

Secure two of the ruler-like sticks used by gasoline stations

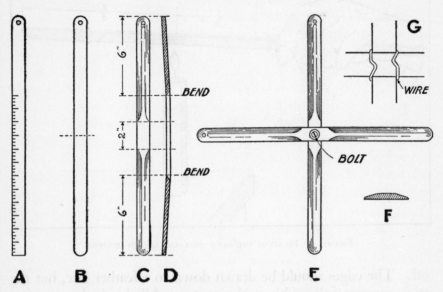

A   B   C D   E

FIGURE 1. A SMALL CROSS-STICK MADE OF GASOLINE STICKS

to measure the amount of gasoline in automobile tanks. These are usually of the right dimensions and made of the right kind of soft wood. Failing here, secure two strips of basswood or other soft wood eighteen inches long, one-and-one-fourth inches wide, and one-eighth inch thick.

Place each stick on the edge of your knife blade and balance it to determine the center of gravity, and mark this point. The center of gravity is used as the center of the stick, rather than the center of measurement. Mark out a two-inch section in the center of each stick as shown in C, Figure 1. With a jackknife, trim off the edges on one side of the stick beyond these lines so that it is roughly convex, as indicated in C, Figure 1, and shown in the diagram of the cross-section, F, in Figure 1. Note that the bottom or back side remains flat, while the top side is roughly rounded

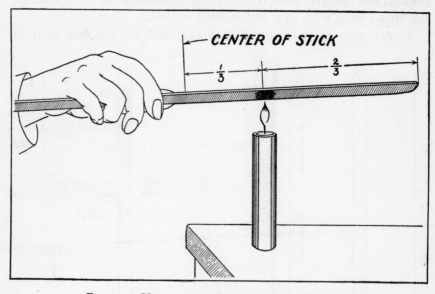

FIGURE 2. HEATING THE STICK PRELIMINARY TO BENDING

off. The edges should be drawn down to a feather line, but the stick remains full width at the center. All this is done with a jackknife and consequently the sticks are somewhat irregularly convex, but so far as efficiency of the boomerang is concerned, this irregularity makes no difference provided the edges are rather uniformly thin. In fact, it is not absolutely essential that the top of the stick be entirely rounded off to a convex shape—it is usually sufficient merely to bevel the edges down to a thin line.

Now each end of the sticks must be given a slight bend upward, that is, toward the beveled or convex side. Figure 1, D, indicates this bend. This is a task for but a moment or two: hold the stick over a lighted candle so that the flame strikes it six inches from the end, as illustrated in Figure 2. When heated hold the stick with the fingers as shown in Figure 3, bend upward slightly, and hold in this position for a few seconds—the curve will then be permanent. A very slight bend is all that is needed—not over a quarter of an inch. Both ends of each stick are bent in the same way; care should be taken in each case to apply the heat at a point the

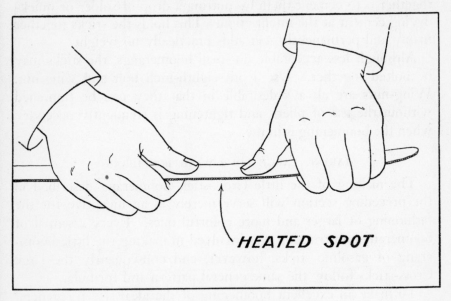

HEATED SPOT

FIGURE 3. BENDING THE HEATED STICK

same distance from the end, and to bend each end about the same amount.

In camp the wood may be bent on a small rock heated in the campfire. When the rock is hot withdraw it from the fire, moisten the stick with the tongue at the point where it is to be bent, then place the moistened spot on the rock and bend to the desired angle. Hold it there for a moment and the curve will be permanently fixed.

To complete the boomerang, place one stick across the other and fasten together, as shown in E, Figure 1—we thus have a flying missile with four wings. Little boomerangs such as this are best held together by wire. Use soft wire that bends easily and run it straight across the stick as shown in G, Figure 1—not diagonally across. When the wire is attached, it may be tightened by grasping it with the pliers and twisting, thus giving it the Z shape indicated in G, Figure 1.

Another very satisfactory method of holding small boomerangs together is to cement them by putting a drop of solder or quick-drying cement at the intersection. This holds the sticks together firmly and permanently, yet adds practically no weight.

Although less acceptable on small boomerangs, the sticks may be bolted together. Use a one-eighth-inch bolt and wing-nut. Wing-nuts are always desirable in that they can be tightened without the use of pliers, and tightening is frequently necessary when the boomerang is in use.

MAKING LARGE FOUR-WING BOOMERANGS

The making of the little Cross-stick Boomerang described in the preceding section will serve merely as an incentive for the fashioning of larger and more colorful ones. Every essential of boomerang construction was involved in making the little boomerang of gasoline sticks, however, and consequently the large Cross-sticks follow the same general pattern and formula.

To make an excellent boomerang of the ideal size for general use, cut two strips of basswood, whitewood, or pine, twenty-four inches long, one-and-one-half inches wide, and one-eighth inch thick. Bevel the edges on the top side throughout the entire length of each stick, bringing them down to a feather line, and round off the top to a roughly convex shape, as described in the preceding section.

The corners at the end of each stick should be trimmed off to the curved shape shown in Figure 4. Note, however, that the end is not cut to a semi-circular shape, but rather, more wood is removed from the left corner of the upper wings than from the right corner—this is true of each wing when it is placed in the upper position. The reason for this is that the left or cut-off side is the point that cuts into the air as the boomerang sails, and likewise it is the point that hits the ground or an obstruction in case the boomerang should fall; the wing is less inclineed to split when

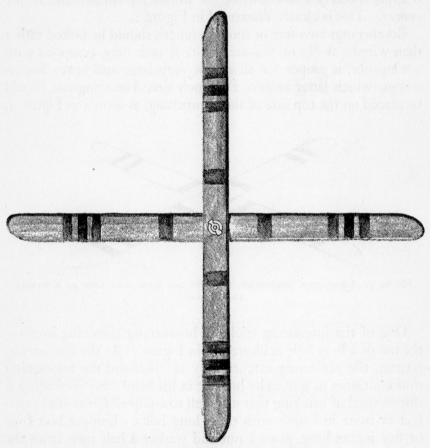

FIGURE 4. A TYPICAL CROSS-STICK BOOMERANG

trimmed off in this way. Do not bevel or thin down the ends of the sticks—the wood should be left at full thickness here to insure all possible strength.

Now hold each stick over a candle at a point eight inches from the end, and when heated, bend it slightly toward the convex or

beveled side, as described in the preceding section (See Figure 3).
Bend each of the four wings in the same way.

Regardless of the size of the boomerang, the point of bending is approximately two-thirds of the distance from the end to the center. This is clearly illustrated in Figure 2.

Boomerangs two feet or more in length should be bolted rather than wired. A ⅛- or ³⁄₁₆-inch bolt, ¾ inch long, equipped with a wing-nut, is proper for all except very large and heavy boomerangs, which latter require a ¼-inch size. The wing-nut should be placed on the top side of the boomerang, as shown in Figure 4.

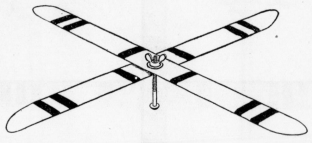

FIGURE 5.   CROSS-STICK BOOMERANG SHOWING THE LONG BOLT USED AS A HANDLE
IN CATCHING

One of the interesting tricks in boomerang throwing involves the use of a long bolt as illustrated in Figure 5. As the boomerang returns, the performer catches it by the bolt and the boomerang thus continues to spin as he holds it in his hand. So fascinating is this method of catching that it is well to equip all Cross-sticks two feet or more in length with these long bolts. Using a bolt four or five inches long, place a nut and washer a half inch from the end, insert the end through the two blades, place a washer on top, and hold with a wing-nut. Figure 5 shows the arrangement clearly. These long bolts should be as light in weight as the size of the boomerang will permit—a three-sixteenth-inch size is large enough for all except extremely heavy boomerangs.

No type of nut is satisfactory for use on boomerangs unless it can be tightened with the fingers, without the use of pliers. Since the nut tends to loosen in throwing and must be frequently tightened, it is a great convenience if it can be adjusted with the fingers. Two types of nuts meet this requirement, the wing-nut (Figure 7) and the toggle bolt and nut (Figure 6). The latter is particularly desirable on large boomerangs.

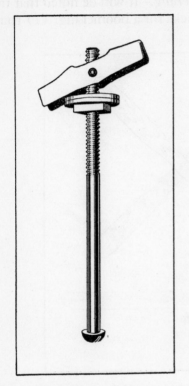

FIGURE 6. TOGGLE BOLT   FIGURE 7. BOLT WITH WING-NUT

When the two sticks are bolted together as in Figure 5, the boomerang is completed and ready to throw.

If the boomerang dives to the ground, or cuts in at you without turning into a horizontal position and floating in easily and gently, it probably is too heavy and needs to be lightened. This is accomplished by gouging out some of the wood on the back or flat sides of the sticks. Use a three-fourths-inch gouge for this. A few chips may be removed as in A, Figure 8, thus lightening the weight slightly, or the entire length of the stick may be gouged out uniformly, making the bottom side concave as shown in B, Figure 8. Most large boomerangs need to be lightened in this way.

The Two Secrets of the Boomerang.—It will be noted that there are two processes in preparing sticks for a boomerang: (1) round-

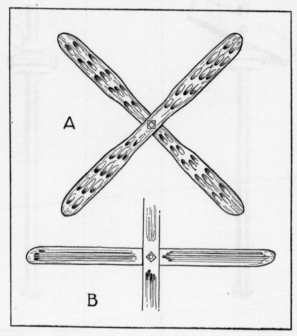

FIGURE 8. WINGS LIGHTENED BY GAUGING OUT THE BACK SIDES

ing off the top side to a roughly convex shape while the bottom remains flat, and (2), bending each wing slightly toward the convex side. *These are the two secrets in boomerang construction.* It is the convex or beveled shape of the top side that is the primary factor in causing the boomerang to return. The bend in the wings causes the boomerang to tend to turn over into a horizontal position and thus to float and sail, staying in the air until it has had time to return. The bend in the wings forms a dihedral angle which helps the boomerang to glide and volplane. An occasional boomerang will be found that will return satisfactorily without the angle or bend in the wings, but this is not often the case—such boomerangs usually tend to dive heavily to the earth before completing the return.

Other "tricks of the trade" in making efficient boomerangs will

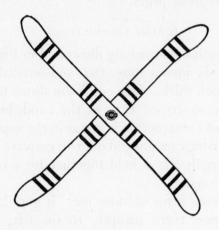

FIGURE 9.   CROSS-STICK BOOMERANG WITH CURVED WINGS

be discussed in describing the larger Cross-sticks in the pages that follow.

CROSS-STICKS WITH CURVED WINGS

Figure 9 shows a favorite boomerang pattern in which the sticks are slightly curved. These are delightful both in appearance and performance. The dimensions are: twenty-four inches long, one-and-three-fourths inches wide, and one-eighth inch thick. In laying out the wing, cut a strip two-and-one-fourth inches wide and two feet long. Draw the curved wing on this strip, making the wing width one-and-three-fourths inches; then whittle it out. A strip of this width will provide just enough curve to the sides of the wing for a graceful appearance.

In making a boomerang thirty inches long, the width of the wings would be two-and-one-fourth inches and the thickness one-eighth inch. Wings of this width should be drawn on a piece of lumber three inches wide.

The sticks having been cut to the curved shape, the boomerang is completed in the same way as are the straight Cross-sticks, described in the foregoing pages.

JUMBO CROSS-STICKS

The big Cross-stick Boomerang illustrated in Figure 10 is made of boards thirty-six inches long, two-and-one-half inches wide, and one-fourth inch thick. One end is cut down to a smaller size, forming a handle so shaped as to fit the hand, but further than this, the method of construction is just as in the smaller sizes. The back sides of the wings are gouged out to a concave shape throughout the entire length. It is held together by a one-fourth-inch bolt, five inches long.

Such a boomerang is for outdoor use. It goes in a straight line for a long distance, turns abruptly to the left, and returns in almost a straight line. It comes in gently, and can be easily caught by the bolt.

TABLE OF DIMENSIONS FOR CROSS-STICKS WITH WINGS OF UNIFORM WIDTH

The Cross-sticks discussed thus far in this chapter are made with sticks uniform in width throughout the entire length. The table of dimensions presented herewith is for boomerangs of this type. Some Cross-sticks are made with wings that are wider at the ends than at the center—these are discussed in the section following.

Whenever the length of the stick is increased, the width should be increased proportionately. For every six inches that the length is increased the width should be increased about one-half inch.

If we assume as the standard proportion, sticks that are twenty-four inches long and one-and-one-half inches wide, to increase the length to thirty inches would necessitate increasing the width to two inches.   This is not a hard and fast rule, since all sorts of odd

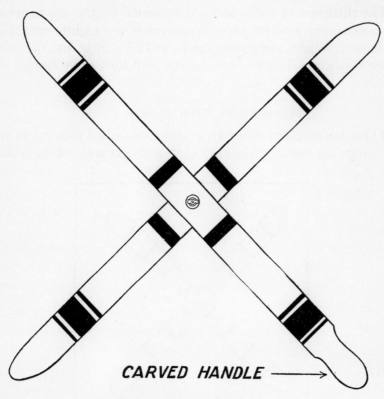

CARVED HANDLE ⟶

FIGURE 10. JUMBO CROSS-STICK

dimensions may be worked out, but these proportions are sure to be satisfactory. If the width is too great for the length, the wings offer too much resistance to the air and the boomerang does not have sufficient carrying power.

The following dimensions are recommended for Cross-sticks with wings of uniform width throughout:

Length	Width	Thickness
18 inches	1 inch	⅛ inch
24 inches	1½ inches	⅛ and ¼ inch
30 inches	2 inches	⅛ and ¼ inch
36 inches	2½ inches	¼ inch

The thickness of the wood is determined by the use to which the boomerang is to be put. Boomerangs one-eighth inch thick are light in weight, cut a small circle, and sail gently into the hands of the thrower. Those of one-fourth-inch stuff carry further and are ideal for outdoor use.

CROSS-STICKS WITH FLARED ENDS

These boomerangs differ from those described thus far in that the wings are wider at the ends than at the center, whereas those

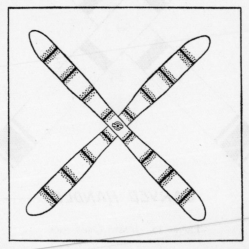

FIGURE 11. THE ENDS OF THE WINGS MAY BE FLARED OUT INSTEAD OF STRAIGHT

described up to this point are made with sticks that are uniform in width throughout. Figures 11 and 12 illustrate flared-end types —they are particularly effective boomerangs. This arrangement lightens the weight and at the same time provides a wide wing at the point where width is needed. Furthermore, with this pattern it is possible to secure the effect that wider wings produce without the danger of too much air resistance which would result if the greater width were continued throughout.

These boomerangs are not only pleasing in their lines but they sail and soar more than those made of uniform sticks, staying in the air longer before returning. From whatever angle we view

FIGURE 12. ANOTHER TYPE OF FLARED-END BOOMERANG

these flared-end boomerangs they prove to be the most efficient and satisfying type of Cross-stick.

The patterns illustrated in Figures 11 and 12 are twenty-four inches long, one-eighth inch thick, two inches wide at the widest point, and one-and-one-fourth inches at the narrow section. Larger boomerangs may also be made in the same designs provided the same relative proportions are maintained.

CROSS-STICKS WITH TAPERED ENDS

This type of boomerang violates a basic principle of wing construction but it serves well the specialized purpose for which it is designed. The wing of a boomerang should be wider at the end than at the bolt, or at least it should be uniform in width throughout, if typical performance is to be expected. All the boomerangs described thus far are of one or the other of these two types. The wings of this boomerang, however, are wider at the middle and taper down to a narrow end. The boomerang thus has very little wing spread and consequently little capacity to stay in the air. When thrown, it follows the typical course of the Cross-sticks but drops quickly and abruptly to the thrower at

FIGURE 13. CROSS-STICK BOOMERANG WITH TAPERED ENDS

the end of the flight; if it is not caught it drops to the floor at the thrower's feet. It is useful only when one must throw boomerangs under conditions where it would be dangerous if the boomerang were not caught but allowed to float past him. An actor on a very small stage is sometimes in such a situation—a boomerang that returns and circles around him and behind him before coming to his hands might hit the back of the stage; others that cut in directly to him might, if not caught, float past him and out into the audience. If made with tapered ends, he can be sure that the boomerang does not have enough carrying power to go past him. Those boomerangs are certainly not to be recommended for any other purpose, and since few people will ever have to meet such a situation, they are of little use at all. A professional of enough experience to be throwing from the stage will be able to so manipulate ordinary boomerangs that they will not get past him.

To make one of these boomerangs, cut from one-eighth-inch stuff two strips two inches wide and twenty-four inches long. Leaving them two inches wide at the middle, taper them gradually down to a width of one-half inch at the end, as shown in Figure 13. In rounding off the top sides, leave them unbeveled for a distance of two inches at the ends. In other respects the boomerang is completed as any other Cross-stick.

THE CROSS

The Cross-stick Boomerangs described thus far are of the balanced type; that is, the wings are of equal length. The Cross is an unbalanced Cross-stick—one stick is placed across the other at a point near one end, thus giving the boomerang the appearance of a cross as shown in A, Figure 14. The shortest wing is one-third of the length of the stick, and the longest wing two-thirds of the length. The dimensions of the sticks are the same as in four-wing Cross-sticks already described.

The Cross flies with a jerky movement, and while it may be lacking in grace of movement as compared to the others, it returns to the thrower just as efficiently.

Variation.—Another type of Cross which acts in much the same way as the one just described is suggested in B, Figure 14. The long wings are twice the length of the short wings.

TWO-WING CROSS-STICK BOOMERANGS

The boomerangs which we shall now describe differ from the Cross-sticks already discussed in that they have two wings instead of four. These are not particularly effective boomerangs. Certainly they do not compare at all favorably with the balanced

Cross-sticks in flying qualities, but nevertheless, they are interesting novelties that will appeal to all who find fascination in boomerangs. Once a person is exposed to boomerang making, he is seldom satisfied until he has made every conceivable type that can be caused to come back to him. These two-wingers will return

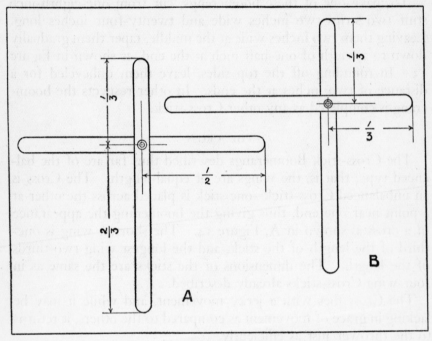

FIGURE 14. TWO STYLES OF THE CROSS

even though they do not possess the precision and the soaring qualities of the other models.

Boomerangs of these types should be thrown higher in the air than is usually the case (see Chapter VIII "How to Throw Boomerangs"). They go straight for a short distance, turn to the left and rise in the air, hesitate, and then glide and volplane down to the thrower. They cannot be caused to make a circular flight as do the regular Cross-sticks.

THE SQUARE

This boomerang consists of two blades arranged so as to form a right angle, as illustrated in A, Figure 15. It is in fact one-half of a four-wing Cross-stick Boomerang. The dimensions are the same as in the Cross-sticks except that the wings are one-half the length plus two inches for overlapping and bolting. Take any

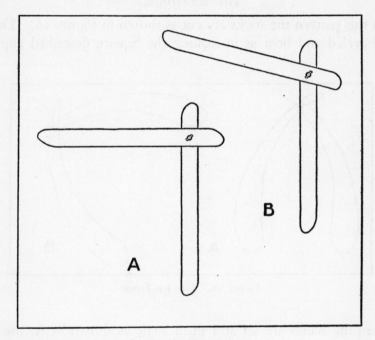

FIGURE 15. THE SQUARE

of the suggested dimensions for Cross-sticks on page 26 and shorten the sticks as here suggested. The sticks are beveled as usual and bent just as in making the regular Cross-sticks, but only in one place, that point being two-thirds the distance from the end to the bolt (see Figure 2). Arrange the wings so as to form a right angle and fasten with a lightweight bolt and wing-nut.

Variation.—A much more effective boomerang than the one

just described is illustrated in B, Figure 15. The dimensions and proportions are the same except that the blades are longer, extending three-and-one-half inches beyond the bolt. The wings are adjusted so as to form an angle slightly greater than a right angle. These boomerangs are somewhat similar in appearance to the curved Australian type, but they are very different in action.

THE ICE-TONGS

In this pattern the sticks are cut as shown in Figure 16. They are beveled and bent as in making the Square described above.

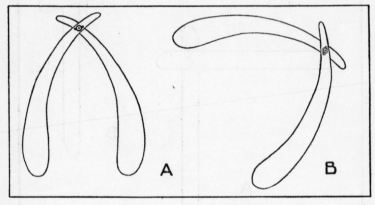

FIGURE 16. THE ICE-TONGS

When the wings are set at a small angle as shown in A, the arrangement takes on the appearance of ice-tongs, hence the name. The wings may also be set at a larger angle as shown in B. These novelties are not particularly efficient as boomerangs but are interesting nevertheless.

THE RAZOR

The sticks are cut to represent a razor, as illustrated in Figure 17. The following dimensions are recommended, the width applying to the widest points:

Width	Length	Thickness
1 ¾ inches	15 inches	⅛ inch
2 ⅛ inches	19 inches	⅛ to ¼ inch
2 ½ inches	22 inches	¼ inch

The sticks are whittled to the usual convex shape on top, and are bent just as in making the Square described on page 31. They

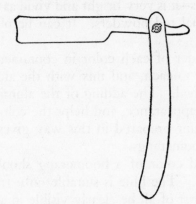

FIGURE 17. THE RAZOR

should be adjusted so as to form an angle a little larger than a right angle.

DECORATING BOOMERANGS

No boomerang is complete until it is painted. Coloring adds immeasurably to the eye appeal both when the boomerang is in the hand and in the air. Properly ornamented with stripes across the wings, the whirling Cross-sticks create vivid circles of color which are strikingly effective.

PAINTING

Do not use ordinary paint or enamel on the boomerangs—it is heavy and creates too thick a layer. Secure some aluminum paint powder together with the oil in which to mix it. The silver effect produced by the aluminum is particularly effective and easily visible against almost any background. It dries quickly and adds practically nothing to the weight. Mix together a little powder and oil, making a thin paste, and paint with it.

Also, secure from a paint store a little paint powder or dry pigment in vivid yellow, ultramarine, and fire red. This powder is very inexpensive. Fire red is the only red powder that is effective on boomerangs—it is very bright and vivid as contrasted to the dullness of the usual red powders. It can be obtained from the larger paint stores.

Put a little powder of each color in containers, add a dash of aluminum powder to each, and mix with the aluminum oil until a thin paste is formed. The adding of the aluminum contributes a luster or frosted appearance, and helps the color to stand out in artificial light. Paint prepared in this way gives a theatrical appearance to the boomerangs.

The background color of a boomerang should be aluminum, yellow, or fire red. The blue is suitable only for striping. The boomerang must first of all be clearly visible in any kind of light, and this is best accomplished by the use of lighter shades for the background color, set off with stripes of darker colors. Paint the boomerang in aluminum and add crosswise stripes to the wings in blue, yellow, or red. Or paint it in yellow or red with stripes of aluminum, edged with thin lines of blue.

Each wing of the boomerang should be painted in the same way or else the design will be lost when the missile is spinning. There are many effective ways of striping the wings. Excellent designs for Cross-sticks are shown in Figures 4, 9, 10, 11, and 12. The possibilities are limitless here and each craftsman will be able to work out many unique and original effects of his own.

ILLUMINATING BOOMERANGS

The attaching of electric lights to boomerangs gives a unique and brilliant effect, producing the appearance of whirling circles of fire. Secure tiny flash light bulbs and batteries. Attach the battery with wire as near as possible to the bolt at the center. Bore a hole through the wing midway between the bolt and the end, set the bulb well down in this hole so that it is protected from damage, and run the wire to the battery. Two bulbs are enough to produce the circle of light as the boomerang spins—they should be placed on wings directly opposite each other, that is, one on each wing of the same stick, equally distant from the bolt. If two circles of light are desired, add two additional bulbs on the other set of wings, placed at a different distance from the ends than the first set.

COLORED STREAMERS

If used at all, colored streamers and trailing attachments must be handled cautiously and very conservatively. Nothing in the way of trailers can be attached to a boomerang without impeding its flight and cramping its style more than one would think. Certainly nothing of this sort, however light it may be, can be attached to the ends of the wings without crippling the boomerang rather completely. It is possible to attach slender and very light colored ribbons to the bolt on the under side of a boomerang provided it is sturdy and buoyant enough to offset the drag. It is not so much the weight of the ribbons that hampers the flight as it is the wind resistance against them as the boomerang flies through the air. Air currents are doubly detrimental when streamers are used, often causing the boomerang to become exceedingly erratic. To be effective, the ribbons should be at least two feet long.

CHAPTER III

Pin-wheel Boomerangs—How to Make Them

If the Cross-stick can be glorified as the most perfect type of boomerang, certainly to the Pin-wheel goes the credit of being the most perfect Cross-stick. That puts it far and away at the head of the list of all the boomerangs. Made of three sticks bolted together in the center, it is a six-wing boomerang such as is illustrated in Figure 18.

Like huge pin-wheels these boomerangs go humming around their circuits. Having more blades than the four-wingers, they are more steady, more exact, more dependable—they find their way back home with the utmost of precision. When one throws a Pin-wheel he knows that it is going to travel exactly the same course in exactly the same way that it did last time—this owing to its many wings, for if one of them should become warped or twisted, there are five others to offset any damaging effects.

One knows, too, when he hurls a Pin-wheel, that it will not come back bluntly, hopping and jerking, abruptly thrusting itself at him. The Pin-wheel has too much refinement for that—by nature it is too gentle, too sensitive. It soars and sails—slowly, gracefully, aesthetically—and floats in to you gently, settling softly into your hands. Herein rests its chief superiority over those with fewer wings, which latter zip about swiftly, cut a close circle, and often dive in to you so suddenly fast that you scarcely expect them. A good Pin-wheel often seems reluctant to come home to you at all—having drifted lightly back it turns and floats away again in another little circle before finally settling into your hands. Indeed, there are some that make three trips away before coming home at last.

Both in precision of returning and in beauty of action, there is no boomerang so satisfying to handle as the Pin-wheel.

36

This chapter will describe first the making of the six-wingers—the typical Pin-wheels—and then it will take up the three-wing boomerangs.

MAKING PIN-WHEELS

The sticks for the Pin-wheels are prepared precisely as for the simple Cross-sticks described in the preceding chapter. It takes three of them to make a Pin-wheel rather than two, but there is

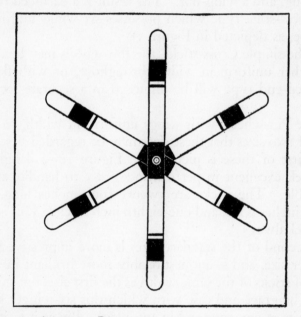

FIGURE 18. A TYPICAL PIN-WHEEL WITH WINGS OF UNIFORM WIDTH

no difference in their preparation. In fact, if one of the sticks of a Pin-wheel should break, we can usually arrange the two remaining sticks at right angles to each other and thus convert the wreckage into a serviceable Cross-stick of the four-wing type.

Since every one should try his luck at making one of the four-wingers discussed in the last chapter before attempting a Pin-wheel, the process of preparing the sticks should by now be familiar to all, but let us briefly reiterate the essentials just as a precaution against any possible oversight: Bevel the edges with a jackknife on the top side of each stick throughout the entire length (see the discussion on page 16 and the illustration in Figure 1). Do not bevel the ends but rather leave them at their full thickness, doing nothing more than to trim off the corners to the shape shown in Figure 18. Bend each wing as illustrated in Figures 2 and 3, and described on page 17. Fasten the three sticks together at their centers with a three-sixteenth-inch bolt, four inches long, and a wing-nut. The result is a balanced boomerang of the cross-stick type which possesses six wings uniform in size and shape, as depicted in Figure 18.

Like the simple Cross-sticks, the Pin-wheels may be made with sticks either uniform in width throughout, or with flared ends. The flared-end type will be discussed in a separate section presently.

Of the Pin-wheels with wings uniform in width, so many are of one of two sizes that these sizes may be regarded as standard:

The first of these is pictured in Figure 18—a delightful little Pin-wheel, excellent in performance, easy to handle, and always dependable. The sticks are twenty-four inches long, one-and-one-half inches wide, and one-eighth inch thick. This is a popular Pin-wheel always.

The second of the standard sizes is more impressive because of its greater size, and is unquestionably more brilliant in action. It is made of sticks of the same width as the first size, but thirty inches long. The grace and ease with which this six-winger sails makes it a favorite at any time and in any place. Big as it is, it cuts such a small circle that it can be thrown in any small gymnasium or hall. The sticks are one-and-one-half inches wide, thirty inches long, and one-eighth inch thick. It is obvious that sticks of these dimensions would not make a very satisfactory four-wing Cross-stick in that they are too long and slender, but since the Pin-wheels have six wings, the sticks used in them may be narrower in relation to the length than is ordinarily the case. Too wide a wing spread will prove unsatisfactory in a Pin-wheel.

JUMBO PIN-WHEELS

Huge size is always an impressive factor in the Pin-wheels. An oversized wheel can be so constructed as to belie completely its weight and its flying distance. Over-large in all dimensions, such a wheel looks forbidding indeed when picked for throwing indoors, yet in reality it may be very light and may cut as small a circle as any young-sized Pin-wheel. These jumbo wheels thrill by their very hugeness when they are held up preparatory to throwing, yet they prove to be as harmless as their tiniest brothers.

Out of one-fourth-inch stuff, cut three boards forty-two inches long, and two-and-one-fourth inches wide. Whittle off the top sides to a convex shape and bend the ends as usual in preparing sticks for a Cross-stick Boomerang. Shape the end of one of the sticks into a handle by cutting it down to fit the hand, as illustrated in Figure 19. Using a one-inch gouge, remove as much wood as possible from the back side of each stick, gouging it out to a concave shape. The gouging should be carefully done so that the stick becomes a thin shell, not more than one-eighth inch through. Bolt the boards together at their center in the usual fashion, using a one-fourth-inch bolt, five inches long.

It is sometimes difficult to fasten these over-large wheels together with a bolt tightly enough so that the wings will not move when thrown. If this occurs, the boomerang either collapses and falls, or nose-dives abruptly to the ground. To guard against such a happening, a very small hole may be bored through each wing about five inches from the bolt and a wire run through them as illustrated in Figure 19. This will preclude any chance of the blades moving enough to influence the flight. Such precautions should always be taken when large wheels are thrown indoors.

Still another style of Jumbo Pin-wheels may be made by flaring out the ends of the wings. Use boards forty-five inches long, three inches wide, and one-fourth inch thick. Divide each board into three fifteen-inch sections; leave the two end sections at their full width of three inches, but pull the center section in to two inches in width. Gouge out the back side and complete the boards as usual.

HEAVY PIN-WHEELS FOR OUTDOOR USE

All the Pin-wheels described thus far in this chapter may be used either indoors or out. A long-flying Pin-wheel for strictly

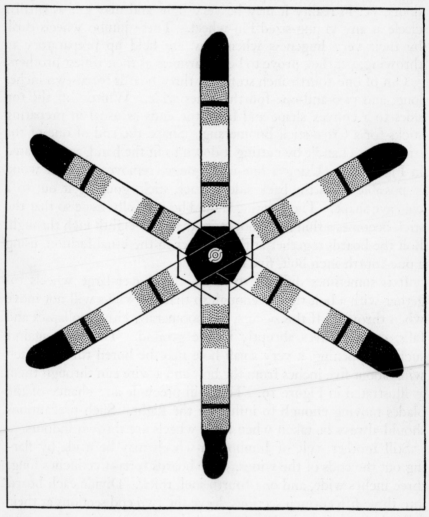

FIGURE 19. JUMBO PIN-WHEEL

outdoor use need not necessarily be large in size but rather must be heavier than the average in weight.

An excellent far-flying Pin-wheel of the larger size may be made from sticks thirty-six inches long, one-and-three-fourths inches wide, and one-fourth inch thick. Leave the sticks unbeveled and at their full thickness for a space of four inches at the center, and whittle them off to the usual convex shape beyond this area. Such boomerangs are impressive in the great distance that they travel, but they do not sail and float so gracefully as the lighter ones.

An equally good long-flyer of the smaller size calls for sticks twenty-four inches long, one-and-one-half inches wide, and three-sixteenths to one-fourth inch thick. Those of one-fourth-inch stuff may be gouged out a little on the back side if it is necessary to lighten the weight for good performance.

TABLE OF DIMENSIONS FOR PIN-WHEELS
WITH WINGS OF UNIFORM WIDTH

Many odd and lawless sizes and shapes are possible in Pin-wheels, but the dimensions set forth in the following table are sure to give satisfactory results. By the time these sizes have all been successfully made, the creative urge that grips all boomerang enthusiasts, once they are really bitten by the bug, will lead to the quick discovery of other proportions.

Length	Width	Thickness.
24 inches	1½ inches	⅛ inch
24 inches	1⅛ inches	⅛ inch
30 or 32 inches	1½ inches	⅛ inch
36 inches	1¾ inches	¼ inch
36 inches	2 inches	⅛ inch
24 inches	1¾ inches	3⁄16 inch
30 inches	1¾ inches	¼ inch
42 inches	2¼ inches	¼ inch
45 inches	3 inches	¼ inch

PIN-WHEELS WITH FLARED ENDS

There could scarcely be an argument on the point that wings with flared ends produce better Pin-wheels than those that are uniform in width throughout. Such wheels take to the air with greater ease, conduct themselves with more charm and gentle grace, yet maintain withal a buoyant and enlivened spirit, all of which results from the fact that there is greater width of wings where width is needed for flying, and less where width serves only as dead weight to be carried.

While no indictment of the excellent Pin-wheels described thus

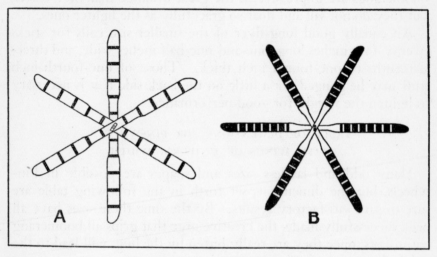

FIGURE 20. PIN-WHEELS WITH WINGS FLARED OUT AT THE ENDS

far in this chapter is meant, the boomerang maker will do well to fix in his mind as the type-perfect model, the wing with ends flared out wider than the center.

Figure 20 shows two characteristic outlines for such widened ends. In A the center area is pulled in gently and with curving lines, whereas in B, the center is cut away more deeply and sharply.

In making such a boomerang, divide the stick into three equal sections, the center third to be cut away to a narrower width. Any of the dimensions for Pin-wheels referred to earlier in this chapter may be used as a basis for the flared-end type. For any one of the dimensions given, merely narrow down the center section a quarter or half inch, leaving the ends at the stated width. For example, if the dimensions of the stick are twenty-four inches long by one-and-one-half inches wide, cut down the center to one inch, leaving the stick an inch and a half wide at the ends.

The boomerang used as a model for the drawing shown in A, Figure 20, is a large and very effective Pin-wheel, measuring three feet across. For a distance of one foot at each end, the sticks are

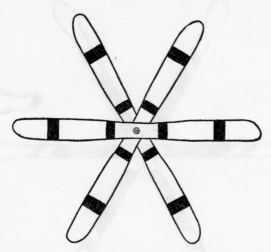

FIGURE 21. AN EXCELLENT, LONG-FLYING PIN-WHEEL

two inches wide, and the one-foot center area is one-and-one-half inches wide. The thickness is one-eighth inch full.

The model for B, Figure 20, is a twenty-four inch boomerang made of slender sticks. They are one-and-one-eighth inches wide at the ends, seven-eighth inches wide at the center. It floats lightly and beautifully.

Figure 21 shows one of the very finest Pin-wheels ever encountered in the experience of this writer. It is a long-traveling wheel with remarkable soaring qualities. When used out-of-doors and thrown with much force, it will travel far, rise high in the air, and will often make three circles before returning. The dimensions of the sticks are: twenty-four inches in length, two inches in width at the ends, one-and-one-half inches at the center, and three-sixteenth inch in thickness. The three-sixteenths thickness gives it a greater weight than most Pin-wheels and consequently greater carrying power. Note the curving lines of the wings.

Figure 22 shows a colorful wheel of good flying qualities which

FIGURE 22. A PICTURESQUE PIN-WHEEL

has the ends shaped and painted to represent birds' heads. The sticks are thirty-two inches long, one-eighth inch thick, and one-and-one-half inches wide except for the heads which are two-and-one-fourth inches wide.

THREE-WING BOOMERANGS

These boomerangs with three wings have one-half the wing support of the Pin-wheels. Their course is a circular one similar to that of the four-wing Cross-sticks and the Pin-wheels, but since they have less wing support than either of these, they move more swiftly, often having a jumpy action, and by comparison are lacking in graceful sailing qualities.

MAKING THREE-WING BOOMERANGS

The sticks are prepared just as in the case of the ordinary Cross-sticks and Pin-wheels—whittled to a convex shape on top and bent

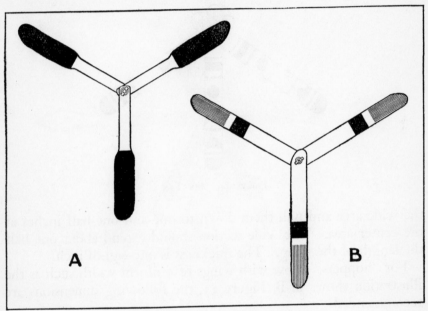

FIGURE 23. THREE-WING BOOMERANGS

—but since each stick constitutes one wing rather than two, it is bent in one place only, that point being two-thirds of the distance from the end to the bolt. When bolted together, the sticks are arranged equidistant from one another, as shown in Figure 23.

These three-wingers may be made either with wings flared out at the ends as in A, Figure 23, or with wings uniform in width throughout, as in B. In boomerangs of this type, the flared ends

are by all odds preferable. Not having much wing support anyway, the widened ends are in many cases essential to good performance. Without them the boomerang zips about with a
hopping motion, making it difficult for the thrower to follow
its course, and it cuts in to him too swiftly to be handled with
ease. Such boomerangs are often called "hoppers."

A good wing length for a three-winger with flared ends is sixteen inches. Make the wings two-and-one-half inches wide at

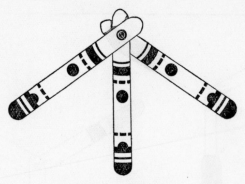

FIGURE 24. THE FAN

the wide area and pull them down to one-and-one-half inches at
the center area. The wide section should extend about one half
the length of the wing. The thickness is one-eighth inch.

For "hoppers," those with wings of uniform width such as the
illustration shows in B, Figure 23, the following dimensions are
recommended:

Width	Length	Thickness
1½ inches	12 inches	⅛ inch
2 inches	16 inches	⅛ inch
2¼ inches	18 inches	⅛ inch

FANS

The Fan, illustrated in Figure 24, is in fact one-half of a Pin-
wheel: if three adjacent wings of a Pin-wheel are cut off near the
bolt, we have the Fan. The three-wing boomerangs in Figure 23

may be converted into Fans by loosening the bolt and adjusting the wings as shown in Figure 24.

While the fans can be thrown so that their flight will be similar to that of the Pin-wheels, their most characteristic action is to sail high up in the air, turn into a horizontal position, and then glide and volplane back in almost the same plane to the thrower.

CHAPTER IV

Boomabirds—How to Make Them

"All birds come home to roost"—and so it is with the Booma-bird. Like the homer pigeon, it invariably finds its way back to its master. Of all the boomerangs, it is the most picturesque, whether held in the hand or flying over the tree tops. As these bird-shaped boomerangs gracefully sail and soar overhead, they look for all the world like living, gliding birds.

It was on one of those calm, peaceful evenings in June when not a breath of air was stirring that I picked up some Boomabirds and went over in the shadow of a great football stadium. Never did the boomers soar so beautifully—the quiet evening was made to order for their liking. There was but one annoyance—a flock of swallows circled and circled overhead, making it difficult to keep one's eye on the Boomabirds. Suddenly as a Boomabird settled into my hands, a swallow swooped down and almost hit me! Then the explanation of it all abruptly dawned—*the swallows were being attracted by the Boomabirds. So realistic were these bird-shaped sticks that they fooled even the birds themselves.*

Since then the birds have joined company with the Boomabirds on many an occasion. They seem to feel that since the Booma-birds keep circling around one spot, there must be some choice attraction there of no ordinary interest to birds and so they proceed to investigate for themselves.

At first blush it would seem that when so much attention is given to the shape of a boomerang as to make it resemble a bird, something in the way of efficiency must be sacrificed. Happily, however, this is far from being the case. These birds have a flying style all their own, but they find their way back to your waiting hands with such unerring propriety, and withal so gracefully, that they must be listed high up in the social register of the boomerang élite. They hold their own among all others in finished etiquette and they excel outstandingly in glamour and personal attractiveness. Their very life-like, bird-like appearance as they glide about enhances their grip on the imagination.

When thrown, the Boomabird goes straight forward for some distance, swings to the left and rises high in the air, then circles over the head of the thrower and around in front of him, reverses its direction and settles gently into his hands. The average Boomabird makes two circles before reaching the thrower, and occasionally one is found that will make three circles.

The author had a small Boomabird at one time that, when thrown from a theater stage, would sail up above the balcony and start back, making a complete circle over the audience before floating up to the stage. As it approached him, the thrower would start off the stage to the right and the bird would follow him out the wings. Such a Boomabird is one in a million, of course, but the Boomabirds in general are noted for their odd and intricate tricks. Their lawless habits make it impossible to predict their conduct until each has been duly subjected to a detailed case study.

A Boomabird is in fact a four-wing Cross-stick Boomerang. It differs from those described thus far in that one of the sticks, the body stick, is much wider and heavier than the stick used for the wings.

MAKING THE BOOMABIRD

Boomabirds require the same light, soft wood described for the Cross-sticks in Chapter II: basswood, tulip (white-wood), or Number 1 white pine.

Figure 26 illustrates the best shape for the body of the bird. The head is usually the same width as the body, but may be slightly narrower. Figure 27 shows another type of body that some may prefer.

An excellent size for all-around use is diagrammed in Figure 25. Cut a board from one-eighth-inch stuff, twenty-two inches long, and three-and-one-fourth inches wide. Draw the outline of the bird on it, as illustrated in A. Note that the body is divided into three parts; ten inches should be allowed for the body proper, and six inches each for the head and tail. Whittle out the shape of the bird with a jackknife (B) and then bevel the edges on the top side, rounding them off to a smooth curve as shown in the diagram of the cross section in F. (See page 16 for a more detailed description of the beveling.) This beveling is carried

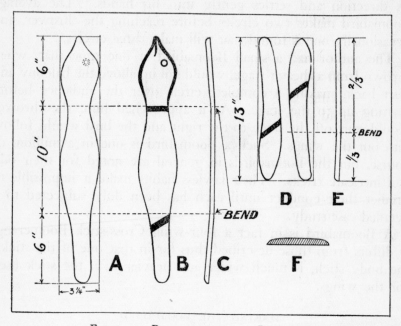

FIGURE 25. PLAN FOR MAKING A BOOMABIRD

all around the body with the exception of the point of the beak and the tip of the tail, which points are left at full thickness.

Now heat the wood at the points indicated in C, Figure 25, by holding over a candle, and give the head and tail a slight bend upward, that is, toward the beveled side. (See Figures 2 and 3, and page 17 for a detailed description of the bending process.)

To determine the point on the body where the hole is to be bored for the wings, place the body on a knife blade until it balances—this point will be an inch or so nearer the head rather than at the exact center of the body.

The wings may be made either of two pieces, as shown in Figure 26, or of one straight piece as shown in Figure 27. The use of two separate wings makes a slightly more attractive Boomabird, but not necessarily a more efficient one.

Let us describe the making of the two separate wings first. As shown in D, Figure 25, each wing is thirteen inches long;

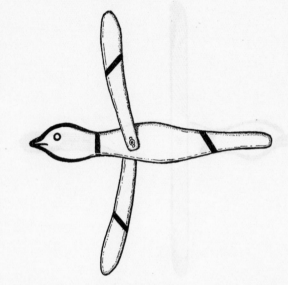

FIGURE 26. A TYPICAL BOOMABIRD WITH SEPARATE WINGS

they are one-and-five-eighths inches wide at the widest point, and one inch at the narrow point. The wings are cut to the curved shape illustrated. Bevel them as in making the body, and bend them at the point illustrated in E—two-thirds of the distance from the end to the bolt.

Bolt the wings in place as shown in Figure 26, using either a short bolt and wing-nut, or a long bolt with which to catch the bird, as described on page 20. Note that the wing on the belly side is placed on the bottom side of the body, and the other on the top side. Tighten the nut very securely.

The wings should first be adjusted so that they are at right angles to the center line of the body. If the bird does not perform perfectly with wings in this position, turn them at an angle, nearer the head as shown in Figure 26. Continue to adjust the wings in this way until the bird flies in the way that you want it to.

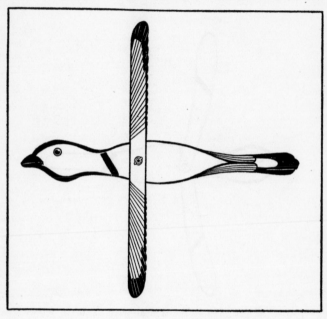

FIGURE 27. ANOTHER STYLE OF BOOMABIRD SHOWING WINGS MADE OF ONE PIECE

If a single stick is to be used for the wings, it should be twenty-four inches long and one-and-one-half inches wide. Bevel the edges, and round off the ends as shown in Figure 27. Bend the ends as before, at a point two-thirds of the distance from the end to the bolt. Place this stick across the top side of the body and bolt securely.

Another type of wing is illustrated in Figure 29. It is one piece of wood cut so as to give the wings a slight curve.

If the Boomabird proves to be too heavy to float well, gouge out the back side of the body throughout the entire length, as described on page 21. It will not be necessary to gouge out the wings in Boomabirds of this size.

TABLE OF DIMENSIONS FOR BOOMABIRDS

Boomabirds can be made in a wide variety of sizes. In the following table of dimensions the thickness of the stick is the same for both body and wings. The width of the wing in each case refers to the width at the widest part.

| | Body | | | Wings | |
	Length	Width	Thickness	Length	Width
1.	15 inches	2½ inches	⅛ inch	17 inches	1¼ inches
2.	18 inches	3 inches	⅛ inch	21 inches	1½ inches
3.	22 inches	3¼ inches	⅛ inch	24 inches	1⅝ inches
4.	30 inches	4 inches	¼ inch	32 inches	2 inches
5.	36 inches	4½ inches	¼ inch	39 inches	2¼ inches

Number 3, the twenty-two-inch length, is the one described in detail in the preceding pages. It and Number 2, the eighteen-inch length, are the two best sizes for all-around use. Number 2 is a delightful little Boomer—it usually has a full bag of tricks which it displays generously when flying. Since no two Boomabirds act in exactly the same way, one can make several of these birds, all of the same dimensions, and be able to display a different brand of stunt flying with each.

Number 4, the big thirty-inch bird made of one-fourth inch stuff, is steady, sure, always dependable in its flight, either outdoors or indoors. It flies slowly and deliberately, and returns with studied precision. The back side of both the body and the wings of this bird should be gouged out to a concave shape throughout the entire length.

All Boomabirds twenty-two inches or more in length should be equipped with bolts four inches long. It is easy to catch the birds by these bolts, but difficult without them. Furthermore, the spinning of the bird in the hand when caught by the bolt adds a colorful touch.

THUNDERBIRDS

The Redman's picturesque thunderbird, glamorous always in its eye appeal, suggests the outline for the Boomabird shown in Figure 28. The dimensions and the manner of making are the same as in the Boomabirds described in the preceding pages. A few liberties may be taken with the recommended dimensions

FIGURE 28. THE THUNDERBIRD—A COLORFUL BOOMABIRD IN THE INDIAN STYLE

in order to gain enough width of body to secure the typical lines of a thunderbird, but if the body is made too wide the bird will coast about playfully in the air without tending to its business of coming home.

The design of the thunderbird is painted on the body and wings. Here, as in the handling of all things Indian, we do better to copy in accurate detail an original Indian thunderbird design. The present-day artist thinks to improve on the Redman's ideas of design, but this invariably to his chagrin, for the Indian's simple figures "make medicine" whereas the white man's "improvement" is often nothing more than so many lines on a page. The Red Artist is supreme in his own field and the wise will copy and not attempt to alter or perfect.

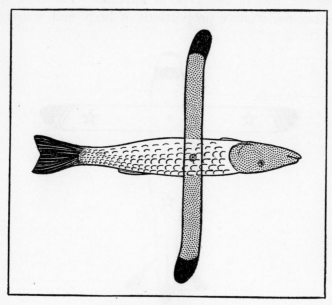

FIGURE 29. A FLYING FISH

FLYING FISH

The flying fish illustrated in Figure 29 is made exactly like the Boomabirds. Any of the dimensions listed for Boomabirds will apply with minor alterations. Here we must think in terms of a long slender type of fish—a northern pike or musky will make a better model than a bass or wall-eye. Use your privilege of artistic license and give the fish long sweeping lines.

BOOMAPLANE

Boomerangs and airplanes somehow seem to go together. People interested in boomerangs are often interested in model airplanes, and aviation enthusiasts usually take to the boomerang hobby wholeheartedly once they are exposed to it. Certainly an airplane suggests a most appropriate shape for a boomerang.

Such a boomerang is represented in the outline of the Boomaplane in Figure 30. Numberless variations in shape are possible, following the lines of any type of airplane. The only requirement is that the relative proportions of body and wings be ap-

FIGURE 30.   THE BOOMAPLANE

proximately the same as in the case of the Boomabirds, and consequently they should be made in about the same dimensions as specified for Boomabirds on page 53. The dimensions may force us to distort the shape of a selected airplane somewhat, but not so much so that the model will not be recognizable.

DECORATING BOOMABIRDS

The preparation of paint for use on boomerangs has already been described on page 34. Remember that light colors are desirable for the main body of the Boomabird in order that it be visible in all kinds of light and against all types of backgrounds —use aluminum, yellow, or fire red. The lines should be in contrasting colors, perferably blue or black. If the blue is used for the body of the bird, ample splotches of aluminum or yellow should be added. Whatever colors are used, a little aluminum powder should be mixed with it to provide luster.

The body of the bird and the wings should be painted in solid color and then outlined in contrasting color. It is wise to paint a stripe across the wings, tail and neck, these serving to create circles as the birds whirl through the air. Spots of contrasting color may also be added to the body. Excellent designs for Boomabirds are shown in Figures 26 and 27.

CHAPTER V

Tumblesticks—How to Make and Throw Them

A Tumblestick is a curious affair—it is essentially a straight stick of wood which when thrown into the air will return to your hands. Since a Tumblestick will come back to the thrower it properly belongs in the category of boomerangs, but certainly it is the most unique and little-known of all the gadgets that can be so classified. Consequently it is the most intriguing type, both to the spectators and the thrower. The Tumblestick never fails to mystify. When one sees a large and elaborate contrivance such as a Pin-wheel, he assumes that there is a mechanism involved that he does not understand which brings it back, but when a straight stick is caused to return the stunt seems so incredible at first exposure as to be baffling indeed.

Every one has seen children throw a slender strip of wood in the air so that it makes a humming sound—whir-r-r-r sticks, the boys call them. These whir-r-r-r sticks resemble a Tumblestick both in appearance and sound, and in fact one is occasionally seen that turns over in the air and makes a feeble effort at returning. Trimmed up perfectly by an expert such a whir-r-r-r stick might conceivably be converted into a dependable Tumblestick.

Because of its very simplicity there is no boomerang so easy to whittle out as the Tumblestick, yet there is no type of boomerang which offers so many difficulties when it comes to producing one of perfect performance—you may make a dozen Tumblesticks exactly alike in size and shape, all out of the same wood, yet find only one that will return accurately and consistently. This delicacy and temperamental quality, however, adds interest to the Tumblestick. One can whittle them out so easily that he does not become discouraged if his first few attempts are unsuccessful, and when at last he finds one that does work, joy is un-bounded! A good Tumblestick is precious indeed and is always carefully guarded! The long search for the right stick may convince one that Tumblesticks are too frail and temperamental to bother with, but this much is beyond question: once a good Tumblestick is discovered, it can be depended upon to do its stunt of returning to your hand every time it is expertly thrown. What more could be asked of any boomerang?

MAKING THE TUMBLESTICKS

Look around until you find a light, straight-grained piece of one-eighth-inch basswood or whitewood. Pieces of the same kind of wood frequently vary considerably in weight. The need here is for as light and as evenly balanced a piece as can be found in the kinds of wood mentioned.

Cut from the one-eighth-inch stuff a strip twenty-four inches long and one-and-one-half inches wide. Bevel the edges and round off the top side to a convex shape just as in making the wings for the Cross-stick Boomerangs described in Chapter II. The bottom side remains flat as usual. Do not round off the ends as in making the boomerangs previously described, but rather leave them square as illustrated in Figure 31.

Now throw the Tumblestick as described later in this chapter, to determine whether or not it will return. If after a thorough trial, it does not come back so that you can catch it without stepping, bend each end of the stick slightly toward the beveled side as is done in making the wings of Cross-stick Boomerangs (see Figure 3, also the discussion on page 17. Each end of the stick should

FIGURE 31. THE TUMBLESTICK

be bent in this way, at a point eight inches from the end. Now throw the Tumblestick again, and if it still does not work, try rounding off the square corners at the ends. Most Tumblesticks, however, work better with square ends. If the Tumble-stick still does not work, try lightening it by shaving off more wood on the top side, making the stick a little thinner. If this fails, use the stick as part of a Cross-stick Boomerang and make another Tumblestick.

It should not be assumed from all these various suggestions that there is anything particularly forbidding and discouragingly difficult about making a successful Tumblestick. They can be whittled out in five minutes. If failure results when the stick is carefully prepared as described, the difficulty probably rests in the wood—it may be too heavy or unevenly balanced. It may very easily happen that you will be fortunate enough to get a first-class Tumblestick in your first attempt.

It will be noted that the Tumblestick is prepared exactly as are the sticks for a twenty-four-inch Cross-stick. It is always possible, therefore, to use those Tumblesticks that fail to function accurately as parts of Cross-stick Boomerangs. This works the other way around, too—if you take apart your Cross-sticks and try throwing the sticks as Tumblesticks you may discover one that is so perfect in performance as a Tumblestick that you will want to save it for that purpose and replace it with another piece in the Cross-stick whence it came.

While Tumblesticks may be made in larger and smaller sizes, the size suggested above will produce the best results. It is difficult to throw a larger size in that the greater width prevents the stick from whirling in the air rapidly enough. In making other sizes, use the dimensions recommended for Cross-stick Boomerangs on page 26.

THROWING THE TUMBLESTICKS

The methods of throwing boomerangs are discussed in Chapter VIII, but since Tumblesticks require a technique all their own, we shall describe the specialized process of throwing them here.

Grasp the end of the Tumblestick in the right hand between the thumb and forefinger, with the beveled or convex side toward

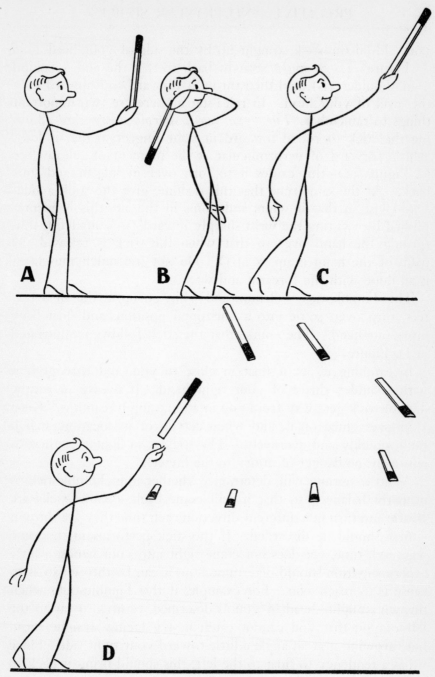

FIGURE 32. HOW THE TUMBLESTICK IS THROWN

you. Hold the stick straight up by the side of your head as in A, Figure 32. Swing it straight back so that the end is behind your shoulder (B), and then throw it forward and upward over the level of your head. In releasing it there are two important things to remember: *Turn your wrist sharply downward* allowing the stick to rotate forward in your fingers so that it leans a little forward of perpendicular at the moment of release (see C, Figure 32)—this causes it to turn over in the air and start back. At the same time that this is done, give the stick a sidewise twist so that it whirs and hums in the air—this is accomplished by twisting the wrist sharply inward (to your left), thus turning the hand over so that when the stick is released the palm of the hand is up as in D. Do not use much muscle—it is all done with the forearm and wrist.

The Tumblestick will hum and whir, go up in the air a few feet, turn over, settle into a horizontal position, and float back into your hand. The course that the stick follows is illustrated in D, Figure 32.

In catching it, let it float in close to you, and then grab it with a sudden thrust of your right hand. It is easy to let the Tumblestick get away from you in attempting to catch it. Keep your eyes glued on it, and when certain of its location, snatch for it quickly and decisively. The stick is so light that there is positively no danger of injury to the fingers.

A little testing will determine whether the Tumblestick is properly balanced so that it will come back. Some sticks are erratic and turn in a different direction each time they are thrown —these should be discarded. If the stick performs in the same way each time, yet does not come right into your hands, a little experimentation should determine how it can be thrown so as to cause it to reach you. For example, if the Tumblestick, when thrown straight ahead of you as described, returns so far to the left of you that you cannot catch it, try facing straight ahead but throwing it at an angle a little toward your right side. Since it has a tendency to float to the left, this should bring it back to your hands. Similarly, if the stick tends to drift too far to your right, throw off in an oblique direction to your left.

Remember that no two boomerangs of any type can be thrown in just the same way. We must experiment with each one to find out what its peculiarities are, and then take pains to throw it in this way each time.

CHAPTER VI

Australian Boomerangs—How to Make Them

While boomerangs of the Australian type will not prove to be as interesting for general recreational use as the types described in the preceding chapters, yet a person who becomes interested in boomerangs as a hobby will certainly want to familiarize himself with them. There are several reasons why the Australian type is not so satisfying and is not recommended for general use: In the first place, these boomerangs are difficult to make—they call for heavy wood that is hard to work, and require a twist or skew which frequently exhausts the patience of the amateur. Secondly, the best of them are not as accurate in their return as the ordinary Cross-sticks and Pin-wheels which can be made in a few minutes. The primary argument against them, however, centers around the greater element of danger in their use: They are heavy and must be thrown with great force, consequently extreme caution must be taken to safeguard against injury to people or property. Their weight and shape make it unwise to attempt to catch them in any way except with the use of a net.

In favor of the Australian Boomerangs, it can be said that their use is excellent exercise. They must be thrown out-of-doors, and one must throw them hard. The fascination of attempting to make them return is such as to furnish incentive enough to keep one at it for a long time.

Certainly an adult or older boy who takes up the boomerang sport seriously will want to learn to make and throw these curved missiles perfected by the far-off Australian Bushmen. As stated in Chapter I there are two types of Australian Boomerangs, the *return type*, and the *non-return type*. Each of these will be described in turn. The methods of throwing Australian

Boomerangs are described in Chapter VIII, "How to Throw Boomerangs."

THE RETURN TYPE

The Australian Bushmen use acacia wood for the making of their boomerangs, but hickory or hard maple will answer the purpose very well. It is a waste of time to try to make boomerangs of this type out of light, soft wood.

The boomerang consists of two straight arms as illustrated in

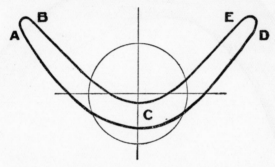

FIGURE 33. DIAGRAM OF AN AUSTRALIAN BOOMERANG

Figure 33. The circle indicates the center of gravity and the rotation of the missile around this center when the boomerang is in flight. It is possible to make boomerangs of the returning type with arms at angles of 70 to 120 degrees, although one seldom sees one with an angle of less than 90 degrees. Those made at angles of 110 to 120 degrees are the most common and the most convenient to use. Sometimes both arms are of the same length, and again one arm is an inch or two longer than the other.

One side, the bottom, remains flat whereas the top side is rounded off to a convex shape. The arms are bent slightly so that the ends (A B and D E in Figure 33) are raised above the plane of the boomerang at C as it lies on its flat side. In addition, each arm has a *skew* also; that is, the extreme end of each arm is twisted two or three degrees from a plane running through the center, so that B is below the plane and A above it, and D below it and E above it. This skew is an all-important factor and no curved boomerang will work without it when thrown from the vertical position.

These boomerangs may be made in lengths varying from eighteen inches from tip to tip up to three feet or longer. For our purpose it is recommended that an eighteen-inch or two-foot

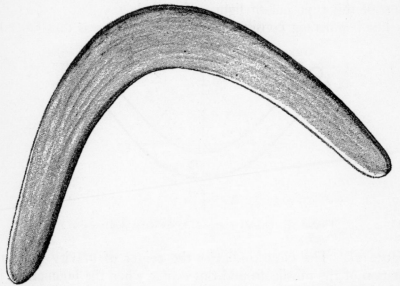

FIGURE 34. A TYPICAL AUSTRALIAN BOOMERANG OF THE RETURN TYPE

length be used. The primitive Australian Boomerang that was used for the model of Figure 34 measures twenty-one inches from tip to tip and weighs one pound. It is three inches wide at the bend, one-and-seven-eighths inches at one end, and one-and-one-half inches at the other end.

Although the proportions vary somewhat, it is a safe guide to say that the length of the wing or arm is six times its width at the widest point, and that the width of the wing is six times its thickness at the thickest point. Most primitive Australian boomerangs will not vary far from these proportions.

HOW TO MAKE THE RETURN TYPE

To make a boomerang out of one piece of wood is a most difficult task, in that it is next to impossible to bend the stick permanently into the proper angle. Once in a long time one may find in the woods a hardwood branch or root which has just

FIGURE 35. A BOOMERANG MADE BY PRESENT-DAY NATIVE AUSTRALIANS, SHOWING BURNT DECORATIONS

the right bend so that if it were stripped up, it would furnish sticks already possessing the angle necessary for a boomerang. If one were to set out to find one of these, however, he might hunt for months without success. The only other method would be to steam or soak a strip of wood and then bend it to the proper angle, keeping it in the bent position until it dries. This requires apparatus that the average person does not possess.

It is possible, however, to make an Australian-type boomerang out of two pieces of wood joined together at the bend. This is the method which we shall describe. If one is fortunate enough to secure a curved piece of wood, the wood can be worked and given the skew in just the same way that will be described for the one made of two pieces.

First make a pattern from a piece of paper twenty-one inches long by twelve inches wide. This pattern is shown in A, Figure 36. Drawn as indicated, the arms should be sixteen inches long, two-and-one-half inches wide near the angle, and one-and-one-half inches wide at the ends. Cut out the pattern, and draw two lines across it near the bend as shown in B, Figure 36.

Place the pattern on a piece of hickory, hard maple, or ash, five-sixteenths inch thick, and trace each arm of the boomerang as shown in E, Figure 36. Cut out each arm with a keyhole saw. The curved section of each arm (between the lines on the paper pattern) must now be cut into a half-lap joint as shown in C.

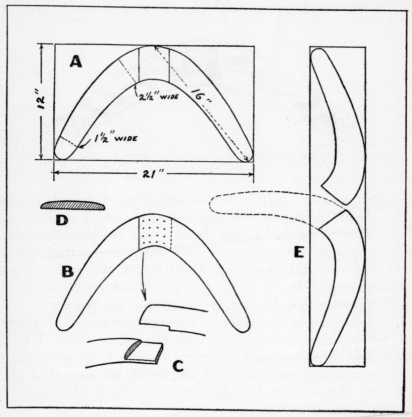

FIGURE 36. PLANS FOR MAKING AN AUSTRALIAN BOOMERANG

This can be done with a hacksaw or miter saw. Glue this joint and set in a press to dry. Then drive in some small nails to give additional support.

Now with drawknife, wood rasp, and jackknife, bevel off the edges on the top side of the boomerang and round off to a convex shape, as indicated in the diagram of the cross section in D, Figure 36. The stick remains at full width at the center, but is pulled down to a feather line at the edges.

The result now has all of the appearances of a boomerang yet it lacks the essential features that cause it to return. The two secrets here are a bend in each arm, and a skew near each end. Both the bend and the skew are so slight that the average person does not detect them in looking at the boomerang.

The Dihedral Angle.—The arms should be bent before they are skewed. The bend consists of a very slight turn upward, that is, toward the convex side. To accomplish this, hold the arm of the boomerang over a flame so that the flame hits it at a point two-thirds of the distance from the end to the curve. When the wood is hot place the heated spot against the edge of a table and press hard, thus bending the arm slightly. The bend thus caused will remain permanently. Bend the other arm in the same way.

After these bends have been properly made each arm will possess a slight dihedral angle. When it is placed on the bench with the flat side down, the ends of the arms will be slightly higher than the middle section of the boomerang. This angle is so slight, however, that a casual observance of the boomerang would not detect it.

The Skew.—It is now necessary to give each end of the boomerang a slight skew. Referring to Figure 33, which represents the convex side of the boomerang, the end must be so skewed that A is above the plane running through the center and B is below it. Similarly the other end must be so skewed that E is above the plane and D below it.

To accomplish this skew, heat the end of the boomerang over a gas burner for a distance of about four inches. When hot, grip the end with a pair of heavy pliers held in one hand, and grip the arm four inches from the end with another pair of pliers held in the other hand. Bend the arm two or three degrees in the desired direction and hold for a moment or so.

Now throw the boomerang and if it does not return properly

increase the skew a little. Continue to experiment by increasing and decreasing the skew until you get the results you want.

Very seldom does one see a description of how boomerangs are made which makes any mention of the bend in the arms or of the skew. Both are essential. It is absolutely impossible to make a boomerang of this type return or even swing to the left with an indication of returning unless the arms are given a skew in the direction indicated above. The secret of the curved boomerang of the Australian type is in the skew.

THE NON-RETURN TYPE

The non-return type of boomerang employed by the Australian Bushmen for hunting and warfare will travel for great distances with uncanny accuracy. As made by the Bushmen, these boomerangs vary from six inches in length to four feet. The big boomerang from Australia which was used for the model

FIGURE 37. A BIG HUNTING BOOMERANG OF THE NON-RETURN TYPE

of Figure 37 measures exactly four feet in length and weighs three-and-one-fourth pounds; it is two-and-one-fourth inches wide at the middle section, this width remaining constant through the greater length of the boomerang; the tapering starts near the ends and comes down to one-and-three-fourths inches near each tip.

It will be noted that most boomerangs of this type are sickle-shaped and do not possess the sharp angle that is characteristic of the return type. This is not an essential feature, however, in that the models with a sharp curve will, if made correctly, perform in the same way.

Non-return boomerangs are made by exactly the same method

described for the return-type with one important exception: the skew at the end of each arm is in the reverse direction from that found in the return type. That is, B in Figure 33 is higher than the plane of the boomerang and A is lower; similarly D is above the plane and E below it. The skew is made by the method already described for the return boomerang.

When thrown in a position vertical to the ground this type of boomerang will travel for a long way without swerving to the right or left. It can be made to come back, however, if it is thrown from a position parallel to the ground as described on page 87, Chapter VIII. In this case it rises at a steady angle to a great height and then glides and volplanes down to the thrower.

CHAPTER VII

Miniature Boomerangs of Cardboard

Like the circus, the little boomerangs of cardboard are supposed to be stuff for the amusement of children, but curiously enough they find an equally robust following among grown-ups, which latter usually make them on the pretext of amusing the children but in fact are equally intrigued by them themselves. Certainly any one, old or young, who finds a hobby in boomerang making and throwing will put in happy hours with these little cardboard floats, while sitting around the house in the evening. Requiring but a few feet of space, they can be safely twirled in any room of the house.

A clever turn may be given to a boomerang-throwing act or demonstration by inserting one or two of these tiny boomerangs between the throws of the big and far-flying wooden boomerangs. The sudden change in size from the huge to the tiny is always a good trick of the stage.

A pair of scissors and a piece of cardboard will make boomerangs of every style described in these chapters, and the making is a task of but a moment or two. Any kind and weight of cardboard may be used, ranging from the thin pasteboard back of a writing tablet up to the very heavy board, the only requirement being that the pasteboard be solid and not of the corrugated type.

The heavier the cardboard the larger the boomerang may be. The dimensions given in this chapter are for pasteboard of the weight customarily used on the back of a writing tablet. If heavier cardboard is used, increase the dimensions accordingly.

CARDBOARD CROSS-STICK BOOMERANGS

On a piece of cardboard eight-and-one-half inches square, mark out the cross shown in Figure 38, making the wings one inch wide. Then cut it out with a pair of scissors. Give each wing a slight bend upward with the fingers at a point about two inches from the end. Do not bend it enough to break or crease

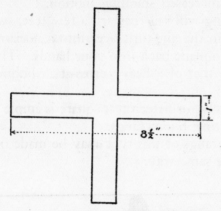

FIGURE 38. A CARDBOARD CROSS-STICK BOOMERANG

the cardboard, but rather just enough to give it a slight curve. This is all there is to it and the boomerang is now complete.

Now to throw it: Hold the boomerang between the thumb

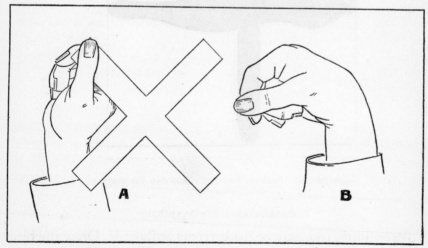

FIGURE 39. THROWING THE LITTLE CARDBOARD CROSS-STICK

and forefinger and turn the wrist back as in A, Figure 39. Throw it by snapping the wrist forward quickly and as you do so let the boomerang rotate forward between the thumb and forefinger so as to give it increased spinning motion.

The boomerang will sail forward a few feet, swing to the left and rise higher in the air, turn over into a horizontal plane, and then glide and volplane back into your hands. The performance is strikingly like that of a heavy cross-stick boomerang made of wood.

A space of twelve or fifteen feet square is ample room in which to throw these tiny boomerangs.

Larger boomerangs of this type may be made of heavier cardboard in just the same way.

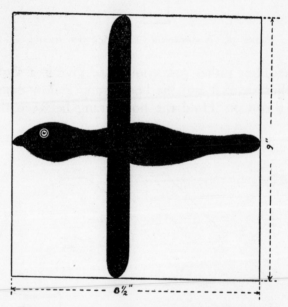

FIGURE 40. DIAGRAM FOR THE CARDBOARD BOOMABIRD

CARDBOARD BOOMABIRDS

Boomabirds, too, may be made from cardboard. Draw the bird on a piece of cardboard measuring eight-and-one-half inches wide by nine inches long, as illustrated in Figure 40. The body of the bird is one-and-three-eighths-inches wide at the widest point, and eight-and-one-half inches long. The wings are about an inch wide at the widest point and measure nine inches from tip to tip. Cut out the bird with scissors and bend the end of each wing, also the head and the tail, upward slightly as was done in making the cardboard Cross-stick described above.

The Boomabird is thrown in just the same way as is the cardboard Cross-stick. Its flight follows a course that resembles quite typically that of a large wooden Boomabird.

It is also possible to propel the Boomabird by snapping it from a book, following the method described for the cardboard Australian boomerang in the following section. Its flight in this case is very different than if thrown with the hand.

CURVED CARDBOARD BOOMERANGS

A cardboard boomerang resembling in outline the curved boomerangs used by the Bushman of Australia is illustrated in Figure 41. When made of light cardboard, the arms should be an inch wide, one of them five inches long and the other about a half inch shorter. No bend or curve in the wings is necessary in this boomerang. Merely cut it out and it is ready to throw.

Lay the boomerang on a book allowing one end to project over the

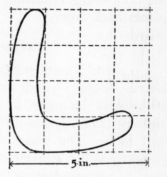

FIGURE 41. "THROWING" A CURVED BOOMERANG MADE OF CARDBOARD

edge about an inch, as shown in Figure 41. Hold the book containing the boomerang in the left hand and a pencil in the right, as illustrated. Give the boomerang a sharp rap with the pencil, thus sending it forward and upward. Or, if you choose, discard the pencil and snap it with the finger.

The boomerang will sail forward and upward eight or ten feet, turn and glide directly back in practically the same plane in which it rose.

It will be noted that this boomerang is not thrown from the vertical position as is the pasteboard Cross-stick Boomerang, nor can it be thrown in this way. Consequently the course of its flight is different. When snapped from the horizontal position, its flight resembles that of a heavy Australian-style boomerang of the non-return type when such a wooden boomerang is thrown from a horizontal position. That is, it sails forward and upward, the boomerang remaining in a horizontal position, and then volplanes back down.

CARDBOARD TUMBLESTICKS

Excellent Tumblesticks may be made from lightweight cardboard. Using a length of eight-and-one-half inches, the Tumblesticks may be made in the following widths: one-and-seven-eighths inches, one-and-three-eighths inches, one inch, and one-half inch. The wider they are the slower they rotate when thrown! When heavier cardboard is used the length and width may be increased accordingly.

No description of how to throw cardboard Tumblesticks is necessary here in that they are thrown in precisely the same way as the large wooden Tumblesticks described on page 62.

If one fails in his efforts to make a wooden Tumblestick return, and thus reaches the decision that a straight missile cannot be thrown so that it will come back, all that is necessary to convince him is to have him try one of the cardboard Tumblesticks. If properly thrown as described in Chapter V, they are practically "fool proof."

CHAPTER VIII

How to Throw Boomerangs

All the sport of boomerang making is but preliminary to the joy of throwing. And any one who has never made a boomerang and thrown it for the first time, can scarcely realize the thrill that results as it comes floating back, circles over his head, and settles in his hands. It is worth many times over the labor required for the making.

Most people have the idea that skill in throwing boomerangs can be developed only by long and arduous practice, yet such is far removed from the fact. The skill rests in the making more than in the throwing. Given a perfect boomerang, any novice of average athletic ability will find himself catching it regularly after a half hour of practice, provided the instructions in this chapter are carefully followed.

There are of course many "tricks of the trade" in boomerang throwing which are acquired only from experience, but such is true in any sport. Each boomerang offers a problem all its own, and varying conditions of space and weather contribute added complications. The veteran sizes up these factors at a glance, whereas the novice must learn by trial and error. But after all is said and done, given a good boomerang and proper air conditions, success comes more quickly than in many sports that might be mentioned. However, it is absolutely necessary that careful attention be given to the fundamental techniques described in the following pages—the veteran performs these without giving conscious attention to them whereas the beginner must study each movement.

For some unexplainable reason, boomerangs will return accurately when thrown so as to curve from right to left but cannot be caused to return satisfactorily or consistently from left to right. It would seem that a good Pin-wheel, for example, which works perfectly when thrown so as to curve to the left, would, if turned around, circle to the right with equal accuracy. Such, however, is not the case, and no one has been able to offer a satisfactory explanation. A left-handed person would naturally reverse the position of the boomerang and throw it with the left hand, and the normal flight of such a throw would be from left to right. Within my experience, however, I have never found a person who was consistently successful with such a throw. The result is that left-handed people either throw with the right hand, or hold the boomerang in the left hand in such a way as to cause it to swing to the left. Occasionally a boomerang is found that can be made to fly in both directions, but after experimenting with countless boomerangs of all types over a long period, the conclusion must be reached that *boomerangs perform accurately and consistently only when thrown so as to curve from right to left.* Mysterious, indeed, but it is a fact nevertheless!

All boomerangs except the Tumblesticks are thrown in practically the same way. Consequently, the instructions in this chapter will apply in a general way to all types—Cross-sticks, Pin-wheels, Boomabirds, and curved Australian Boomerangs. Where there are exceptions, attention will be called to the fact. The instructions for throwing Tumblesticks are given in Chapter V, "Tumblesticks—How to Make and Throw Them."

Before any thought can be given to the methods of throwing, we must first think about any elements of danger that may be involved. No one would want to be responsible for hurting a bystander or injuring property, not to mention breaking his boomerang which probably would be the result if it collided with an object.

AVOIDING ACCIDENTS

First off, let the fact be clear that this book does not recommend the general use of curved boomerangs of the Australian type. The Cross-sticks, Pin-wheels, and Boomabirds are safe and harmless when used with a little ordinary common sense such as is exercised in archery, swimming, horseback riding, shot putting, and scores of other sports. The heavy Australian Boomerangs are dangerous except when used by mature and careful people. Their use should be confined to large, open areas, and to times when none but the throwers are present. Except under very careful supervision, they have no place on playgrounds, in camps or similar areas. *Substitute for them the light and safe Cross-sticks and Boomabirds—they are more efficient and more enjoyable anyway.*

Assuming that the boomerangs are of the type recommended in these chapters, there is no more danger in their use than in most other sports provided the same degree of precaution is exercised. There is some danger in any game in which a ball is thrown, but this does not prohibit ball games—neither should it rule out boomerang throwing. With common sense in the driving seat, boomerang throwing may safely take place either in a gymnasium or outdoors.

In the interest of safety, common sense dictates that the following regulations should always be carefully observed:

1. Always have the spectators and bystanders gather in a group to your right. The boomerangs curve from right to left, and consequently offer no danger to those who are gathered to the thrower's right. If a boomerang does reach them it will be on its return trip and its force will be spent—it will settle down gently and harmlessly.

2. *Never throw when people are scattered about the area,* even though they all know the throw is coming and are watching. Since a boomerang curves, the spectators cannot always judge which way it will turn. Even though these light boomerangs probably would not do serious damage, *safety first* is the rule always. An expert performer can manipulate boomerangs around people, even to the point of throwing them from the stage of a theater, but such stunts are not for novices.

3. *Never throw without first yelling a warning* so that every one is informed and can watch.

4. *Never throw a boomerang in a strong wind.* The wind will carry it far from where you intend it to go.

5. *Tighten the bolt securely before throwing*—if it loosens, the boomerang may fall unexpectedly.

6. *Never throw a boomerang near a building*—it may find a window.

THROWING

The would-be boomerang thrower immediately comes face to face with a most serious problem: the wind blows his boomerangs all over the lot. And if there is much breeze blowing, there is no way to prevent such a happening. Some of the heavy curved boomerangs of the Australian type are at their best in a breeze since they are not accurate enough to return without the help of the wind, but not so with the Cross-sticks, Pin-wheels, and Boomabirds—these are made to return perfectly when the air is calm, and so cannot be expected to stay true to their course when buffeted by the breeze. Even an expert performer would appear to a bad advantage if forced to work in the wind.

For perfect performance and complete satisfaction, a large gymnasium is the boomerang thrower's dream. All but the large and heavy boomerangs can be thrown in the average-sized school gymnasium. In the theater, the circus tent, and the gymnasium there is no wind to defeat us. Given a calm day when the air is still or the breeze very slight, there is great joy to be had in outdoor boomerang throwing, particularly in using the Boomabirds. Usually there is less movement of the air in the evening than at other times of the day. When a new boomerang is being tried out, it is better to test it in a gymnasium or when there is perfect calm outdoors; otherwise one cannot tell whether it is made just right or not.

This leads us to the first two important rules of throwing boomerangs outdoors: First, pick a calm day when there is little or no breeze; and second, always throw directly into the breeze—handled in this way, the devastating effect of a slight breeze can be quite effectually overcome. The boomerang of course moves with greater force on its outward journey than on its return. When thrown against the wind, the wind assists rather than blocks it in making its turn. An absolutely calm day very seldom occurs. The leaves may be motionless and the lake like a mirror, yet there are air motions that a delicate boomerang will instantly register. The direction of the breeze may be located by wetting one's finger and holding it up in all directions. Better still, throw a light boomerang of perfect action once in every direction. This will settle the matter beyond controversy—it will come back more perfectly when thrown in one certain direction and that direction should be used for all throwing at that time.

THE STANDARD OR VERTICAL THROW

Throwing the Cross-sticks and Boomabirds.—Hold the boomerang in the right hand, gripped rather loosely but securely as near the end of one wing as possible. Place it in the straight up-and-down position shown in B, Figure 42, directly perpendicular to the ground. The beveled or convex side must be toward you. If you are left-handed, either try to throw the boomerang from your right hand, or hold it in the left hand with the beveled side *away* from you.

From the position shown in A, Figure 43, draw the arm back to the position in B, being careful not to tilt the boomerang side-wise. Throw it straight forward as in C, and just as you release it, turn the wrist and forearm sharply downward as in D, the latter movement being made in order to give the boomerang as much spin as possible. A great deal of muscle is not necessary, but it is usually essential that you give it an emphatic spin by turning your wrist downward in releasing. The entire throwing movement is more one of the forearm than of the entire arm, especially in handling boomerangs of ordinary size.

If the boomerang fails to return as it should, it may be that you are unconsciously turning it or "slicing" it at an angle in releasing it. This is a common fault among beginners. People who play tennis seem to be particularly troubled in this respect at the start—they are often inclined to give their forearm a slight turn as in cutting the ball while serving in tennis. This of course turns the boomerang and the throw goes awry. Check to see that you are throwing straight forward and releasing the boomerang without tilting or twisting it.

If, after a thorough trial, the boomerang does not return, try holding it at one of the angles shown in A and C, Figure 42.

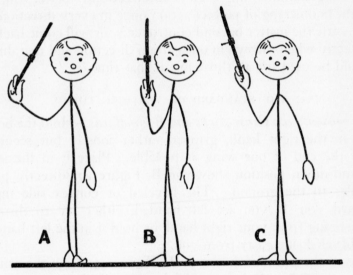

FIGURE 42.   ANGLES AT WHICH BOOMERANGS ARE HELD IN THROWING

Which of these angles to use is determined by how the boomerang acts when thrown from the vertical position. If the boomerang cuts in too soon each time and falls in front of you, it must be thrown from the position in C—tilt it slightly *away* from you when you throw it and it should return directly to you. On the other hand, if the boomerang does not cut in soon enough and is of the type that persists in swinging around behind you and falling to the ground, it should be thrown from the angle in A—tilt it slightly *toward* you.

Remember that no two boomerangs can be thrown in precisely the same way. We must become familiar with each boomerang and determine by experience just how it must be thrown for best results. It is no reflection on the worth of a boomerang if it cannot be thrown from the up-and-down position shown in B, Figure 42, but requires one of the inclined positions in A and C. Many of the finest of boomerangs require one of these slanting throws. Once you discover the proper angle, make a note on the back side of the boomerang so that you can tell at a glance what to do with it.

Now the type-perfect Cross-stick or Boomabird must be

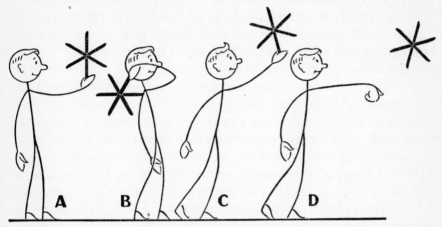

FIGURE 43. THROWING THE PIN-WHEEL, ILLUSTRATING THE VERTICAL THROW USED FOR MOST TYPES OF BOOMERANGS

thrown straight out at the level of the head and parallel to the ground. It will rise higher of its own accord as it starts to turn and will then settle down within easy reach of the hands on its return. If thrown higher into the air, it will sail over the head and out of reach. However, individual boomerangs differ as much here as in any other respect. Some must be thrown at an angle of at least forty-five degrees into the air. Experimentation is the only rule in discovering the proper angle, and once it is determined, it should be noted with pencil on the back of the boomerang.

Similarly, some boomerangs must be thrown with great force,

some with average speed, and others very gently. And once this item is ascertained, a note to that effect should be made on the boomerang.

There are thus three items that should be recorded with pencil on the back side of the boomerang: (1) the angle at which it should be held, whether A, B, or C, as shown in Figure 42; (2) the angle at which it should be thrown into the air, whether high, medium or low; (3) the speed with which it should be thrown. The notations are not only a great convenience always, but are indispensable when one is throwing a number of boomerangs, one after the other, as in an exhibition of boomerang throwing. A glance at the back and we know definitely how to handle each boomerang and what to expect of it. The spectators of course are not aware that any notations are being used. Since typical performance would require the straight up-and-down position (B, Figure 42), average speed, and a throw straight out and parallel to the ground, these can be taken as standard, and notations made only on the boomerangs that depart from this pattern. If no notations are to be seen, we assume that the boomerang is held and thrown in the usual way. And again, if only one of the three items is noted, the assumption is that the boomerang is handled typically in the other respects. Thus, if the penciled notation reads "C, high, easy" we know that it must be tilted slightly outward, and thrown gently at a high angle into the air. Whereas if the notation merely said "A," we assume that if it is held so that it is tilted slightly inward, it will come back if thrown straight out and with average speed.

Once in a long time a boomerang that is usually dependable will fly forward a few feet, turn suddenly to the right, and nose-dive to the ground. This is called "back firing" and is a bad fault against which definite precautions must be taken. It is due to the fact that at the moment of release the boomerang was held so that the front wing was pointed a little to the right rather than straight ahead, and the force of the throw caused the air to catch it and turn it to the right. Boomerangs two feet in size or smaller can usually be grasped between the thumb and forefinger at a point an inch or two above the end of the wing. Held in this way, the pressure of the thumb against the bevel of the wing turns the front wing a little further to the left and prevents any possibility of "back firing." With experience, a person develops the knack of throwing the boomerang in such a way that "back firing" seldom if ever occurs. However, if a boomerang "back fires" often, *discard it*. It could not have a worse fault. Like some horses, some boomerangs will always remain obstreperous and persist in bucking when you least expect them to. Such are good only for kindling wood.

It is the glory of a good boomerang that you can depend upon it to travel in precisely the same way every time it is sent forth.

Throwing the Curved Australian Boomerang.—The curved Australian Boomerangs of the *return* type are thrown just as described above except that they must be hurled with great force as compared to the other types, and are given the spin or revolving motion in a different way. Just as the boomerang is released, the hand is given a sharp upward jerk. This sharp jerk is important because without it the boomerang will spin lazily at the start and will not have enough revolving motion to make the return journey. Most Australian Boomerangs will perform correctly if thrown from the straight up-and-down position illustrated in B, Figure 42. It is seldom necessary to throw from the positions shown in A and C.

The average boomerang of the return type will go forward thirty to fifty yards before swinging to the left, then rise high in the air, and volplane back.

The *non-return* type is thrown in just the same way if the object is to hurl it accurately at a target some distance away. It is possible to throw these non-return boomerangs so that they will come back, but this method is described in the following section on the horizontal throw.

THE FLAT OR HORIZONTAL THROW

Throwing the Cross-sticks and Boomabirds.—Hold the boomerang in the right hand parallel to the ground, that is, at an angle of forty-five degrees in respect to the ground, with the beveled or curved side up, as shown in Figure 44. Throw it forward and upward, giving it as much spin as possible with the wrist in releasing it. It will sail high up into the air, hesitate, and then glide and volplane back in practically the same plane as in the ascent. This is not as spectacular a throw as the vertical but it is interesting as a variation. Not all boomerangs will work when thrown in this way. Occasionally a balanced Cross-stick is

FIGURE 44. THE FLAT OR HORIZONTAL THROW

found that can be thrown from either the vertical or horizontal position. Usually, however, a Cross-stick designed to be thrown from the horizontal position should be made with shorter and wider wings, and the wings should have only a very slight upward bend or none at all. An ideal size is made of two sticks eighteen inches long, one-and-one-fourth inches wide and one-eighth inch thick.

Some boomerangs must be thrown in a way that is a cross between the vertical and horizontal methods. They must be tilted at a wide angle away from you, much wider than that illustrated in C, Figure 42, yet not so far as to be in the horizontal position shown in Figure 44. The Two-wing Cross-sticks (Figures 15, 16, and 17) and the Fans (Figure 24) are of this type. In flight, these boomerangs follow the typical course of the boomerangs thrown from the horizontal position—they sail out and up at an angle of about forty-five degrees, then volplane back in practically the same plane.

Throwing the Curved Australian Boomerangs of the Non-Return Type.—The curved Australian Boomerangs of the *non-return* type may be caused to return by throwing them from the horizontal position. When thrown from the *vertical* position they go straight forward with great accuracy, wavering not at all to the right or left, but when thrown from the *flat* or *horizontal* position, they go high up in the air and then glide back to the thrower in essentially the same plane. These boomerangs have a reverse or backward skew in the arms, as described in Chapter VI, which accounts for the difference in action.

Frequently one finds in the stores commercial boomerangs supposedly of the *return* type which have all the appearances of good Australian Boomerangs but which fail to return when thrown in the normal way from the vertical position. These boomerangs usually are at fault in that they do not have a skew in the arms. As a rule these can be thrown somewhat successfully from the flat or horizontal position.

CHARACTERISTIC FLIGHTS OF BOOMERANGS

No two boomerangs perform in exactly the same way. Each has a temperament of its own and certain habits of flight that give it a personality differing from all others. This is one of the chief reasons why people become so thoroughly absorbed in boomerangs as a hobby. They keep on making more and more, knowing that each one will differ slightly from all others in its ways of behaving, and that these ways cannot be anticipated accurately until the boomerang has been thrown and its habits studied.

Figure 45 shows typical courses followed by boomerangs in their flight; there are of course endless variations of each of these.

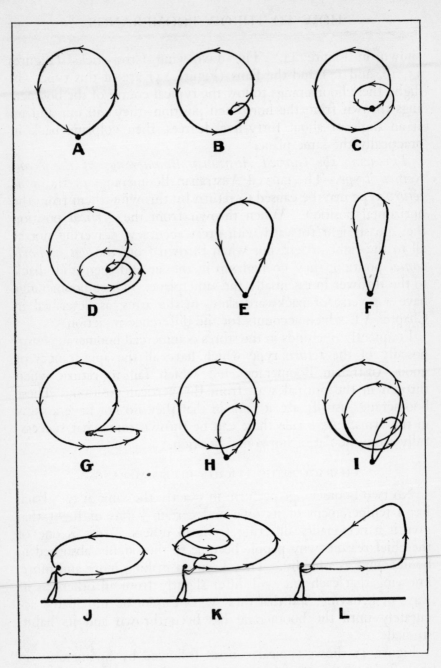

FIGURE 45. CHARACTERISTIC FLIGHTS OF BOOMERANGS

Some boomerangs are inclined toward circular flights as shown in Figures A to D, while others tend toward an oblong or somewhat of an egg-shaped flight as illustrated in E; still others go a long distance, turn around rather abruptly, and come back in almost a straight line, as diagrammed in F.

Light-weight Cross-sticks follow a circular course as a rule. Some cut a circle in front of the thrower and come in to his left side as shown in A. Others will swing around and come up behind him, or come in from his right side, as shown in B. Still others will make a circle and a half before reaching him and come in from his left side, as in C.

Light-weight Pin-wheels act much like the Cross-sticks. A, B and C illustrate their typical courses. Those with short wings are inclined to follow the patterns in A and B, whereas those with the long wings often stay in the air longer and follow the course shown in C.

A heavy Pin-wheel with short wings, similar to that illustrated in Figure 21 on page 43, frequently follows the delightful course shown in D, rising high in the air and circling three times before reaching the thrower.

Very heavy Cross-sticks and Pin-wheels with long wings tend toward the more oblong courses shown in E and F.

The Boomabirds with their wide bodies rotate slowly and stay in the air a long time, their flights forming the patterns shown in G, H, and I. G shows a very characteristic flight of a Boomabird when given a gentle throw. Forceful throws will often send them through the courses of H and I.

The curved Australian boomerangs go straight forward for a long distance, swing to the left and cut back, following a course similar to that shown in E.

Diagrams A to I in Figure 45 show how the flights of boomerangs would appear if one could look down on them from above. Boomerangs also perform differently, one from another, in the elevation from the ground that they reach in the course of the flight.

The light Cross-sticks and Pin-wheels go forward vertically

for some distance at the level at which they were thrown, then circle to the left, turn over on the flat side and rise slightly in the air, remaining at the higher level until they near the thrower. Viewed from a point to the right of the thrower, the flight appears as shown in J, Figure 45. The Boomabirds and the heavier Pin-wheels go forward in much the same way, but as they turn to the left they often rise high in the air, turn over on the flat side, circling and double circling, and finally settle down to the thrower —Figure K illustrates such a course as it would appear viewed from the right of the thrower.

The Australian boomerangs, although varying in detail, all follow a rather characteristic, parabolic course. They go forward a long way in almost a straight line, turn rather abruptly to the left and at the same time rise high in the air; at the highest point they turn over so that they are parallel to the ground, flat side down, and then glide and volplane down to the thrower. Figure L indicates this course as it would appear from the right side of the thrower.

CATCHING BOOMERANGS

No matter how accurately a boomerang returns, if the thrower does not catch it, the impression created is one of failure. To "muff" it is worse in its effect than if the thrower had to walk a few steps to reach it—the spectators may not notice the steps in that their eyes are probably on the boomerang, but they cannot fail to see the miss in catching.

The method used in catching depends upon whether the boomerang is held together with a long or short bolt. Given a short bolt, it is caught by the wings, whereas with a long bolt, it is caught by the bolt. There is a third method sometimes used for curved Australian boomerangs—that of catching them in a net. Nets are useless for other types of boomerangs. A trick method of catching boomerangs on the head is described later in this chapter under the section on "Trick Stunts."

CATCHING BY THE WINGS

Do not attempt to catch the boomerang with one hand. To do so presents two hazards: the odds are in favor of missing it in that the spinning wings are hard to judge and to secure, and

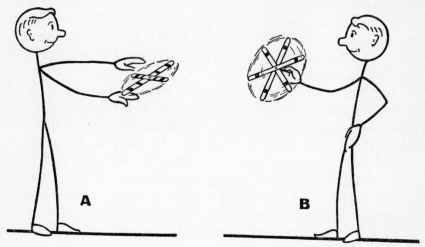

FIGURE 46. TWO WAYS OF CATCHING THE CROSS-STICKS

there is danger of bruising the fingers if they are thrust into the circling wings.

To catch it, *hold one hand above it and the other below it, and clap the hands together*, as shown in A, Figure 46. It is pretty hard to miss by this method if the boomerang is within easy reach, and the danger of injury is so negligible as to be practically non-existent. This method is safe and sure.

CATCHING BY THE BOLT

The presence of a four-inch bolt (see page 20) simplifies greatly the process of catching the boomerang, and at the same time adds much to the picture since the boomerang continues to spin after it is caught. The average spectator will not detect the bolt and consequently wonders how the boomerang is being held so that it continues to spin. True, the bolt is small and is often hard to see, but nevertheless it offers less grief and insures more consistent success than otherwise, and withal is more spectacular and picturesque. Happily, most Pin-wheels and Cross-sticks, as they approach you on their return, turn the flat or back side toward you, and consequently present the bolt in a position that is very easy to grasp.

As the boomerang comes in, keep your eye glued on the bolt but do not reach out with your hand until it is in position to catch. Merely hold your hand up and in readiness. When the boomerang is where you want it, shove your hand out quickly and grab the bolt firmly and emphatically. To reach out with your hand and follow the motion of the bolt with it often results in the boomerang getting away. When you are sure you know just where the bolt is, snatch it suddenly. In doing so, however, be careful not to stop the flight too abruptly; rather, let your hand move along with the boomerang a foot or so and then swing it around in front of you with a graceful curve and at the same rate of speed at which the boomerang was moving. The Pin-wheel in B, Figure 46, has just been captured by the bolt.

CATCHING WITH A NET

There is no way to catch an Australian Boomerang of the curved type in the hands with anything approaching safety. They are as dangerous to the thrower as to the spectators. Better let them alone entirely. However, if they are used, do not attempt to catch them in any way except with a net. Secure a net frame of the size of a large butterfly net, equipped with a three-foot handle. Attach a net made of heavy mesh, such as is used in tennis nets. If the Australian Boomerang comes close enough to you, snatch it in the net. Do not bother with nets in catching other types of boomerangs.

TRICK STUNTS

Here are some interesting trick throws that are excellent for use in boomerang-throwing exhibitions. These will require long practice but can be easily mastered by those who are familiar with the goings and comings of boomerangs and the techniques of throwing and catching.

THROWING TWO BOOMERANGS IN SUCCESSION

Pick out two Pin-wheels that are mates in size and in action, each having a long bolt with which to catch it. Hold one boomerang in each hand. Throw the boomerang that is in the right hand, immediately transfer the other to the right hand, and throw it as quickly as possible. The first boomerang will return a few seconds before the other—catch it by the bolt in the right hand and then catch the other in the left. Allow both boomerangs to continue to spin in your hands after catching.

This is not a difficult feat to learn. Be sure to throw the second boomerang just as quickly as possible after the first in order to give yourself time to get your bearings and get set for the catch. When both boomerangs are in the air, do not glance at the second until the first has been caught—if you do you will probably catch neither of them.

THROWING TWO BOOMERANGS AT ONCE

Select two small Cross-sticks that are perfect mates in size and action. Each should be held together with wire, rather than a bolt, as described on page 18. Lay one boomerang on top of the other and grasp both in the right hand. Throw the two just as if only one was being hurled. Shortly after they leave the hand they will separate and follow separate courses, but both will return and within a second or two of each other. If they are close enough together when they return (which isn't apt to happen), catch both at once by slapping them together with the hands. Otherwise, catch the first to return by clapping the hands on it, and, letting it lie on the lower hand, catch the second in the same way on top of it.

Sticks eighteen inches long, one-and-one-fourth inches wide, and one-eighth inch thick will make boomerangs that are ideal for this stunt.

FOUR IN THE AIR AT ONCE

This is the combination of the two preceding stunts. Four small Cross-stick boomerangs are needed of the size described in the foregoing paragraph for throwing two boomerangs at once. Arrange the boomerangs in pairs, one on top of the other, and hold one pair in the right hand and the other pair in the left. Throw the pair in the right hand, immediately transfer the pair in the left hand to the right, and throw them in the same way. Catch the boomerangs as they return by slapping the hands together on them. In catching, hold the left hand above the right, and let the boomerangs remain in the right hand after they are caught, catching each succeeding one on top of the others. To perform this one, you must be alert and do some fast grabbing.

FIGURE 47. CATCHING THEM ON YOUR HEAD

CATCHING A BOOMERANG ON THE HEAD

Secure a tin-can cover that is about five inches in diameter. Attach it to a piece of elastic that is just long enough so that when the cover is placed on the top of the head, the band will slip snugly under the chin. A rivet will hold the cover and elastic together.

Select a slow-floating Pin-wheel that returns at a height a little above the level of the head and settles gently down. It should be held together with a long bolt.

Place the cover on the top of the head and throw the boomerang in the usual way. As the Pin-wheel returns, place the head under it and catch the bolt in the can cover, as shown in Figure 47. It will continue to spin on top of the head with a most picturesque effect. The stunt requires a boomerang that habitually returns at just the right level. At best, it will require practice.

Fred Stone, the famous and versatile comedian, performed this stunt spectacularly with a heavy Pin-wheel thrown out over the audience in the theatre.

PLAYING CATCH WITH A BOOMERANG

In this interesting feat, two people stand a few feet apart. One throws a boomerang so that it circles and is caught by the other on its return trip. This stunt can easily be done on the stage—the performers stand on opposite sides of the stage, as far front as possible, and the one at the right throws the boomerang out over the heads of the audience so that it is caught by his partner on the left of the stage.

Much experimentation will be necessary to find the boomerang that will do this stunt. In trying out new boomerangs, we sometimes find one that for some reason will not return all the way back but drops far over to the left and behind the thrower. Such a boomerang should be excellent for this stunt. Then, too, there are the boomerangs that are perfect in action, but which circle all the way around the thrower before returning, passing him far to the left on the first backward flight. These also are usable.

Experimentation will also be necessary to determine just how far apart the two partners in the stunt should stand for any particular boomerang. This distance should be at least fifteen feet if the stunt is to be at all impressive.

BOOMERANG THROWING CONTESTS

Playgrounds, camps, clubs, and schools that feature boomerang making and throwing in their programs will find that a boomerang-throwing meet will be enthusiastically received and will serve as an excellent climax to the period devoted to the making and practicing. The following events will prove suggestive for such a competition.

In all these events, a participant should not be permitted to use boomerangs that he did not make himself.

The events should take place in a large gymnasium, or if outdoors, on a very calm day. Remember that there is usually less breeze in the evening than during the day.

ACCURACY THROWING CONTEST

Mark a circle about one foot in diameter on the floor or ground. With one foot in this circle, the contestant throws his boomerang and catches it when it returns. He is not permitted to remove his foot from the circle, although he may turn around at will in following the course of the flight.

Each contestant is given ten throws in succession and is awarded one point for each catch. The one making the highest score wins. In case of a tie, the winners throw again.

Any type of boomerang may be used and a contestant may change boomerangs during the contest if he chooses.

CONTEST IN THROWING TWO BOOMERANGS AT ONCE

One boomerang is placed on top of another and the two are thrown as one (see page 93). Each contestant is given ten attempts and scores one point each time he catches both boomerangs. To catch only one counts nothing. The conditions are the same as in the Accuracy Throwing Contest.

CONTEST IN THROWING TWO BOOMERANGS IN SUCCESSION

The contestant throws two boomerangs, one immediately after the other, and then attempts to catch them both, as described on page 93. Each is allowed ten throws and one point is scored each time both boomerangs are caught. In other respects, the conditions described for the Accuracy Throwing Contest apply.

LONGEST FLYING BOOMERANG

This contest determines the boomerang that can stay in the air the longest time. Some boomerangs float for a long time, circling and double circling before returning. These are the ideal type for this contest.

The event is best conducted out-of-doors. A stopwatch is used to record the time from the second the boomerang leaves the thrower's hand until he catches it. Since this is a contest between boomerangs, a contestant may enter several boomerangs, if he chooses. Each contestant is given five throws with each boomerang, and is credited with his best time. The thrower must keep one foot in a circle twelve inches in diameter, as in the Accuracy Throwing Contest above, and if he fails to catch the boomerang legitimately, the time is not recorded although it counts as a trial.

FARTHEST TRAVELING BOOMERANG

This contest is to determine the boomerang that can travel the greatest distance from the thrower and then return to him so that he can catch it. Of course it is not possible to do more than to estimate the distance approximately. Establish a throwing spot one foot wide on which the contestant must keep one foot. The judges are scattered parallel to the line of travel. When the contestant throws, the judges mark the farthest spot over which the boomerang passed in its flight. Each is given five throws and is credited with his greatest distance. No throw is measured unless the thrower catches the boomerang.

"PLAYING CATCH" CONTEST

Two partners "play catch" with a boomerang, throwing it from one to the other, as described on page 95. The partners stand as far apart as they choose, provided there is at least fifteen feet between them. One throws the boomerang so that it reaches his partner on its return trip, who catches it. Ten throws are made and one point is credited each time a throw is caught. The pair with the highest score wins.

BOOMERANG WITH MOST UNIQUE ACTION

Some boomerangs perform peculiar stunts in the air and follow unusual courses, stunts that other boomerangs will not do. This event is won by the contestant whose boomerang, in the opinion of the judges, performs the most unique stunts in the air, or completes the most circles before returning. Each participant continues to throw until the judges are satisfied as to the characteristic action of the boomerang.

BEST STUNT WITH A BOOMERANG

This contest is won by the contestant who, in the opinion of the judges, performs the most unusual and unique stunt in throwing and catching a boomerang. Such stunts may be used as catching the boomerang on the head, throwing and catching while sitting down or lying in a prostrate position, having four boomerangs in the air at once and catching them all, and so forth.

MOST UNIQUE TYPE OF BOOMERANG

Boomerangs may be made in all sorts of unusual and bizarre shapes, based upon the standard types described in the preceding chapters. This contest is won by the contestant who, in the opinion of the judges, displays the most unique type of boomerang. No boomerang is considered unless the thrower can catch it without stepping, at least five times out of ten trials.

BIGGEST BOOMERANG

The biggest boomerang that can be caught by the thrower without stepping wins this contest.

SMALLEST BOOMERANG

This contest is won by the contestant who displays the smallest boomerang made of wood, provided he demonstrates to the satisfaction of the judges that it will come back to him when thrown. The boomerang must be thrown and not snapped from a book or other object (see page 75).

PART II

THE COWBOY'S SECTION

Ropes and Whips

CHAPTER IX

Ropes and Roping

I've tried to find the cause of it, but I can't. All I can say is that I'm infected with roping fever, and it is a hopelessly incurable malady. Not that it is unpleasant in its effects or an affliction of which one would want to be relieved—rather the opposite is the truth of the matter, so deliriously happy is one under its spell. But I've been told that it is an unwholesome and pernicious disorder, for it twists the mind in such a way as to cause all things else to seem of trifling importance as compared to making a noose spin and jumping through it. And once you are through it, the most important thing in the world seems to be to get back on the side from which you just came. All of which takes time and energy away from worthwhile things. (At least, so the normal ones say.) But I know that I've got it and can't be cured of it, so I've long since quit trying to stop and just keep trying to rope. And *trying* to rope is the way to put it, for no one can rope perfectly—all he can do is to try and keep trying.

And I know, too, that this roping fever is contagious. For I can name hundreds of people that caught it from me, and are as bad off as I am. And I hope to keep on contaminating folks with it, knowing full well that they will contaminate others. While they may get less work done, they will nevertheless be happier.

However the mind may be affected by it, I am certain on the point that the roping infection has absolutely no injurious physical results. It means work—endless months and years of work. And strenuous work, too, for this matter of twirling the noose of a lariat is vigorous and lusty business. Being gripping and compelling, you drive hard toward your goal of mastery, and quit only when too weary to continue. Now, interesting physical effort never hurt any one—and if exercise is beneficial to the human system, then roping goes down as a bodily tonic *par excellence*, for no one ever roped without getting a workout.

The germ of this whole roping business came from the wild and woolly West of the American plains and mesas. True enough, ropes for catching stock antedate the American West some many years, but the lariat in its present form, and the method of handling it, are a product of those tempestuous, melodramatic days when the West was new and each man a law unto himself. And right here rests perhaps the major reason why roping possesses such an undeniable glamour for boys and men, girls and women—the rope is a symbol of all that rugged and romantic Western picture. And where is there a boy or girl in America whose pulse does not beat a little more rapidly at the thought of those gloriously picturesque days?

But there is something else to roping besides romantic symbols. Minus all this glamour of its early history, it would still compel. Explain it how you will, it gets into the blood and stays there—and this because of something intrinsic in the sport itself. The spinning noose is pleasing to the eye—gracefully floating, rhythmic, circling on and on effortlessly. It makes folks want to be the cause of the spinning themselves. There is an aesthetic something about it.

Furthermore, it is intricate—there is nothing about roping that can be easily picked up. While a few simple tricks may be quickly learned, they but pave the way to the regular feats of the art. If one devotes years to it he will still have much to learn, and will be discontented and impatient with himself for not succeeding more swiftly and fully. I have never known a roping artist of the stage, circus, or rodeo, who felt that he had mastered all there is to roping, and who did not have some other tricks in the back of his mind that he hoped some day to figure out.

The result of all this is that roping is a lifetime task. One never learns it all. Every new wrinkle he learns opens the way to still more wrinkles that he did not know existed before. It challenges and challenges, and refuses to be defeated. This all goes to label roping as a hobby with scarcely an equal. To serve its full func-

tion a hobby must be rich enough in content to furnish incentive
for a lifetime of effort. This definitely admits roping to the select
class. And roping is not one of those quiet intellectual types of
hobbies—when one ropes, he not only ropes his way to joy but to
health and strength.

You can spin the rope almost any place and any time, and the
only equipment needed is your ropes. And you do not need
others to help you—it is a one-man sport. You can even practice
in the drawing room of your home if you do not have much respect for your furniture, draperies, and the light fixtures! However, it wouldn't be quite advisable to rope in clothes that you
expect to use for any other purpose, unless you do not care
about the size of your dry-cleaning bill. Ropes have a way of
accumulating all the dirt on the lot, and transferring it to clothing
or other things that are usually expected to be kept clean.

Enough of the advantages of rope spinning as a sport or a
hobby! There is no better exercise, no more compelling and gripping individual sport, no similar play activity quite so filled with
intricacies as to challenge one to effort for a lifetime.

Rope spinning, however, can be of no practical importance to
the average person, other than for the recreation it supplies. It
will never increase his supply of stocks and bonds. Neither has
it been of any practical worth to the cowboy of the ranges—in
fact, it has often been a detriment to him, for when a perfectly
good cow-hand who can rope his steers and catch his calves,
begins to learn to spin his noose, the fever infects him to the point
where handling stock seems mundane indeed. And to make
matters worse, the other cowboys are immediately contaminated
by him until loops are whirling all over the place. Now the ranch
boss cares not at all for all this spinning business—he wants ropers
who can catch the stock and figures on them tending strictly to
the business at hand. And if too much time is consumed with
Wedding Rings and Butterflies and Ocean Waves, likely as not
the boss will issue an order that none of this rope spinning is to
be tolerated on the premises. Many a good catch-roper has moved
along to seek a new job because of his fancy for spinning nooses.

Of course, the dude ranches today have rope-spinners aplenty, which fact gives the impression that such ropers were always common in the serious life of ranching. But not so—lariat throwing is business, but rope spinning is play.

While rope spinning may have no practical use in itself, lariat throwing is replete with practical applications. Aside from its value in handling stock, it trains a person so that he can manipulate any rope effectively for any purpose. For example, a life line can be handled accurately and efficiently by a boy who can rope without any additional or special practice or training. Life buoys can be tossed more efficiently because of lassoing experience. Knots can be quickly tied and ropes thrown and handled in professional style for sailing or other purposes. The lariat itself can be used in life-saving—there are many instances on record of a drowning person being saved by the noose of a lariat being thrown over his struggling body—and this is more pleasant and certain of results than diving into the water after him. Sportsmen sometimes use their lariats in hunting—mountain lions and even polar bears have been captured by means of nothing more formidable than a lass-rope.

It should be apparent by this time that rope spinning is one thing and catch-roping is something else. The equipment is different and the movements have little in common. A head-line catch-roper might be entirely helpless with a spinning rope, and similarly, a stage rope-spinner might not be able to rope a calf if his life depended on it. There is one respect in which the two arts are interwoven—the so-called trick-and-fancy roping of the circuses and rodeos involves catching horses after a preliminary display of rope spinning. The roper spins his lariat in an Ocean Wave, jumps through it a time or two as the horse approaches, and then ropes him without stopping the spinning noose. While the two arts must be regarded as separate, yet they are similar enough in nature to go hand in hand for recreational purposes, and people interested in learning one would certainly want to know something of the other.

Ancient as the catch-rope is, rope spinning is a new wrinkle.

It was a Mexican named Vincenti Orespo who first displayed a spinning loop in this country. This was shortly before the turn of the century, and he was signed up forthwith by Buffalo Bill for his Wild West show. Orespo was a crack catch-roper but did only a few spins, which latter were sufficient, however, to claim for him the honor of originating modern rope spinning. This Mexican would be amazed today, could he see the intricacies of the modern roper's art, for the American cowboys were not slow in taking to this sport, once they got the idea.

I can wish you no greater joy than that which will result if the roping fever catches you. And I hope these pages may be the cause of your catching it and spreading it among others.

So good luck, and good roping!

PLACE IN THE SCHOOL AND RECREATIONAL PROGRAM

Any vigorous and compelling activity of the type that is apt to carry on as recreation· and beneficial exercise throughout life has a place in a school's physical-education program. Similarly, any wholesome activity that brings joy at the moment and, once the skills have been developed, gives promise of continuing to bring joy in the future, has a place in a recreational program. That roping possesses these qualifications to the majority of those who have come to know it has already been indicated—it grips and compels peculiarly. Its fascination seems never to wane. It possesses such endless variations that one never masters them all—it challenges throughout life. In short, roping instruction constitutes excellent education for leisure.

At the time it is being learned, and as long as it is practiced, roping is better exercise than the average gymnasium and playground activity in which one can engage alone and without playmates. It fills the need for strenuous physical activity. The desire for mastery is there, always serving as a driving force to vigorous effort, yet complete mastery seems never to be achieved. As a beneficial physical exercise, roping has much to recommend it.

Rope spinning is of particular interest in the field of correctives.

It is ideal exercise for that group of individuals who because of physical handicaps cannot wisely enter whole-heartedly into the team games of the average student. It can be participated in as strenuously or as leisurely as the individual desires, and can be enjoyed whether alone or in the presence of companions. The compelling interest it develops leads to practice at home as well as in the gymnasium. Roping tricks may be selected that furnish desirable exercise for the improvement of most posture mal-adjustments.

With all its other attributes which recommend it to physical education and recreation, roping has that priceless asset, *appeal to the imagination*. It brings delight beyond and above that which comes from performing a vigorous and difficult feat. It takes the roper in imagination to those romantic days of the old West that the rope invariably symbolizes.

Not only is the roper's imagination stimulated in these ways, but the spectators are similarly inspired. This being the case, roping serves admirably as a feature for exhibitions and demonstrations in the physical-education and recreation program. Few spots on the program will carry so much glamour as will a dozen or more rope spinners on the floor or field, all spinning their ropes in colorful and intricate fashion. Roping can be worked into demonstrations, pageants, and dancing exhibitions in many and intriguing ways.

Roping falls in line with the present-day trend in physical education to include new and colorful activities that have strong imaginative appeal. Few activities will have as strong a romantic touch and at the same time be as beneficial from the standpoint of wholesome exercise.

PARTS OF A ROPE

First off, let us familiarize ourselves with the parts of a lariat and the terms applied to the various sections of a spinning rope and catch-rope.

A rope used in catching animals is variously called a lariat, riata, lass-rope, catch-rope, or soga, but those who use it regularly are

inclined to call it just a rope. The term "lariat" is seldom applied
to a spinning rope—men who handle both types refer to one as a
spinning rope and the other as a catch-rope. "Lasso," coming
from the Spanish *lazo*, is seldom used as the name for a rope—it is
more commonly used as a verb referring to the act of throwing a
lariat. The word "lariat" is derived from the Spanish "la riata."

Both the spinning rope and the catch-rope, although made of
different materials, are constructed according to the same prin-

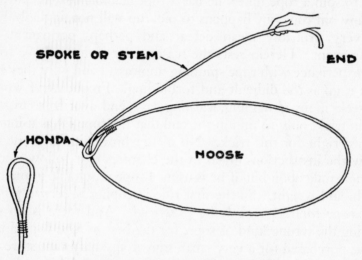

FIGURE 48. PARTS OF A SPINNING ROPE

ciple. One end of the rope is doubled back to form a small loop
or eye about two inches long—this is called a *honda* (see Figure
48). When the other end of the rope is passed through this
honda, as in Figure 48, the large loop thus formed is called a *loop*
or *noose*, and the section from the honda to the end is called the
stem or *spoke*.

THE SPINNING ROPE

Practically every boy and man has tried at some time to learn
to spin a rope. And the handiest rope being the ever-present

clothesline, it was usually pressed into service as a spinning rope. But the clothesline refused to spin! There is nothing unusual about this, for a clothesline would refuse to function in the hands of even the most expert of ropers. Often a ready-made lariat of the type designed for roping steers is secured from a western supply store by the aspiring rope-spinner. It, too, refuses to spin —and rightly so, for it is not made for spinning.

There is nothing more certain than the fact that one will never learn to spin a rope unless he has a rope suitable for the purpose. Just any old rope one happens to pick up will not fit the bill and will very probably mean defeat and perhaps permanent discouragement. Herein rests the reason why so many have found their experience with rope spinning unpleasant and why they have given it up as too difficult and forbidding. Frequently I worked for weeks in my struggling, learning days, endeavoring to master a certain trick, only to find in the end that the rope I was using was not just right for this trick. No matter how faithfully one may follow the instructions given in the chapters that follow, success will not smile upon him if he is using a rope unsuitable in material, length, and weight. So the first rule in roping is, *secure just the right rope for the trick being practiced*. And there is no need of using the wrong kind of rope, for the best of rope for spinning can be purchased for a very small sum at any hardware store.

Ordinary Manilla rope is useless for rope spinning. A good roper may be able to make it spin, but he certainly cannot do many tricks with it. Both for learning purposes and for expert performance, it is out of the question.

The rope that is needed is *braided cotton sash cord, three-eighths inch in thickness*. Of the several qualities of sash cord, the best type of *spot lariat cord* is required—the name "spot cord" is commonly given this rope because of the colored spots it contains. There are two qualities of this cord, one called *spot cord* and the other *spot lariat cord*, the latter being a harder braid manufactured especially for spinning which does not loosen up and become softened with use. Either of these cords will answer the purpose well for the average roper. Most of the larger hardware stores carry spot cord of the quality needed. Be sure to secure the three-eighths-inch thickness—this is commonly called Number 12.

The length of the rope depends upon the trick we are trying to learn or do. The flat spins described in the next chapter, which are the tricks that the beginner should learn first, require a twenty-foot rope and a fourteen-foot rope. If only one rope can be afforded, it should be twenty feet long.

Made-up spinning ropes may be purchased at a cost very slightly in excess of the cost of the rope required for making them, but there is really no need of buying a ready-made rope in that any one can prepare the rope for spinning in ten minutes.

First, it is necessary to make the honda.

MAKING THE HONDA

Double one end of the rope back, making an eye or loop, the opening of which is about two inches long. Make the loop secure by wiring it tightly with medium-weight copper wire, as illustrated in A, Figure 49. Three to six strands of wire should be sufficient to hold it—more wire may make the honda too heavy. Now wrap a strand or two of wire or a little adhesive tape around the other end of the rope to keep it from unraveling. Insert the straight end through the honda and the rope is complete and ready to use.

Many ropers prefer to use the rope without protecting the end against unraveling until it has unraveled four or five inches. They then wire it to prevent further unraveling. This produces an unraveled tassel at the end of the rope that has a nice appearance and in no way detracts from the rope's usefulness.

Some roping artists desire to protect the end of the honda from wear and so wrap it with copper wire as shown in B, Figure 49, or sew a piece of leather around it as in C. Such hondas are also often used when it is desired to give the rope a little additional weight for certain tricks. The average roper will find no use for such protected hondas, however, and certainly they should be avoided by beginners. The ideal honda is shown in A, Figure 49.

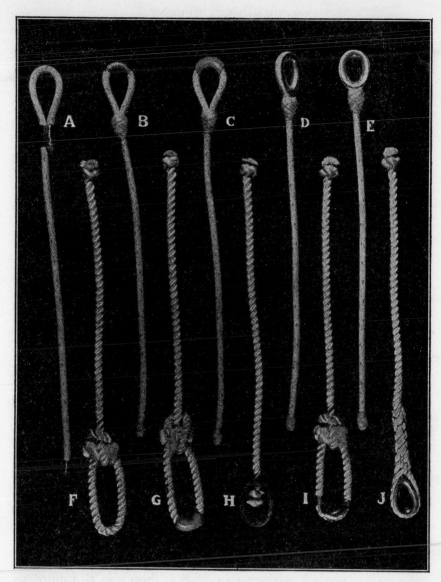

FIGURE 49. VARIOUS TYPES OF HONDAS: *A to E, Spinning Rope Hondas:* A, plain light honda; B, same with end wrapped with wire; C, same with end wrapped with leather; D, aluminum honda; E, brass honda. *F to J, Catch-rope Hondas:* F, standard honda made with lariat-loop knot; G, same with end wrapped with leather; H, rawhide honda; I, Hogue's Honda or brass half-honda; J, standard brass honda, spliced.

All hondas prepared by Hamley & Co., Pendleton, Oregon.

The hondas shown in B and C have the wiring covered with a plait of leather. Pleasing as this is to the eye, it should be avoided for the reason that it adds weight that is a hindrance in the tricks for which these light-honda ropes are used.

METAL HONDAS

Some ropers prefer to use the light aluminum honda illustrated in D, Figure 49. These are so light that they add very little weight to the honda, but there is really no purpose in using them. In fact, they make more difficult the performing of most roping tricks and certainly should not be used by beginners. When one develops skill and can do many tricks, he will possess several ropes and may then want one equipped with an aluminum honda which he may find useful for certain stunts. But this must be determined by experience—on the start, use the simple, unweighted honda described in the preceding section and do not attempt to use the aluminum type until you have learned all the fine points of the roping game. And even then, you probably will find no place for it.

The heavy brass honda illustrated in E, Figure 49, however, is used regularly in rope spinning, but only in the more advanced tricks which require a heavily weighted rope. In the hands of a beginner learning the flat spins, one of these heavy hondas would render the rope useless. It is used chiefly in the vertical spins described in Chapter XI, and here it is indispensable. Do not attempt to use one until you are ready to learn these difficult vertical spins. The finest of ropers could not do the flat spins successfully with a brass honda, and the flat spins are the tricks with which a beginner must start.

Brass hondas for spinning ropes may be purchased at very small cost from any manufacturer of spinning ropes or any western cowboy outfitter. Wrap the end of the rope around the honda and wire the end to the standing part of the rope very tightly with copper wire. With such a heavy honda, the wiring may be covered with leather if desired, as shown in C, Figure 49. Some ropers prefer to sew the end to the standing part with heavy linen thread instead of wiring it, but this makes a delicate rope that is not suitable for any one except an expert who handles his rope skillfully and gently. A beginner, of necessity, subjects his rope to hard usage because of his lack of skill in handling it, and consequently the honda should be wired in place. Wired hondas are used by ninety-nine out of every hundred ropers anyway.

THE THROWING LARIAT

While there is only one kind of rope usable for rope spinning, there are many kinds of ropes that do service in lassoing. And which of these is best depends upon the purpose for which it is to be used. Actual roping of steers and horses on the range calls for one kind of rope; trick-and-fancy catching in the circuses demands another type; learning to throw a lariat requires still another. And since these pages are designed for those who are learning the skills of the lariat, we shall consider first the practice rope, and then discuss each of the other types in turn.

MAKING A PRACTICE ROPE

In learning to throw a lariat there is no better rope than ordinary three-eighths-inch Manilla rope obtainable at any hardware store. It serves better than the special hemp lariat rope from which the catch-ropes of the ranches are made, in that the latter are too heavy and stiff for the beginner to handle easily. Once the knack has been mastered with an ordinary Manilla rope, the regular lariats can be easily and skillfully manipulated.

Secure thirty-five feet of three-eighths-inch Manilla rope. The honda may be made in several ways: The easiest, quickest, and best way is to tie the lariat-loop illustrated in Figure 50. This is the method commonly used on the plains in making a temporary lariat out of rope. Simply tie an overhand knot about ten inches from the end of the rope, leaving it loose as illustrated in A, Figure 50. Then tuck the end through the knot following the course indicated by the arrow. Tie an ordinary overhand knot with this end to prevent it from pulling out, then jam the whole knot as tightly as possible. The honda then appears as in B, Figure 50. The lariat-loop makes a nicely shaped honda that stays open all the time, and the weight of the knot gives the Manilla rope just the right amount of weight to enable it to be easily handled. The hondas shown in F, G, and H, Figure 49, are made in this way.

Hondas may also be made by wiring the end to the standing part as in making the honda on a spinning rope (A, Figure 49),

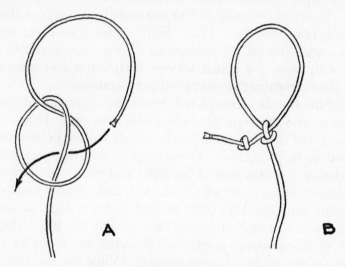

FIGURE 50. HOW THE LARIAT-LOOP IS TIED

or by splicing the end into the standing part with an eye-splice. Splicing makes an excellent honda but for some reason was seldom used in making lariats on the ranches. Wiring does not make nearly as strong a honda on a catch-rope as does the lariat-loop.

Never use metal hondas on a practice rope. Occasionally the catch-ropes of the ranches have a small brass honda such as shown in J, Figure 49, but such hondas weight the rope too much for practice purposes. Furthermore, they are dangerous: it would be very easy to injure a person by throwing at him a lariat equipped with one of these brass weights, and many a horse has had an eye knocked out by them.

If it seems necessary to weight the honda slightly so that the noose will carry better or to protect it from wear when thrown, wrap the end half of the honda with copper wire of the medium-heavy size, or cover it with leather as illustrated in G, Figure 49.

Another device often used on the ranges is the metal half-honda shown in H, Figure 49. This is a curved piece of brass which is slipped inside the end of the honda loop and hammered tightly onto the rope. Such a device is called a Hogue's honda. It increases the weight somewhat but not nearly so much as does the full-sized brass honda. These half-hondas, however, are not recommended for use by beginners. Those who desire to equip lariats with them for actual service with cattle and horses may obtain them from any western saddlery company.

When the honda is completed, insert the other end of the rope through it, and the rope has been converted into a lariat. With use, the end of the rope opposite the honda will, of course, unravel and needs to be protected. To accomplish this, many a cow-hand has tied a knot on the end of his lariat and this to his sorrow, for came the day when he roped a frisky colt and found it necessary to release the rope quickly, only to find that the rope persisted in staying with him and dragging him around the lot. The knot caught in his clothing somehow, as knots are wont to do, or perhaps on the saddle or its trappings. While the average person just learning to rope will not be throwing at temperamental colts, yet as a matter of principle, the end of the rope should be wrapped with a strand or two of wire so that it will slip out of the hand quickly and freely whenever it is given a sudden jerk.

CATCH-ROPES

The catch-ropes used in the work-a-day life of the cowboys are usually made of an extra quality hemp rope that is exceptionally smooth and hard in finish. Some of these ropes are specially treated so that they are not affected by atmospheric changes and can be handled as easily in damp weather as in dry. This is important to cowboys in that ordinary Manilla rope becomes stiff and kinky when damp, and is often limp and lifeless after it has been dried out. Made-up catch-ropes of these types, and rope in bulk for the making of lariats, may be secured from any western saddlery company or cowboy outfitting concern. Such ropes are essential for actual roping of steers and horses, but as stated in the preceding section, are not as desirable as ordinary cheap Manilla rope in the hands of a beginner who is just starting to learn the art.

Professional catch-ropes come in several sizes. For roping calves, the three-eighths inch scant or the three-eighths inch full size is preferred. For small stock, the seven-sixteenths-inch scant size makes a good all-around rope. Steer and horse roping calls for the seven-sixteenths-inch full size or the half-inch size, which latter will stand any emergency that can arise in roping, but is too heavy to handle conveniently and is usually utilized only when extra heavy strain is anticipated. The average catch-rope is seven-sixteenths inch in diameter.

Catch-ropes vary in length from thirty-five to fifty feet. Forty feet is about the right length for normal conditions.

In regard to hondas on catch-ropes, four types are in common use. The lariat-loop described in the preceding section, (Figure 50) is often seen, but is almost always covered with leather to protect the rope, the leather being wrapped around the rope in the honda loop and sewed along the outside edge as illustrated in G, Figure 49. The brass honda is occasionally utilized but only on heavy ropes and under conditions where the lariat must be thrown long distances. Its use is limited to steers almost entirely, it being seldom desirable in handling horses. The metal half-honda illustrated in I, Figure 49, is not common, but is preferable to the full-sized brass honda in that it furnishes sufficient weight and protection for ordinary conditions, yet does not offer such a great hazard to animals. Still another honda often used on catch-ropes is the rawhide honda, shown in H, Figure 49. It consists of an eye of heavy rawhide attached to the rope in such a way as to enable it to revolve. This honda is light and serviceable, and entirely harmless to any living creatures that it may hit. Such rawhide hondas can be secured from any western cowboy out-fitter.

While each of these special types of hondas has its use in the work of the cowboys, they are scarcely necessary when the lariat is used for recreational purposes. Here, a lariat-loop is all that is needed; it may be wrapped with leather or wound with copper wire if it is to be subjected to an unusual amount of use.

THE MAGUEY ROPE

The maguey lariat is the rope used by all the professionals of the circuses, rodeos, and vaudeville stage for trick-and-fancy catches. It is the finest of all ropes for expert trick roping but is not recommended for regular lariat purposes in handling stock on the ranges.

The maguey rope is made by hand in Old Mexico from agave fiber. It is a handsome rope with a very smooth and hard finish, and as contrasted to the Manilla ropes, it never becomes raggy and soft with use. Because of its unusually hard surface and firm nature it permits a more finished performance and holds a loop better than any other lariat made. Furthermore, it can be thrown with greater precision and accuracy than regular lariat ropes. The trick-and-fancy roping acts of the circuses and rodeos involve both rope spinning and trick catching. The maguey rope spins beautifully for the vertical spinning tricks used in these maneuvers, and at the same time is the finest of catch-ropes.

The maguey rope is thoroughly to be recommended to every one interested in learning to handle a catch-rope accurately. However, it is not the rope with which a beginner should receive his first initiation into the art of roping. Its stiffness will prove confusing to him until after he has used an ordinary Manilla rope for a while.

The maguey rope has one rather serious shortcoming for every one except an expert, and one that often proves distracting even to the professionals: in damp weather it becomes exceedingly stiff and wiry. To guard against this, it is well to keep the rope in a warm place when the weather is damp, taking it out only when needed.

Since the maguey rope is a four-strand rope, a special type of honda is used on it. Run a marline spike through the rope twelve inches from the end, thus separating the rope with two strands on each side of the spike. Through this opening force the end of

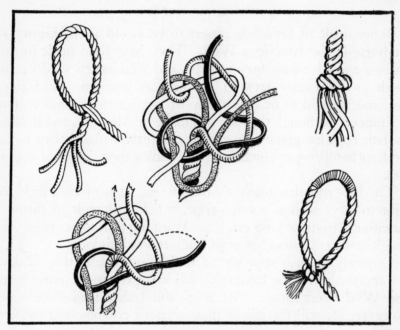

FIGURE 51. HONDA FOR A FOUR-STRAND MAGUEY ROPE, USING THE TUCKED WALL KNOT

the rope, making a loop two-and-one-half inches long as shown in Figure 51. Then unravel the strands of the end and tie a tucked wall knot, following the method clearly shown in Figure 51. The honda may be wrapped with a little copper wire at the end, or may be covered with leather. There are other more complicated methods of making a honda on a maguey rope, but the one described above is the more common and answers every purpose.

Maguey ropes are remarkably inexpensive considering their fine quality. They may be obtained from any western saddlery or cowboy outfitting company for less money than good hemp catch-ropes will cost. They range in length from thirty-five to fifty feet, the smaller sizes running about three-eighths of an inch thick. By specifying a professional grade of maguey rope, an extra long and large size may be obtained. Since maguey ropes are hand-made, they vary a great deal in size and workmanship.

HORSEHAIR ROPES

Ropes made of horsehair appear to be as old as the history of the horse in the American West. They have been made by the Indians and Mexicans for centuries and were much used by the cowboys of the early days. They were not uncommon in Europe also, and are said to be used today by peasants in various regions of France. Although they are still made by Mexicans and Indians, the hair rope has given way almost completely in America to the modern hemp rope which is by all odds a more efficient roping tool.

The hair rope has many shortcomings. It is often a little too light to serve well as a catch-rope, it being difficult to throw it far enough to make long catches. With use it becomes raggy and rough, and at all times has a tendency toward kinking.

Certainly the hair rope served well its purpose in the old days, but the modern riatas have relegated it largely to the curio stores and Wild West shows. Mexican- and Indian-made hair ropes, however, are still for sale at most western cowboy and saddlery outfitters, and are an interesting novelty to add to a roper's collection of lariats.

THE RAWHIDE LARIAT

As is the case with the hair ropes, the rawhide lariats belong largely to yesterday. They were the standard and almost universally used rope for hard use in the early days of the West, but today have been supplanted by modern hemp ropes not only because of the labor and time required in making rawhide sogas, but because of the greater efficiency of the hemp lass-rope.

As compared to the modern hemp ropes, rawhide riatas are

heavier and more unwieldy, and do not retain a loop as well. Then, too, while they are unusually strong and tough throughout the most of their lengths, they often have a weak spot which will give way at the time when strength and dependability are most needed. Once a strand is broken the entire rope is rendered useless.

In the old days the rawhide ropes were made from buffalo hide, or from buck or elk. Buck hide is still used by the Indians today and makes an especially fine rope. In making the rope, the hide is cut into one long strand about a half inch wide by going round and round the hide. Four strands are braided together by hand into the rope. The making of a good rope is a long and tedious process requiring endless hours of rolling and pounding to make it even and round, not to speak of the boiling and greasing to waterproof and soften it.

Like the hair ropes, the rawhide lariats belong largely to the Wild West shows and the western curio stores, although they are still made by the Mexicans and can be purchased through western cowboy outfitters.

CARING FOR A LARIAT

Every rope must be broken in before it will work effectively. New rope is stiff and full of kinks as a rule. The perennial method of conditioning a rope in the West is to tie it on behind a wagon, or to the saddle, and thus let it drag for a half a day on the ground. Another method commonly used is to lay it over a post and pull it back and forth strenuously with the hands. Braided cotton rope used for rope spinning does not require this kind of breaking in— a half hour of use will properly loosen up such a rope. However, in initiating new hemp and maguey ropes much time will be saved if they are conditioned by one of the two methods described above.

Once the rope has been broken in and is adjusted so that the roper can use it himself for the tricks that he does, he will want to take particular care of it and use it only for this purpose. Otherwise it will soon become unbalanced and inefficient. Every professional roper guards his ropes with great caution and does not permit any one else to use them. Spinning ropes particularly are temperamental affairs, each one seeming to have an individuality of its own. To use a spinning rope as a lariat and throw it at some one is to abuse it in a way that no spinning rope should be treated. Use the spinning rope as a spinning rope only and do not allow other people to handle it. Once you get a good rope that will do intricate tricks for you, you may try a long time to find another that will do these stunts as well. A roper invariably becomes attached to his ropes and it usually happens that the oldest and least attractive of the ropes is the one that the roping artist prizes the most.

Dampness is not good for any rope. Untreated hemp rope becomes limp and lifeless as compared to its condition before wetting. Even though the better quality of catch-ropes are specially treated with water-proofing, yet they should not be subjected to undue dampness. Maguey ropes are so susceptible to dampness that they are not a practical rope in sections of the country where the climate is consistently damp. When there is dampness in the air, they become exceedingly stiff and wiry, but when dried out, show fewer ill effects than most other ropes. A wet spinning rope is extremely difficult to handle.

A spinning rope can be washed in soap and water when it gets dirty. Cotton ropes pick up so much dirt, and soil everything they touch to such an extent, that they should be cleaned often. The washing does not damage them at all.

Always coil your ropes carefully when you are through using them and hang them up or store them away in a dry place.

CHAPTER X

Rope Spinning—The Flat Spins

While catch-roping involves the throwing of a lariat in such a way that the noose encircles and tightens on an animal or other object, rope spinning consists of manipulating a short rope in such a way that the loop becomes dilated and remains open in circular form as long as it is revolved. This loop is swung around the body of the roper in various tricks and stunts. When the loop is revolving the centrifugal force keeps it open so that it remains dilated and in circular form in the air. The friction of the honda against the spoke prevents the noose from collapsing.

The various rope-spinning tricks are of two general types, the *flat spins* and the *vertical spins*. In the flat spins, the loop spins in a horizontal plane, that is, parallel to the ground, whereas in the vertical spins, the loop revolves in a vertical plane, perpendicular to the floor. The flat spins are much easier to learn and do than are the vertical tricks, and certainly must be learned first. This chapter describes the flat spins—the vertical maneuvers are presented in the chapter following.

There are two fundamental flat spins which are the basis of all the tricks in flat roping. These are called the *Wedding Ring* and the *Flat Loop*. The difference lies in the fact that in the Wedding Ring the roper stands *inside* the spinning loop, whereas in the Flat Loop, he stands outside the loop and spins it in front of his body or manipulates it around himself. Both of these tricks are very simple and easy to learn—they are the first tricks to be undertaken, being basic to the more intricate maneuvers.

There is a number of tricks based on the Wedding Ring, and these are presented in the pages that follow under the heading, The Wedding-Ring Series. Similarly, there is a number of stunts based on the Flat Loop which are presented under the heading, The Flat-Loop Series. Then there are several tricks combining the Wedding Ring and the Flat Loop—these are described under the heading, The Combination Series.

As stated in the preceding chapter, braided cotton sash cord is the only rope usable for rope spinning. This is commonly called spot cord (see page 108).

GRADED LIST OF FLAT SPINS

Roping tricks vary a great deal in complexity and difficulty. They build up one upon another, the skills learned in one opening the way to the learning of another, which latter would be much more difficult were it not for the ability developed in the preceding. To attempt too difficult a trick before the proper foundation has been laid will probably result in failure and perhaps permanent discouragement.

The following list indicates the recommended order in which the tricks should be learned:

1. Flat Loop
2. Wedding Ring
3. Hand-shaking
4. Hand-shaking around One Leg
5. Lying Down
6. Jumping into the Flat Loop
7. Jumping Out
8. Up and Over
9. Merry-go-round
10. Two-handed Merry-go-round
11. Tapping In and Out
12. Juggling
13. The Bounce
14. Juggling Up and Over
15. Hand-shaking around Alternate Legs
16. Hurdling
17. The Big Loop
18. Lift onto Body
19. Lift onto Arm
20. The Skyrocket
21. Spinning Two Ropes

THE TWO FUNDAMENTAL SPINS

The two fundamental spins in flat roping are the *Flat Loop* and the *Wedding Ring*. Once these two spins are perfected so that they can be performed easily and without conscious effort, the road is wide open to all the spectacular tricks that involve a flat loop. Without perfection in these two fundamentals, however, the others are impossible.

THE FLAT LOOP

Rope—fourteen feet long with a light honda.

In the Flat Loop a small loop is spun in front of the body so that the plane of the loop is parallel to the ground, as illustrated in Figure 52. This is the simplest of all tricks and the easiest to learn, and, although not as fascinating as the Wedding Ring, it is the trick that should be learned first in most cases.

Use a fourteen-foot length of Number 12 spot lariat cord

FIGURE 52. SPINNING THE FLAT LOOP

with a light honda (see page 109). While this trick can be done with a rope of any length, the ideal length for learning is fourteen feet. Arrange the rope as shown in A, Figure 52. The roper in this picture is using a longer rope and consequently the end extends over into his left hand—if a fourteen-foot length were used the right hand would grip the spoke at its very end. The reason why a fourteen-foot rope is preferred in learning is because we are not troubled with this long end extending over into the left hand.

Note that the spoke goes straight through the honda and is

not doubled back—Figure 53 shows the right way and the wrong way to arrange the rope preliminary to spinning.

In arranging the rope as in A, Figure 52, the end of the rope is held between the thumb and forefinger of the right hand, the other fingers of the right hand being used to hold the loop. The left hand merely holds the loop open. Note that the spoke ex-

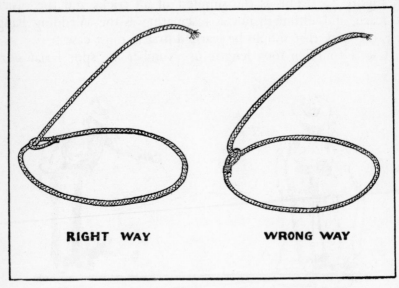

RIGHT WAY   **WRONG WAY**

FIGURE 53. RIGHT AND WRONG WAY TO ARRANGE THE NOOSE

tends from the hand nearly down to the floor—the correct length for the spoke is about one half the diameter of the loop. Note also that the roper is leaning slightly forward at the hips with his hands well below the level of the waist.

With everything all arranged as in A, Figure 52, we are ready to spin the loop. Keeping the left hand just where it is, throw the loop over to the left with the right hand. Do this a few times without attempting to spin it. Then throw it over to the left as before and, as you do so, release the rope with the left hand and give it a circular spin from right to left (counterclockwise) with the right hand, releasing the loop with the right hand and keeping hold of the end of the spoke only.

There is no magic in rope spinning—the rope will not spin of its own accord and you must actually give it its initial spin in such a way as to start it spinning. In starting the spin, the right hand must cut a *circle* in the air of approximately the same size that the spinning noose is to be. *Do not release the loop with the right hand too soon*—you should retain hold of the loop until the hand has cut almost a complete circle in the air. Then release it and keep it going by means of the spoke held in the right hand. After making the initial spin of the size of the loop, raise the right hand slightly, and continue to cut circles in the air with it, each circle being a little smaller than the preceding, until the arm at last becomes stationary, the rope being spun with a gentle wrist motion. In making each succeeding circle smaller, the hand follows a spiral course as shown in Figure 54.

FIGURE 54

In giving the loop its initial spin, it is as if the wheel of a bicycle lying on the ground were being turned—the hand would grasp the tire and would of necessity make a circular movement around the circumference of the wheel. Before releasing the loop, the hand must make just such a circular movement of about the same size as the loop.

Care should be taken not to throw the rope away in giving it the initial spin—the arm should move very slowly, more slowly than the speed necessary to spin the rope once it is going. After releasing the loop, increase the speed steadily but be careful not to jerk it. Once you get the loop spinning, *take it easy*—relax and spin it gently and slowly. It is a wrist rather than an arm motion. Every beginner wants to spin the loop rapidly, using a vigorous arm motion. This not only tends to collapse the loop but produces a choppy motion of the rope that is unattractive to the eye. Most of the failure during your learning days will be due to jerky arm movements resulting from overanxiety and the use of too much muscle.

Rope spinning is *rhythm*. Once the loop is spinning, keep it going in perfect time. Counting as you spin will help to keep the rhythm constant, but with experience this will be unnecessary in that you will be able to feel the rhythm of the rope as the spoke passes a certain spot. If the rhythm is to be increased or decreased, the change must be made very slowly and gradually. The most graceful spinning loops result from a rather slow and gentle motion.

Preventing the Spoke from Twisting.—The spinning of the loop naturally twists the spoke and unless definite precautions are taken the rope will become so twisted and kinky in a moment or two that it will refuse to spin. To guard against this, grip the spoke very gently and allow it to turn in the hand as it chooses. If you open the hand for a fraction of a second each spin, the spoke will turn of its own accord. Or you may find it easier to turn the spoke with your fingers with each revolution of the loop.

If the rope becomes twisted it is a waste of time to try to spin it—stop the spinning and untwist it before continuing. Never try to straighten out a kinked rope by stepping on it and pulling—untwist it by swinging it in the air in the opposite direction to that used in spinning.

Increasing the Size of the Loop.—All that is necessary to increase the size of the loop is to increase the speed of the spinning. This tends to throw the honda up nearer the hand and shorten the spoke. If there be some excess rope extending over into the left hand, increase the speed of the spinning and, as you do so, open the spinning hand and let some of the excess rope slip out. In this way the loop can be increased to the extent of the rope.

Decreasing the Size of the Loop.—Decreasing the size of the loop is not quite so easy as increasing it. Slow down the speed of the spinning, lower the spinning hand a little, and then jerk it back up to its original position again. The loop will become smaller and the spoke proportionately longer.

If you wish to decrease the size of the loop and also shorten the spoke, slow down the speed of the spinning, slip the spinning hand down a few inches toward the honda, thus shortening the spoke, and then increase the spinning to the normal speed again.

Spinning with the Left Hand.—Having mastered the Flat Loop with the right hand, the next move should be to spin it with the left hand. The mark of a finished performer in any kind of roping is the ability to work as efficiently with his left hand as with his right.

The quickest way to learn·left-handed spinning is to start the Flat Loop as usual with the right hand, and when it is going nicely, transfer the spoke from the right to the left hand, and then keep it going with the left hand. Once the left hand has acquired the "feel" of the spinning noose, it is no problem at all to start the spin from the beginning with the left hand. Preliminary to spinning, the loop is held just as in A, Figure 52, except that the hands are crossed: the left hand reaches over and holds the end of the spoke and loop in the position of the right hand in Figure 52, and the right arm crosses under the left and holds the loop open in the position of the left hand in Figure 52.

The Clockwise Flat Spin.—In the Flat Loop as described above, the loop is spun in a counterclockwise direction—this is the standard type of spin and the direction in which the rope is revolved ninety-nine per cent of the time in all rope spinning. However, the beginner should learn to spin each trick in the opposite or clockwise direction as he goes along. After the counterclockwise spin has been mastered, it is but a task of a few minutes to learn to spin the loop in the opposite direction.

Arrange the loop as in A, Figure 52. Then reverse the position of the loop, turning it over so that the arms are crossed, the right hand as it holds the end of the spoke being in front of the left leg, and the left arm crossing behind the right with the left hand in front of the right leg. From this position proceed to spin it in a clockwise direction. It will be easy if you have already learned the standard Flat Loop.

Clockwise Spin with Left Hand.—When spinning with the right hand the counterclockwise spin is the normal and natural movement, whereas with the left hand, the clockwise spin is the natural spin. Arrange rope as in A, Figure 52, except that the sides are reversed, the left hand holding the end of the spoke. Proceed exactly as described above for the standard Flat Loop except that all movements described for the right hand are performed with the left and the direction of the spin is reversed.

THE WEDDING RING

Rope—twenty feet long with a light honda.

Simple though it be, there is no more attractive and appealing trick in roping than the Wedding Ring. When properly done

it is graceful and beautiful indeed. And happily, it is one of the easiest tricks to master—many even feel that it should be learned before the simple Flat Loop is undertaken. The Wedding Ring is a flat loop inside of which the roper stands and which he spins around his body as illustrated in Figure 55. It is sometimes called the Crinoline or the Body Spin.

The Wedding Ring calls for a twenty-foot rope. Arrange the rope exactly as shown in A, Figure 56. Note that the end of the spoke is held in the right hand and that the honda is about at the level of the ground—this

FIGURE 55. THE WEDDING RING

produces a spoke of just the right length regardless of the height of the roper. Note also that the left hand merely holds the loop open.

Keeping the left hand at the level of the waist, pick up the loop with the right hand and turn it back over the head as shown in B, Figure 56. Let it fall around the body and drop to the level of the waist as in C, Figure 56. Move slowly and deliberately in turning the rope back over the head, *and be sure to keep the left hand low*. Every beginner is inclined to raise the left hand, thus throwing the rope wildly behind the back. Make this movement several times before attempting to start the spin.

When the rope has dropped to the level of the waist, as in C, Figure 56, give the noose a hard spin *around* the body from right to left with both hands as indicated by the arrow—be sure that

FIGURE 56. STARTING THE WEDDING RING

the motion of the hands is a *circular* one around the body. As you do so, release the loop with both hands retaining hold of the end of the spoke only, and raise the right hand around behind the head and then up over the head, keeping it going with a gentle motion of the wrist. Figure 57 shows the finished trick.

Two things you must watch, for your failure in starting the spin will probably be due to one of these factors: do not raise the left hand as you toss the rope back over the head with the right hand, and secondly, do not use too much muscle in lifting the rope with the right hand. Either of these mistakes will throw the rope away. Take the starting movements very slowly and gently and give the loop plenty of time to settle down to the level of the waist. In learning, one naturally is over-anxious and tense, and as a result he uses too much muscle and hurries too much. *Relax and take it easy.*

Once the rope is spinning, keep the right hand directly over

FIGURE 57. THE COMPLETED WEDDING RING

the top of the head and spin with the wrist. Whatever you do, guard against a wide swinging motion of the arm. Keep the wrist relaxed and flexible. Try to guide the rope with the thumb and forefinger of the right hand—it is such a delicate and gentle movement that the thumb and finger are all that are needed. Sway the body gently, almost imperceptibly, with the rhythm of the spinning noose—this in itself is enough to keep the spin going, thus relieving the wrist of any important part in the process, once the spin is under way. The tendency always is to speed up the spin and to use the arm to accomplish it; this results in a choppy motion that hurls the noose against the body. If the loop hits the body while being spun gently, the chances are that you are not keeping your right hand directly over your head—if the rope touches you in front, move the hand farther forward, whereas if it touches you behind, move the hand back.

Try to spin as smoothly and gracefully as possible. A slowly spinning, floating loop is always the goal in good roping.

As in all roping tricks, the Wedding Ring must be spun with perfect rhythm. It is well to count during the beginning days, saying *one* and, *two* and, etc., as the loop rotates. If the rhythm is to be increased or decreased, the change must be made gradually without jerks or sudden movements.

Remember that the spoke must turn in the hand or the rope will become so twisted and kinked that it will stop spinning. Hold the end loosely in the hand all the time and relax the grip entirely for a fraction of a second with each spin, thus enabling the spoke to revolve of its own accord. You may even turn the spoke with your fingers each time the loop makes a revolution, but this should not be necessary if you are handling the end lightly enough—the spoke should be so held as to revolve in the hand of its own accord. If the rope is guided by the thumb and forefinger there is little danger of gripping the end too tightly or using too much arm motion in spinning.

At first you will succeed in doing no more than wrapping the rope around your neck. But do not be discouraged—if you give up easily you will never be a roper. There is no easy road to roping—the ropes are stubborn and can be trained and controlled only by practice and still more practice. You may be sure that every roper has purchased his tricks by endless hours of labor—joyous labor, but labor nevertheless. So keep at it—success will come suddenly and when you least expect it. Some day when you are repeating the motions over and over, apparently hopelessly, you will let out a shout of exultation for without warning the rope suddenly begins to spin.

There are so many separate movements to watch in getting the knack of roping. We spend considerable time learning one movement, then another, and so on, without being able to do the thing as a whole. Then we suddenly succeed in integrating these component movements and mastering the whole set in one or two trials. So when you are most discouraged, success may be very much closer than you think possible. Without warning you will start spinning the rope, and from then on the trick is yours.

Another Method of Starting the Wedding Ring.—Here is a simple method of learning the Wedding Ring that is popular in some places. While it is seldom used by good ropers, some teachers of roping prefer to use it when giving beginners their first initiation, feeling it is more certain of success than the regular method, and that the standard method can be picked up easily later on.

The question puzzling the average beginner in figuring out the Wedding Ring is how to get inside the spinning noose. Arrange the rope on the ground in just the position that it would be when spinning, allowing about three feet of rope for the spoke. Then stand in the center, pick up the end of the spoke and the loop in the right hand, and hold up the loop with the left hand. Now turn the body suddenly to the left, raising the hands slightly —this will lift the noose off the floor and start it floating around the body. A turn of about forty-five degrees is all that is necessary to set the loop in motion. As you turn, release the noose with both hands, and raise the right hand gradually up in front of the face and behind the head, and then up to its normal position directly overhead. Don't jerk the hand up too suddenly— jerks of all kinds are fatal in roping. Once the rope is spinning and the hand is overhead, the process continues as described for the standard method of starting the Wedding Ring.

Wedding Ring with the Left Hand.—When the Wedding Ring is going nicely with the right hand, transfer the spoke to the left hand and continue spinning. This is a good way to rest the right arm when one is forced to spin the rope for a long period.

The Clockwise Wedding Ring.—In the Wedding Ring as described above, the rope spins in counterclockwise fashion, this being the standard direction in all flat spinning. To spin it clockwise, start it with the left hand holding the spoke, following all the instructions given above except that the directions are reversed. When the rope is spinning with the left hand guiding it, the spoke may be transferred to the right hand.

THE WEDDING-RING SERIES

Now that we have the Wedding Ring well in hand and can do it smoothly, rhythmically, and effortlessly, with both the right hand and the left, we are ready to undertake the following tricks which use this fundamental spin as a basis. Don't try to put the cart before the horse by getting into these maneuvers before you claim the Wedding Ring entirely as your own. To do so will immediately put you in water over your head. Here, as in every athletic sport, success depends on a thorough-going schooling in fundamentals. In a sense the following tricks are frills which dress up and make more exciting the standard Crinoline. If you leave no question about the smoothness of your Wedding Ring, many of these stunts can be learned in a half hour.

The ideal length of rope for any trick is affected by the height of the roper. In each of the following stunts, the recommended length of rope is for an adult of average height. A shorter or taller person than the average may require a slightly shorter or longer rope for the best results.

HAND-SHAKING

Rope—twenty feet long with a light honda.

This trick, sometimes called the Hand-around, consists of dropping the Wedding Ring to near the floor and keeping it spinning there by passing the spoke from hand to hand around the body. Figure 58 shows it. The trick is one of the easiest to learn and is quite spectacular.

Get the Wedding Ring going smoothly, and then, just as the spoke is passing your left shoulder drop your right hand down across the front of the body to the level of the waist in front, thus allowing the spinning noose to drop within a few inches of the floor. Immediately grab the spoke in the left hand and carry it around behind the back. As you do so move the right hand around behind to meet the left, and quickly grab the spoke with the right hand and carry it around in front. Here grab it in the left hand and take it around in back again. Continue this process as long as you desire to keep the trick going.

This trick will take some fast grabbing with the hands but

FIGURE 58.   HAND-SHAKING

otherwise is not difficult. There is just one danger—in your eagerness to pass the spoke from hand to hand, you may break the rhythm of the spinning loop. If the loop collapses or hits you it is probably because you have jerked it as you passed the spoke around you. Try to keep time with the spinning noose, and if necessary, count to yourself to help keep the rhythm. It is imperative that the hands be kept close in to the body throughout, even brushing the hips as they are moved back and forth.

An excellent way to practice this trick is to use a stick about three feet long, passing it around you rapidly from hand to hand.

The stick should extend downward from the level of the waist and should be passed with the hands at the waist level. The hands must be kept as close to the body as possible.

You will need a smooth floor on which to learn the Hand-shaking trick. The rope is sure to touch the floor at times and a rough or irregular surface will slow up the spin or stop it, whereas the loop will slide over a polished floor and not be affected. A gym floor is ideal.

Hand-Shaking to Wedding Ring.—The Hand-shaking trick should be concluded by raising the loop into the Wedding Ring again. To accomplish this, bring the spoke around in front with the right hand as usual but instead of transferring it to the left hand, raise the right hand up across the front of the body and around behind the left shoulder and then overhead. If this is done without jerking and rushing, the loop will be lifted to the level of the waist and will continue to spin in the Wedding Ring.

Hand-Shaking Clockwise.—Hand-shaking can be done backward or in clockwise fashion by starting the Wedding Ring in the clockwise direction and then dropping the rope into the Hand-shaking trick. The clockwise Wedding Ring is described above in the detailed discussion of that trick.

HAND-SHAKING AROUND ONE LEG

Rope—twenty feet long with a light honda.

The spectacular aspect of this trick belies its simplicity. It is strong in its appeal to spectators, giving the impression of being most difficult, yet it involves nothing more in the way of rope spinning skill than Hand-shaking. Any one who can do the Hand-shaking trick easily and smoothly can learn this one in five minutes.

The stunt consists of standing on one leg, holding the other leg out to one side, and performing the Hand-shaking trick around one leg—Figure 59 shows it. While the twenty-foot rope with the light honda will do the trick, it is a little easier for most people, and a little more spectacular, if done with a twenty-five-foot rope equipped with a brass honda. This is the so-called skip rope described on page 167. With the hands held near the floor, as they must be in this trick, the light rope tends to collapse more easily than it would if it had the weight of a brass honda to keep it open.

To do this trick, get the Hand-shaking spin going smoothly and rhythmically and then quickly raise the left leg far out to one side, stoop well down, and continue to spin the rope with the hands at about the level of the knee. See Figure 59. The Hand-shaking can be done from this position just as easily as when

FIGURE 59.   HAND-SHAKING AROUND ONE LEG

standing upright. Pass the hands around as close to the leg as possible. Since the circumference of the leg is so much smaller than that of the body at the hips, the lowering of the spoke from the high angle to the low does not alter the length of the spoke to any material degree and consequently the sudden transition from the standing to the stooping position does not alter the size of the loop enough to break the spin.

The higher the left leg is raised the more finished and spectacular the trick appears. The leg should be held at right angles to the standing leg if possible.

Having spun the rope around the right leg a few times, lower the left leg, raise the right, and repeat the trick around the left leg.

Before attempting the trick with the rope, it is well to raise the left leg and go through the motions with the empty hand a few times.

Remember that a rough surface will be a severe handicap in learning this trick. Use a polished floor.

Variation.—Another method of Hand-shaking around One Leg consists of raising the left leg forward rather than sidewise. The body is bent slightly forward at the hips so as to enable the hands to reach low enough to pass under the raised leg. The knee of the raised leg is kept stiff. This method is neither as convenient for the performer nor as satisfying to the spectator as the first method—it seems strained, forced, and awkward.

HAND-SHAKING AROUND ALTERNATE LEGS

Rope—twenty-five feet long with a brass honda, or twenty feet long with a light honda.

Although this excellent and spectacular trick can be done well enough with the twenty-foot Wedding Ring rope it is best performed with a twenty-five-foot rope equipped with a brass honda (see the description of the skip rope on page 167). Before attempting the trick with the skip rope, it will be necessary to practice the Wedding Ring a few times with this rope, since the heavy honda will add complications for a person who is familiar only with the light-weight rope.

Get the Hand-shaking trick going nicely, then bend far down and raise the left leg forward, allowing the knee to bend, and pass the spoke around the right leg once as in Handshaking; immediately drop the left leg and raise the right, then pass the spoke around the left leg. Continue to raise the legs alternately in this way, passing the spoke once around each leg each time. Figure 60 shows the trick in action.

This trick should not be attempted until Hand-shaking around One Leg can be done easily. It will offer no serious difficulty provided the raised foot is placed as near as possible to the stationary foot each time it is put down. If a straddling motion is used, the feet being placed far apart, the hands will be forced to jerk the rope so much that the spin may be broken. This trick is a little more difficult to learn and perform than those discussed thus far in this chapter.

Be sure to practice on a smooth floor while learning.

Variation.—In performing this version of the trick described above, stand erect while doing the Hand-shaking trick, then swing the left leg up in front, keeping the knee stiff. With the left leg

FIGURE 60. HAND-SHAKING AROUND ALTERNATE LEGS

in this position, pass the spoke around the right thigh once, using the same motion as in Hand-shaking. Immediately place the left leg down and swing the right leg up, passing the spoke around the left thigh, and so forth.

This trick is a little easier to perform than the first method described above, but it is not at all comparable in the effect it creates. It is interesting only as a little variation which one can throw into a demonstration of the Wedding-ring series of spins.

LYING DOWN

Rope—sixteen feet long with a light honda.

This trick is interesting always and involves nothing more in the way of rope spinning than the Wedding Ring. It consists of lying down with the spinning rope and taking it easy as the roper is doing in Figure 61.

While standing, start the Wedding Ring in the usual manner. When it is going nicely, drop slowly down to the knees and then to a sitting position, working the legs slowly and carefully out under the spinning noose. When everything is under control, ease the body down onto one elbow as the roper in the picture is doing. This is enough to make a good stunt out of it, but if your rope is of the right length, it will be possible for you to drop the head down to the ground and lie completely prostrate.

The difficulty presented by this stunt centers around preventing the spinning noose from touching the body. Speeding up the spinning tends to elevate the noose and lift it away from the

FIGURE 61. LYING DOWN

body. The speed should be increased gradually, however, and care taken not to break the rhythm suddenly.

Success in this stunt depends on having a rope that is just the right length for the individual who is using it. The sixteen-foot length recommended may be too short for a very tall person and too long for a short person. The rope must be long enough to make possible the Wedding Ring while standing erect. When lying down, if the spinning loop hits the body in spite of all that can be done the rope is obviously too long and must be shortened. Study what happens when you do the trick, and then experiment with the rope until just the right length is determined. Different lengths are required by different individuals.

RETIRING

Rope—sixteen feet long with a light honda.

This spectacular variation of Lying Down savors of the Wild West shows and circuses. While it can properly be done by a stunt roper, it more appropriately falls under the duties of the clown cowboy who apes the ropers' antics.

The trick consists of taking off your coat and ten-gallon hat while spinning the Wedding Ring, then lying down and using the coat as a pillow while you keep the rope spinning. Spin the Wedding Ring as usual with the right hand. With the left hand throw the coat off the left shoulder and work the left arm out of the sleeve; then transfer the rope from the right hand to the left, and slip the right arm out of the sleeve. This accomplished, sit down as described in Lying Down, roll up the coat, take off the hat, and proceed to lie down, resting your head on the coat. After spinning the rope for a moment or two in this position, sit up and put on your hat, pick up the coat, get on your feet and put on the coat again. Of course the rope must be kept spinning throughout.

THE JUGGLE

Rope—twenty feet long with a light honda.

We now come to one of the more colorful tricks of roping, much used by the expert performers. It really is not a separate spin in itself, but a flourish of the loop used in connection with the Wedding Ring. It consists of floating the Wedding Ring up and down from near the floor to over the head. Figure 62 indicates the up-and-down movement of the loop. The Juggle is beautiful and graceful indeed when skillfully done.

Using the twenty-foot rope with the light honda, get the Wedding Ring going as smoothly and rhythmically as possible. Now lower the right arm until the elbow hits the ribs in front of the right side of the body—do not turn the forearm down but keep it in a perpendicular position or nearly so. This lowering of the arm drops the loop to the level of the knees. Here give

it a spin and then raise the arm up to full length, thus throwing
the loop up overhead. When the loop is at the highest point
give it a spin to help it along, then drop the arm again.

The rope makes four spins in the process of its up-and-down
motion—one at the level of the knees, the second at the level of
the waist as in the Wedding Ring, the third over the head, and the
fourth at the level of the waist again. Figure 63 may serve to
make this series clear. The lowering and raising of the arm

FIGURE 62. THE JUGGLE

must be done in rhythm with the spinning noose—if it is jerked
or forced the loop will go lopsided or touch the body.

This is not the easiest of tricks to learn and the time required
by many to get the knack of it proves disconcerting. Do not
attempt to float the loop to the full extremities of the up-and-
down motion at the start of the trick, but rather work into the
motion gradually. In lowering the loop the tendency is to
drop the right arm down to the side of the body with the hand
at the level of the waist. When we recall that the right hand
is held directly over the head in the Wedding Ring, it becomes

obvious that throwing the hand down and to the right side of the body carries it far away from the center of the loop, with the result that the loop hits the body. In lowering the arm bring the elbow down so that it is against the ribs in front of the right side; then turn the wrist down and lower the forearm just enough to give the loop a spin, whereat the arm is raised to full

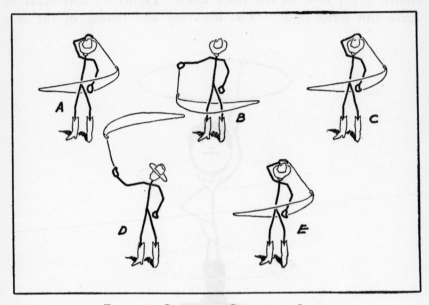

FIGURE 63. SEQUENCE OF SPINS IN THE JUGGLE

length upward with the hand directly over the head. It is well to rise on the tiptoes as the loop is lifted.

Do not try for too much speed. Set the rhythm with the Wedding Ring and then keep this rhythm constant. Remember that the loop makes four spins in completing its circuit, and there is no way to increase the speed of the up-and-down motion without increasing the rhythm of the spinning. When this trick is properly done the loop floats gracefully and smoothly up and down. To rush it unmakes the graceful picture.

THE BOUNCE

Rope—twenty-five feet long with a brass honda.

The Bounce is nothing more than the Juggle done more rapidly with a heavy rope. Using a twenty-five-foot rope with a brass honda, proceed just as in the case of the Juggle. The heavy honda makes possible a much greater speed. In dropping the right hand in this trick, lower it to the level of the waist and immediately swing it to the left and up behind the left shoulder. It is then carried to its full extent overhead where it gives the loop a spin and starts down again. In other words, the hand follows a corkscrew course up and down. The rope should go from the level of the knees up to the full length of the spoke overhead. There is a spring in the spoke of a spinning rope which is utilized in throwing the loop up and down.

With practice it will be possible to bounce the rope in two spins, one near the knees and the other overhead, rather than in four as in Juggling. Done rapidly and vigorously in this way, the loop zigzags up and down in most spectacular fashion.

THE HURDLE

Rope—twenty-five-feet long with a brass honda, or twenty-one-feet long with a medium-heavy honda.

Here is one of the finest tricks of roping—in fact, it shares the spotlight with the Skip (Chapter XI) as one of the two feature attractions in any roping exhibition. It is a strenuous, rugged stunt with much of athletic appeal—an exhilarating feat for the best of men. The cowboys in some parts call it Jumping the Spoke.

Opinions vary regarding the best rope for this trick. My own taste is for the skip rope, twenty-five-feet long equipped with a brass honda (see page 167). This makes a fast and spectacular stunt of it. It can be done with a rope of about twenty-one feet, with a medium-heavy honda, and some feel that such a rope makes the trick easier to learn and to do. The medium-heavy honda is made by wrapping copper wire around the light honda on the

Wedding-Ring rope. My advice is to try the trick with the skip rope first.

The Hand-shaking trick should be mastered before this one is undertaken. Start the Wedding Ring and when the rope settles down to smooth action, drop the loop to near the floor just as was done in the Hand-shaking. The time to drop it is just as the spoke goes past the left shoulder on its way around behind

FIGURE 64. HURDLING THE SPOKE

you. At the same time that you drop your arm, bend well down and as the honda comes around, step over it with the left foot, throwing the right leg up behind. As the spoke comes around again, step over it with the right foot, and so on. Continue to jump the spoke in this way as long as you care to continue the trick. Figure 64 shows how the stunt appears.

You will have to bend down quickly at the start in order to be ready for the spoke when it comes around. The chief difficulty in this trick is getting it started—if you succeed in making the first jump, the rest will go along easily.

The spinning hand is held about a foot above the floor during this stunt, consequently the body is bent well down and the back foot is thrown high behind at each step. The heavy honda makes the rope spin rapidly, thus requiring some fast stepping. It is possible to travel across the floor and back while hurdling the spoke, or you can run in a circle around the spinning hand as a pivot.

At the end of the trick, stand erect and bring the loop up into the Wedding Ring.

If a light-honda rope is used, the speed of the spin is slowed up considerably. In this case, it is not necessary to bend down so far, the spinning hand being held about midway between the knees and the hips.

Be sure to practice on a polished floor.

Variation.—In this version of the Hurdle, the spoke is jumped with both feet, rather than stepped over with one foot. The procedure is exactly as described above except that the body is not bent forward at the hips, but rather crouched a little at the knees, the trunk remaining upright. The spinning hand is held a few inches above the level of the knees. As the spoke comes around, spring in the air with both legs, throwing the legs high up behind and allowing the spoke to pass underneath. As the feet come down, both strike the floor simultaneously.

This trick is much used by the stunt ropers but it is not quite so graceful and pleasing as the standard Hurdle described in the preceding section.

SPINNING THE BIG LOOP

Rope—seventy to one-hundred feet of Number 10 spot cord with a brass honda.

Here is one of the greatest of the roping tricks in the thrill it invariably gives the spectators. No matter how many or how varied the tricks in a ropers' repertoire, none of them will be more certain to "bring down the house" than the Big Loop. And like so many roping tricks, its spectacular qualities give the impression of its being much more difficult than it really is. This one calls for nothing more intricate than the Wedding

Ring, although it does require muscle and endurance, and these in plentiful quantities.

The length of rope an individual will be able to spin can be determined only by experimentation, the idea in this trick being to spin the longest rope possible. Here we use Number 10 spot cord (cotton sash cord)) instead of the Number 12 size, which latter is standard in all other roping tricks. Being lighter, a longer rope can be handled in the Number 10 size. Secure one-hundred feet and try to spin it, and when you determine the amount of the rope you can let out without breaking down, cut off the

FIGURE 65. BIG LOOP

excess. It will take a rangy and very strong man to spin one-hundred feet of rope—seventy feet will offer trouble aplenty for the average person. The section trimmed off from the hundred-foot length can be used to make a light-weight skip rope (see page 167).

A rope of this length will require a very heavy honda. Secure a standard brass honda (Figure 49) from any western cowboy outfitter or spinning-rope manufacturer, and double the end of the rope around it so that there is an overlapping end of six or seven inches. Wire this end to the standing part with copper wire, wrapping the wire tightly and closely together all the way from the honda to the end. The weight of the wire and of the overlapping rope, added to that of the brass honda, will provide weight enough to dilate the big loop.

Now to spin it: Hold on to the honda and throw the rope out across the floor so that it lies straight, is free from kinks, and is unhampered by any obstructions. Form a loop about ten feet in diameter and start the rope spinning just as in the ordinary Wedding Ring. No difficulty should be encountered in starting it although much more force will be required in giving it the initial spin than is ordinarily the case. As soon as your right hand is overhead, start letting out rope *immediately*—it is necessary to move quickly here because the honda is so very heavy that it will collapse a small loop. Continue to let out rope with each spin until the entire rope is out and spinning. With the heavy honda pulling as it does, the letting out of rope is very simple, easier in fact than keeping the loop of uniform size. With each spin release the spoke momentarily and a foot or so of rope will slip out.

This is one stunt in which it is necessary to swing the right arm vigorously in a wide circle around the head until the rope is out. A decided sway of the entire body is necessary to keep the rope going. If the loop seems to get out of control as you are increasing its size, stop letting out rope and give it a few spins until it is subdued and is acting normally again.

Put this spin on with all the showmanship you have. Work hard and let the crowd know you are laboring. Even though you can do the stunt easily, it never pays to let it appear to be easy— that cheapens the trick. This principle does not hold in doing the graceful spins with a light rope; then the opposite is true, but in this heavy stunt it goes far to make the feat impressive. The mistake many professional ropers make is to perform their heavy-rope stunts with too little effort, which makes the maneuvers appear lighter and easier than they really are. The average roper will have no difficulty on this point, because he will be working plenty hard enough to show it in doing the Big Loop—and for reasons.

An elevation of some sort will make possible the spinning of a longer rope than can be accomplished on the level of the ground. A gym horse or a low stepladder will serve very well. Here a nice effort can be obtained by having a number of people stand inside the loop.

Big Loop on Horseback.—Standing on the back of a horse, it is easily possible for a strong man to let out one-hundred feet of rope, the big loop encircling the horse and spinning near the level of the ground.

The most flashy spot in a Wild West show is when a roper spins the Big Loop while standing on horseback, and then rides the horse around the arena at full gallop. This is a stunt that only the best and most athletic of ropers can do.

THE FLAT-LOOP SERIES

In the tricks described in the preceding section the roper stands inside the spinning loop. The maneuvers in this section differ in that the roper stands outside the loop and manipulates it around his body.

Prerequisite to the learning of these tricks is a thorough-going mastery of the Flat Loop by both hands (see page 123).

THE MERRY-GO-ROUND

Rope—fourteen to sixteen feet long with a light honda.

Here we have an interesting and colorful trick that every roper will want to learn. It is not only a good feature in itself but is much used as a transition from one trick to another in a rope-spinning exhibition. It consists of carrying the Flat Loop all the way around the body as illustrated in Figure 66.

While the trick can be done with the fourteen-foot rope used in learning the Flat Loop, a sixteen-foot length will be the better size for the average person, this being the length needed for the tricks in the Combination Series which follows, in which series the Merry-go-round plays an important part.

Start the Flat Loop, counterclockwise as usual, in front of the body and wait until it is going slowly, smoothly, and rhythmically. Then carry the loop around to the left and past the left side where it is given one spin. Then allow it to continue around past the back of the body and over to the right side. Here it is given another spin and is brought around in front again where

the series is started over.   The rope should make four spins in
making the circuit of the body, one in front, one at the left side,
one at the back, and one at the right side—A, B, C, and D in
Figure 66 indicates this sequence of spin.

There are several things to watch in learning this trick: First
off, all movements must be made smoothly and gently.   There is
always the fear that the rope will not get past the back of the body

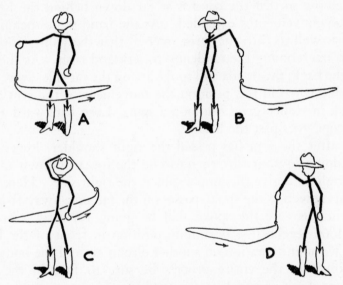

FIGURE 66.   THE MERRY-GO-ROUND, SHOWING THE SEQUENCE OF SPINS

before it stops spinning, with the result that it is given a quick
jerk to hurry it past, and this, of course, breaks the spin.   You
will probably hesitate when you get the rope to the left side of
the body, holding it while you give it several turns to increase the
speed of the spinning so that the loop will carry past the back.
There is no more certain way to defeat the trick.   The slow
rhythm of the loop as it spins in front of the body must be maintained throughout.   The rhythm of this spinning determines the
speed at which the loop should be carried around the body; that

is, the speed of the spoke as the loop revolves sets the speed for carrying the loop around the body.

As the loop reaches the left side give it one gentle spin, this spin being given as the spoke *goes back* and is on the *far* side, the side *away from the body*. With this same motion carry the spoke around in back. Don't worry about the rope getting past the back—its momentum will carry it past easily. When the loop is behind the back the arm is arched back over the head, being bent at the elbow so that the hand is as far down behind the head as it can be conveniently extended. As the hand passes behind the head it is well to turn the wrist over so that the palm is up—this helps in overcoming the tendency to jerk and rush. As the loop passes the back, the honda and spoke are on the far side, away from the body—when in this position the movement of the arm across the back in reality gives the loop a spin. Lean backward a little as the rope goes past the back.

Just after the arm has passed the right shoulder, lower your elbow down to your ribs, then extend the forearm down and out to the right and give the loop a spin at the right side. Here again the spin is given as the spoke passes on the far side, away from the body—in this case the spoke will be going forward. As soon as the loop reaches the beginning position in front of the body, start it without hesitation on another circuit around the body.

Throughout the entire process be sure to face in the same direction—don't succumb to the tendency to turn with the rope.

This trick should be practiced until it can be done easily and without conscious effort. It is a beautiful, graceful maneuver when properly done. The effort should always be for grace of movement rather than speed. Between tricks in an exhibition of flat spins, the Merry-go-round is used as a rest movement and in order to make the transition from trick to trick appear smooth and unforced. This being the case, it should be so completely mastered that it requires no attention or strained effort, and can be done with the utmost grace and ease.

With the development of skill it will be possible to carry the loop around the body in three spins instead of four.

Some may find the learning of this trick a little discouraging, but here, as in all roping, there is only one possible way to defeat discouragement and that is to practice. It is not considered a particularly difficult stunt. Study your movements carefully as you practice and try to find out just what your arm is doing. Then read these instructions over again. Soon you will be surprised to find yourself doing the trick.

Backward Merry-Go-Round.—Once the Merry-go-round is perfected as described above, it will require but very little practice to do the trick with the left hand carrying the loop around the body in the opposite direction. In this trick the rope is spun as usual in the counterclockwise direction.

It is also possible to spin the rope backward (clockwise) and carry it around the body in both directions.

TWO-HANDED MERRY-GO-ROUND

Rope—sixteen feet long with a light honda.

This is a delightful variation of the Merry-go-round, which one can claim as his own in half an hour of practice, once the basic Merry-go-round is mastered. It consists of carrying the spinning loop around the body below the level of the waist by passing the spoke from hand to hand.

Start the Flat Loop with the right hand. Transfer the spoke to the left hand, and with this hand carry the spinning loop over to the left of the body and around behind the back, keeping the hand below the level of the waist. Here take it in the right hand and bring it around in front, where the left hand takes it again and carries it around in back. After the left hand takes the rope it is necessary to give the loop one spin at the left side before carrying it around to the back.

Backward Two-Handed Merry-Go-Round.—Spin the rope in the opposite direction—clockwise—and carry it around the body in the opposite direction.

THE COMBINATION SERIES

It will be noted that the Wedding-Ring Series consists of a number of tricks in which the roper stands inside the spinning noose, whereas the Flat-Spin Series is made up of maneuvers in which the roper is outside the loop. The Combination Series consists of stunts in which the roper is inside the loop part of the time and outside part of the time. These tricks are made up of both the Wedding Ring and the Flat Loop.

JUMPING INTO THE FLAT LOOP

Rope—sixteen feet long with a light honda.
The first thought that comes into one's mind when he can do the Flat Loop is to jump into it, thus turning the Flat Loop into

FIGURE 67. JUMPING INTO THE FLAT LOOP

the Wedding Ring. And this is by no means difficult provided the jump is made at just the right moment. Unless you jump at precisely the right instant the spoke will be in the way and will hit you.

The rope in A, Figure 67, is in the right position for the step in. Note that the spoke is on the *far* side, away from the roper, and is just starting toward him. If you step when the honda is in this position, it will have passed you and be out of the way by the time you actually enter the loop.

It is a case of *stepping into the loop,* not of jumping up and pulling the rope under you, which latter movement would throw the loop lopsided. Spring lightly over into the loop as the roper is doing in B, Figure 67, the rope remaining in the same place throughout. Once you are in it, raise the right hand overhead and do the Wedding Ring.

With practice you will be able to tell when the jump should be made by the feel of the rope in your hand, thus making it unnecessary to watch it.

A polished floor will be a decided help in learning this trick.

JUMPING OUT

Rope—sixteen feet long with a light honda.

After you have jumped into the Flat Loop and are thus spinning the Wedding Ring, the next move is to jump out again. To accomplish this, drop the loop down to the floor and then step backward and out of it, continuing to spin the rope in the Flat Loop in front. The time to lower the rope is just as it passes your left shoulder. As you step back and out, lean well forward so as to be in position to do the Flat Spin.

Remember that it is a case of stepping out of the loop, not of jumping up and pulling the loop forward from under you. The loop is spinning in the same position after you are out as it was before.

When you have learned to jump in and jump out, you can go in and out in rapid succession. As soon as you are in, give the Wedding Ring one spin and then step out, whereat the Flat Loop is given one spin and you step in again.

An interesting variation here is to do the Hand-shaking trick instead of the Wedding Ring after stepping in. When the spoke comes around as you step in, take it in your left hand and carry it around as in Hand-shaking. As soon as your right hand takes the spoke, step out again. In this maneuver the loop is not raised more than a foot from the floor throughout.

TAPPING IN AND OUT

Rope—sixteen feet long with a light honda.

This maneuver involves nothing more in the way of roping than the ordinary Flat Loop but it is an interesting and spectacular maneuver. It consists of stepping into the Flat Loop with one foot and immediately withdrawing it to let the spoke pass. This trick should be easy enough once it is possible to spin the Flat Loop and jump into it. It should not be attempted before jumping into the Flat Loop is learned.

Spin the Flat Loop in front of the body. Lean well forward and raise the right foot in readiness to step forward. The time to step is the same as in Jumping into the Flat Loop—just as the spoke reaches the far side and starts toward you; it will be past and out of the way by the time you have stepped. Keep your eye on the spoke constantly and get its rhythm. At the proper second, shove the right foot in and tap the floor, immediately withdrawing it to let the spoke pass. As soon as the spoke passes, insert it again, tapping the floor with it as before. Practice until you can tap it in the loop regularly without a miss or without losing the rhythm.

When you can tap the right toe in the loop in this manner, try stepping in and taking the weight on the right foot, then immediately withdrawing it. Do not lift the left foot from the floor at first, but merely throw the weight on the right foot. Later, do the finished trick by stepping in with the right foot and at the same time throwing the left foot high up behind. Then step back on the left foot and raise the right to let the spoke pass. This is a spectacular stunt when done rapidly. It is extremely effective if time is kept to music.

We now come to the third method of doing this trick, and it is by all odds the most colorful one, not to say the most difficult. Step in with the right foot, placing the weight on it but keeping the left foot on the floor. As the spoke comes around, jump in the air with both feet, reverse the position of the feet, and land on both feet with the left foot in the loop. The spoke passes while you are in the air. As soon as you land, leap up again, reverse the position of the feet and land with the right foot in the loop.

This trick will furnish lots of interest and plenty of exercise. It is within the capacity of every athletic person and can be learned early in one's roping experience, in that it calls for nothing more in the way of roping skill than the Flat Loop and Jumping In. Be sure to practice it on a polished floor.

UP AND OVER

Rope—sixteen feet long with a light honda.

We now come to one of those tricks that give character and spectacle to the flat spins. It consists of jumping into the Flat

FIGURE 68.   UP AND OVER

Loop and immediately throwing the loop up over the head, then down in front to the Flat Loop again.   Figure 68 shows it.

Spin the Flat Loop a little faster than is normally the case and get it going smoothly with the loop directly parallel with the floor.   Give it a good spin as you step into it and immediately throw the arm up over the head—this throws the loop high up in the air as in B, Figure 68.   Give it a spin while it is at its highest point, then throw it sharply down to the floor in front and pick up the Flat Loop again as in C, Figure 68.   Figure 68 is misleading to the extent that the roper does not turn around in throwing the rope to the floor as C would indicate, but rather faces in the same direction throughout and throws the loop down to the same position it was in before the jump was made.

As in every complicated trick, there are several items to watch in this maneuver: Be sure the Flat Loop is spinning briskly before you step into it—if it is moving slowly and lazily it will not have momentum enough to keep going as it is thrown up. The last spin before you step must give it the force to carry it, but be sure that this last spin is a *circular* spin—there is always danger that you will pull it toward you and upward instead of spinning it perfectly. When you step into it, raise your back foot high and pull it in quickly or it will catch the rope. Further, keep your hand and arm close in to your body as you throw the rope up. The hand normally goes diagonally across from the right hip to the left shoulder, then up past the left side of the head to a point directly overhead, following a sort of corkscrew course as it goes up.

When the rope is overhead, look up at it and give it one spin there as the roper is doing in B, Figure 68, then immediately throw it down in front. Be sure to practice on a polished floor. While learning, throw the loop down directly onto the floor, then jerk it up immediately into the Flat Spin. As skill is acquired, you will be able to stop the loop in the air by starting the Flat-loop motion with the arm as the loop comes down.

JUGGLING UP AND OVER

Rope—sixteen feet long with a light honda.

This trick starts from the Wedding Ring and terminates by the rope being thrown up overhead, then down in front to the Flat Spin. It is a variation of the Up and Over.

Start the Wedding Ring and go into the Juggle (page 141), taking plenty of time to get the loop under control. When the loop is at the lowest point, give it a good spin and throw the arm up over head just as in the Up and Over. Aside from the start of the trick, it is in no respect different from the standard

Up and Over. The details of the Up and Over are discussed in the preceding section.

LIFT ONTO BODY

Rope—twenty feet long with a light honda.

The two Up-and-Over tricks just described are in reality "lifts" in that the noose is carried upward, but they differ from the present one in that in those tricks the roper is inside the loop, whereas in this one, the loop is spun in front and is thrown up and then down around the body. This is a difficult trick to learn, so much so that it is well to delay it until after the Skip described in the next chapter is learned.

We must now give attention for the first time to a principle of roping concerning which we shall have much to say in the chapter on the vertical spins, and one which must be understood before success in this trick will be possible.

If you were to spin the Flat Loop in front of you and then suddenly throw the loop a few feet straight upward, it is obvious that the loop would hit your spinning arm and as a result fall to the floor collapsed. But if, as you raise the loop, you would carry the right hand and the spoke to one side, the loop could pass upward unhampered. You could then reach inside the spinning loop from underneath and continue the spinning from within. Here you have the idea of this trick and also an understanding of a movement necessary in many of the vertical spins. As a matter of fact, the two Up-and-Over tricks just described involve this principle—when the loop is thrown from its highest point down to the floor there is a possibility that the loop will hit the spoke. However, the downward throw tends to pull the spoke over to one side without the roper's paying any attention to the process, and consequently there is no need of discussing the matter in that connection.

A twenty-foot rope should be used with an end of three feet extending over into the left hand, thus making the length of the spinning section about seventeen feet. Start the Flat Loop in the usual way and turn so that the loop is to the right side of the body. Take plenty of time to get the spin going in perfect rhythm and try to absorb the feeling of its rhythm yourself. Lean forward, keeping your eye on the position of the honda. Just as the honda starts forward (toward the direction you are facing) raise the right hand smartly, *first upward and then toward the left,* so that it comes to rest directly in front of the forehead and an inch or two above the level of the head, the arm extending well out to the front. This movement of the hand will carry the spoke

FIGURE 69. LIFT ONTO BODY

outside the loop and at the same time will throw the loop up above the right hand. Now, by bending the elbow, pull the right hand sharply toward the forehead until it almost touches it, and at the same time give the loop a spin with the wrist. The result will be to pull the loop down over the head into the usual Wedding Ring around the body. Figure 69 may help you to understand the movements.

No, this trick will not be performed the first time it is tried—that would be nothing but an accident. It will take repeated practice coupled with constant study of the reasons for failures.

Do not spin the Flat Loop too rapidly at the start of the trick.

When the moment arrives to lift it upward, however, do not hesitate—it must be thrown up smartly and definitely. From the time the loop is lifted until it falls over the head, it makes only one revolution, and consequently there is no time to be wasted. The lift is not a question of sudden, forceful jerks—in fact, but very little muscle is used—but rather of perfect timing and decisive action. There is a spring in the spoke of a spinning noose that is utilized here to send the loop upward sharply, and then to pull it down over the head with equal definiteness. The whole movement, however, must be done in the same rhythm as set by the Flat Loop at the start—try to get the feel of the rhythm from the spoke as it moves around and to swing the hand upward with about the same rate of speed with which the honda revolves. Once you are sure your movements are correct in detail, experiment with the speed of the lift, for it is this question of timing that will require the most practice.

Keep at this trick. It can't be purchased cheaply.

LIFT ONTO ARM

Rope—sixteen feet long with a light honda.

In this trick the Flat Loop is lifted and then dropped around the right arm and spun there, rather than around the body—Figure 70 shows it clearly. What really happens is that after the loop is lifted, the Wedding Ring is spun around the right arm instead of around the entire body. Do not attempt this trick until the Lift onto Body has been learned.

Using a sixteen-foot rope, start a small Flat Loop in front of the body, not over two-and-one-half feet in diameter, allowing the excess rope to extend over into the left hand—see A, Figure 70. Raise the loop directly upward, timing the lift exactly as in the Lift onto Body. As the loop comes up, move the hand a little to the left, thus drawing the spoke out so that the loop does not hit it. Then shove the hand abruptly under the loop and into the center of it—the loop will drop around the arm and a tiny Wedding Ring will be spinning. Figure 70 shows the general movement.

To throw the little Wedding Ring into a Flat Loop again, drop the right arm suddenly and withdraw the spoke. When the loop has fallen, pick up the flat spin in front of the body as usual.

FIGURE 70. LIFT ONTO ARM

THE SKYROCKET

Rope—sixteen feet long with a light honda.

This is a spectacular and none-too-easy flourish of the rope in which the Flat Loop is lifted and carried over the top of the head and down to the opposite side of the body. It differs from the Lift onto Body in that the loop, once lifted, is not dropped over the body into the Wedding Ring but, rather, is carried across the top of the head and then dropped into the Flat Loop again. It is a good trick to learn after the Lift onto Body has been mastered, but will be confusing indeed if attempted before.

Using a sixteen-foot rope, spin the Flat Loop in front of the body, counterclockwise as usual. Carry it over to the left side of the body and let it settle down into a steady rhythm there. Just as the spoke is passing backward (that is, when it is on the side of the loop away from the body) raise the right hand directly upward with a decisive movement. By the time the lift can be made the spoke will be on the near side of the loop and moving forward. Raise the right hand first straight upward, then a little to the right so as to draw the spoke out of the way of the loop. This throws the loop up over the level of the head to the left of the body. With this same movement of the hand to the right, shove the right arm across over the top of the head—this will carry the loop across also. Immediately drop the right hand down to the level of the waist, thus pulling the loop down to the right side of the body into the usual Flat Loop.

As in all the Lifts, the arm must be raised sharply and definitely, yet without jerks. There can be no hesitation from the start of the trick to the finish. The swinging of the right hand up across the head and down is done with one continuous sweep. The rhythm of the spoke in the Flat Loop sets the speed of the hand as it lifts the loop—this same speed is continued as the hand moves up, over the head, and down. The loop makes one spin as it crosses the head, and one as it falls.

A little difficulty may be encountered in preventing the loop from hitting the spoke as it falls to the right, but by studying the position of the spoke as one practices, the proper movement can be easily figured out. By the time one has mastered the art of withdrawing the spoke in the Lift onto Body, he will understand the principle well enough to apply it in this trick.

As soon as the rope has dropped to the right side in the Flat Loop, carry it around to the left side again and start the trick over.

English literature on roping refers to this stunt under the title of Sun-fishing.

SPINNING TWO ROPES

Some trick ropers of the stage and circuses spin two ropes at once, one rope being held in each hand. Some of these stunt performers display a delightful degree of skill in handling the two ropes. On the other hand, some of the best ropers refuse to take up these two-rope stunts, maintaining that if a roper handles one rope well he is doing plenty. I am inclined to string along with this latter point of view. Attempting to handle two ropes militates against good roping rather than contributing to it—the same time spent in perfecting the handling of one-rope tricks would lead to more satisfying results. If a person can handle one rope expertly he does not need to resort to two-rope stunts for a good act.

However, to those who want to experiment with the use of two ropes, the following suggestions may prove interesting.

TWO FLAT LOOPS

Rope—sixteen feet long with a light honda.

Start a Flat Loop, counterclockwise as usual, with the left hand and when it is going nicely start a similar Flat Loop with the right hand, keeping both ropes going with the same rhythm at the same time. This is not a difficult trick and any one who can spin a Flat Loop should be able to learn it in a few minutes.

By keeping the left-hand rope close in to the body, the Merry-go-round can be spun with the right-hand rope. After carrying the Merry-go-round around the body with the right hand a time or two, stop it and continue the Flat Spin with the right hand, then carry the left-hand rope around the body in the Merry-go-round.

Another interesting maneuver is to tap in and out of the loops. Tapping In and Out is described on page 154. Tap the right foot on the floor inside of the right-hand loop and immediately withdraw it. Then tap the left foot on the floor inside of the left-hand loop. With practice this tapping can be carried on at a rapid rate of speed.

WEDDING RING AND FLAT LOOP

Ropes—sixteen feet long and twenty feet long, both with light hondas.

Hold the sixteen-foot rope in the left hand and the twenty-foot rope in the right hand. Start the Flat Loop with the left hand and when it is going nicely start the Wedding Ring with the right hand. It will be necessary to keep the Flat Loop in as close to the body as possible.

While spinning the Flat Loop in the left hand start a slight Juggle with the right hand.

While spinning the Wedding Ring in the right hand, do the Tapping-in-and-out trick in the Flat Loop.

WEDDING RING AND HURDLE

Rope—twenty feet long with a light honda.

Start a Wedding Ring around the body with the left hand, then start a large Flat Loop with the right hand in front of the body. Jump into the Flat Loop and immediately start stepping over the spoke as in the Hurdle. This is a difficult but very spectacular feat.

CHAPTER XI

Rope Spinning—The Vertical Spins

This chapter opens up the second stage in a roper's learning experience, the first stage being confined to flat spins described in the last chapter. In the vertical spins, the rope is spun so that the loop is perpendicular to the floor.

So spectacular are these vertical spins that every beginner is eager to master them as early in his roping experience as possible, and rightly so, for here is roping at its best. More than anything else the vertical spins label one as a master of the art of roping and entitle him to the classification of being out of the amateur stage.

Yet it will be obvious to all who know the first rudiments of handling a rope that these vertical maneuvers are much more difficult than most of the flat spins and consequently cannot be taken up too soon. True, some of the intricate flat spins, such as the Lifts, may prove to be more confusing than any vertical, yet the fact remains that a rather thorough schooling in flat spinning is essential before the tricks in this chapter can be undertaken with any degree of satisfaction. It would be a mistake to jump to the conclusion that these tricks are so forbidding that none but a professional can hope to learn them, for that is far beyond the fact. Once one can do a number of the flat spins these vertical stunts may offer no more of a problem than was encountered in learning the simplest of the flat tricks. Yet if they are attempted before the flat spins, they will be difficult indeed. The result would doubtless be permanent discouragement.

At the beginning of the preceding chapter, a graded list of flat spins was presented, suggesting the order in which the tricks should be learned. It need not be assumed that all of these flat spins must be learned before the various stunts in this chapter are undertaken. After one has learned six or eight of the flat spins he may be familiar enough with the problems offered by the lariat to be able to pick up rather easily the famous Skip, which is not only the feature stunt of vertical spins but the most spectacular of all roping tricks.

GRADED LIST OF VERTICAL SPINS

Assuming that most of the flat spins described in the preceding chapter are well in hand, the vertical tricks presented in this chapter should be taken up in approximately the following order:

1. The Skip	7. The Zigzag
2. Vertical Raise onto Body	8. Vertical Raise onto Arm
3. The Butterfly	9. The Ocean Wave
4. Forward-and-Backward Butterfly	10. The Running Skip
5. The Arrowhead	11. Skip and Turn
6. Rolling Butterfly	12. The Rolls

THE SKIP

Rope—twenty-five feet long with a brass honda.

The Skip is the greatest trick in roping, barring none. Thrilling and spectacular to the onlookers, it is the perfect finale to a roping act. Vigorous and robust, it the best of exercise for the performer. It consists of spinning a large loop and jumping through it as the roper is doing in Figure 71.

I like the Skip—I like to watch it done and I like to do it. It seems to symbolize for me the art of roping. The flying loop as it zigzags back and forth, encircling the jumping roper, is beautiful and invigorating to behold. This is a rugged, lusty stunt— you may be sure that the person who does it is not only a roper but an athlete. It is one of those heavy tricks in which the movements are full, vigorous, and hard. There is none of the delicate and precise wrist motion that is so exasperating in many of the light tricks. Right here is one of chief reasons for its popularity —the heavy, vigorous stunts are always more satisfying to perform than the delicate ones and certainly they carry a greater appeal to the onlookers. For example, the Skip is an easier trick to learn than the delicate Butterfly, yet it is so much more spectacular and appears to be so much more difficult that it completely over-shadows the Butterfly in any roping exhibition. From the stand-point of showmanship there is no comparison between the light and heavy maneuvers—those artists who confine themselves to the delicate tricks are better ropers than they are showmen.

No, the Skip is not too difficult for one with average athletic

FIGURE 71. THE SKIP—GREATEST OF ALL ROPING TRICKS

ability. But it will take work to perfect it. That is why it is so highly valued among ropers—since it cannot be purchased cheaply, few possess it. Yet it probably is the easiest of the major tricks in this chapter, easier certainly than the Butterfly and the Rolls. In comparison to these, the vigorous, muscular characteristics of the Skip belie the ease with which it is learned. It requires just one thing—*practice*. But however much in the way of time it may cost you, it is worth it.

The Skip is really four tricks in one, and each of these stages must be learned separately: (1) the vertical spin, counterclock-wise; (2) the jump through; (3) the backward or clockwise spin;

(4) the jump back. Before we take up each of these stages in turn, however, we must discuss the making of the skip rope.

The Skip Rope.—The Skip calls for a twenty-five-foot rope with a brass honda. Ropers refer to this as the skip rope. Use Number 12 braided cotton sash cord (spot lariat cord). Occasionally an expert uses the smaller Number 10 size for the Skip, but this rope is too fast for a beginner. The Number 12 size spins more slowly and deliberately, giving the roper more time to gauge the time to jump. Secure the brass honda from any cowboy outfitter or spinning rope manufacturer. These hondas are not to be confused with the light metal eyes sold for use on ropes by hardware stores, which latter are useless for our purpose. Send for a standard brass honda made for the purpose—it should weigh at least an ounce and a half. Double the end of the rope around the honda and wire with six or seven wrappings of medium-heavy copper wire, as shown in Figure 72 and described on page 111.

FIGURE 72. BRASS HONDA FOR THE SKIP ROPE

After experimenting with the rope, if you find it so long that the spinning loop is too large for your height, either cut it down to the proper length for you, or let the end extend over into the left hand. Cut off a few inches only and try out the rope again—a few inches make a considerable difference in the size of the loop.

The Vertical Spin, Counterclockwise.—Arrange the rope as in A, Figure 73. Note that the right hand holds the loop up and that the end extends over into the left hand, thus making a rather small loop. The spoke extends about half way from the right hand down to the ground.

Give the loop a hard spin by throwing the right hand forward and downward in a semicircular course, and as you do so, release the loop with both hands, retaining hold of the spoke only. Keep the loop spinning by whirling the right hand briskly in a circle about a foot in diameter. Just the second you see that the rope is actually spinning, start letting out rope with each spin until it is all out and spinning as in B, Figure 73. It is imperative that you let out rope quickly because the honda is so heavy that it will collapse the small loop, whereas when the rope is all out the weight

FIGURE 73. STARTING THE VERTICAL SPIN

of the honda will keep the loop open and spinning steadily in the vertical position.

Weighted as the honda is, the initial spin must be much harder and more decisive than is the case in any of the light-rope tricks. In fact, more force must be used throughout the entire trick because of the greater weight of the rope, but once the rope is all out, the spinning is done entirely with the wrist, not the arm.

Beware of wild and violent arm motion. Each time the spoke comes around, give it an emphatic spin with the wrist. In a heavy vertical spin like this, one of the chief concerns is to keep the loop from dropping low enough to touch the floor. Consequently the spin is given each time that the spoke comes *up*—this tends to lift the loop up at the same time that it revolves it.

The heavy honda keeps the rope spinning in this position much more easily than one might expect. Once going, the honda does much to carry the spin. One of the reasons why a heavy trick like this is easier to do is that slight jerks which would destroy a delicate spin have no disastrous effects—the weight of the honda is great enough to overcome these irregular movements and the loop goes right on spinning.

The skip rope can be spun with great speed, and the beginner usually delights in whirling it as rapidly as possible. Here, as in all roping, however, we must practice the spin slowly, evenly, and rhythmically

Care must be exercised to keep the loop spinning in a perpendicular plane. There is often a tendency for the loop to settle down over one's head and gradually fall into the Wedding Ring. Keep the spinning arm extended almost at full length, and be sure that the wrist throws the spoke straight upward with each spin.

Do not rush into jumping through the loop. Take plenty of time to perfect the spinning before trying the jumping. You will get there more quickly if you do.

Jumping Through.—Spin the rope as described above and turn your left side toward it, reaching your right arm across in front of your body, as the roper is doing in B, Figure 73. Slow down the spinning as much as possible. Now it is a case of perfect timing: unless you jump at just the right time the spoke will hit you. The time to jump is when the spoke is going *down*. The spoke is in just the right position for the jump in A, Figure 74. By the time you have jumped, it will be going up as in B, Figure 74, and thus will be out of the way. If you wait until the spoke is going up before jumping, you will be unable to get through before it will be going down and thus be in the direct line of your jump.

As the spoke starts down, jump in the air and pull the spoke sharply toward you, thereby carrying the loop around your body and over to the other side, as shown in B, Figure 74. After you have jumped, the loop will be spinning on your other side, as in A, Figure 75.

It is not a case of jumping over into the loop, but rather of jumping straight up and pulling the loop past you. There is a spring in the spoke of a spinning loop that sends the loop flying past you when you pull it.

Here are the items to watch in learning this trick: As you pull

FIGURE 74. JUMPING THROUGH—FIRST MOVEMENT IN THE SKIP

the loop toward you, keep your hand close in to your body. Your hand goes right across the pit of your stomach and must be so close that it almost brushes it. Be sure to give the loop a hard spin on its last revolution before you jump, and then forget about the spinning. In pulling the rope to you, your hand goes straight across, or, if anything, rises a little. Beginners usually throw the loop down toward the floor for fear that it will hit the feet if they do not. There is never any danger here—the problem is to keep it up high enough so that it will not hit the floor. Jump off the floor at the same second that you pull and raise your feet high. If you give the rope an emphatic pull, draw your hand straight across and keep it close in to your stomach, and at the same time pick your feet up high, the rope cannot fail to sail past without hitting.

Don't worry about spinning the rope on the other side once you have jumped through. That is another trick and can come later. Keep practicing the spin and the jump. Practice each movement separately, and before you know it, you will be putting them all together in the completed trick.

True, the honda is heavy and moves swiftly, and if it should hit you squarely it might hurt a little. Knowing that the heavy honda is there, it takes a little courage to jump into the loop. But that is part of the game and you can be sure that the honda cannot do any severe damage.

With practice you can tell by the feel of the rope in your hand when the time arrives to jump. Then you will be doing the trick automatically and with no conscious attention.

Be sure to practice on a polished floor.

When you can spin the rope as described you have learned one half of the Skip. The next task is to learn the clockwise spin and jump back.

The Second or Clockwise Spin.—After you have jumped through the loop, the rope is spinning in the opposite direction, in respect to your position, from what it was before you jumped. It is actually spinning in the same direction, but it is going in the opposite direction *in relation to the roper*, and that is the factor that counts. Before you jumped the loop was being spun counterclockwise and after the jump, clockwise.

Since there is no need to know how to do the second or clockwise spin until you can jump through the loop, the easiest way to learn it is to jump through and then try to keep the spin going on the other side. This should offer very little difficulty because the rope is already spinning. If you were careful not to let the loop hit the floor too hard when you jumped, it should still be revolving vigorously and the only worry will be to pick up the spinning motion with your arm before the loop has slowed down too much. Having jumped, the rope is spinning on your right side. As soon as you gain your footing, look toward the rope and gain control of it as quickly as possible. Remember the emphasis in the spinning should be on the *upward* stroke; otherwise the loop will sink down and hit the floor.

No detailed instructions are necessary here. The loop is already spinning and a little practice will discover the means of keeping it going.

Jumping Back.—As with the first jump, the time to jump is when the spoke is going down. However, in this case it seems easier for most beginners to put the emphasis on the upward

FIGURE 75. JUMPING BACK—SECOND MOVEMENT IN THE SKIP

motion. As the spoke starts upward—when it is in the position shown in A, Figure 75—give it an emphatic spin and then wait a second until it has time to start downward. At this point jump in the air and give the spoke a sharp pull toward you. It will pass around you as in B, Figure 75.

The same points must be remembered here as in the first jump: Keep your right hand close in to your body, bringing it past the pit of your stomach, and pull it straight across or a little upward to prevent the loop from striking the floor. Be sure to pick your feet up high.

The Finished Skip.—Now that we have learned all the elements, we are ready to do the complete Skip. Keep the body facing in the same direction throughout, turning only the head and shoulders toward the rope. At first, spin the rope three times on each

side, that is, pull the loop across in the third spin. This makes a
reasonably fast trick, yet gives you time to get your bearings after
each jump. As soon as you are able, do the trick by spinning the
loop twice on each side, jumping on the second spin. This is the
standard rhythm for the trick. In case the loop gets out of control at any point, stop jumping and spin it until it settles down
again.

The Skip relies on the spring in the spinning loop for aid in
pulling it back and forth. After the jump the loop flies as far to
the side as the length of the spoke will permit, and here it seems
to spring back of its own accord. When done in the proper
rhythm of two spins on each side, the spring back starts it on its
way across again, and consequently less force is needed than otherwise would be the case.

Alternative Method for the Skip.—The Skip can be done by
spinning the rope in the opposite direction from that described
above. That is, when the loop is on the left side, spin it clockwise,
and when on the right side, counterclockwise. The general procedure is the same for both methods and any one can learn this
method from the points presented above in the detailed discussion
of the first method.

SKIP AND TURN

Rope—twenty-five feet long with a brass honda.

Here is the most brilliant version of the Skip. It should not
replace the standard Skip but rather be used as a finishing flourish,
and as such, it constitutes a dazzling finale.

Start the rope spinning in the usual way preliminary to skipping,
and face the loop squarely with the body instead of turning the
left side to it as in the standard Skip. Jump and pull the loop past
you as in the Skip but as you do, turn in the air, doing a right-
about-face so that when you land on the floor you are facing the
opposite direction and are still facing the loop squarely as it spins
on the other side. Now jump back as in the last half of the Skip,
but turn to the right in the air again so that you are once more

facing the loop as it spins on the original side. This gives a surprisingly effective flourish to the stunt.

But there is still more color to be added: Keep your feet together as you jump and land on your toes, springing right back up in the air again. Jump through the loop on every second spin, that is, spin it once and jump through on the next spin. After the jump, spring up in the air from your toes for a height of three or four inches, this spring being in time with the spin of the loop in front of you. As soon as you land from this spring, jump high and pull the loop past you. You are thus springing up in the air with every spin of the loop, skipping it on every other spin, and turning an about-face in the air as you skip. That is action enough to add spectacle to any stunt.

If this sets too fast a pace for you, jump the rope on every third spin. Certainly you will need to do that in learning.

Note that all turns in the air are made to the right. Thus when you have completed the two jumps of the full Skip, you have turned in a complete circle. The tendency is to do a left-about-face in making the second jump, but this is wrong. The first jump will offer no difficulty because, in turning to the right, the left side of the body is turned toward the loop and thus is in exactly the same position as in the standard Skip. The jump back, however, offers its problems because, in turning to the right, the left side of the body is presented to the loop whereas in the standard Skip the right side is toward it. Learn this second jump by practicing it with the standard Skip, minus the turning in the air—after you have made the first jump of the Skip, turn the *left* side toward the rope and try to jump back. Be sure to keep your rope hand close in to your body as you jump, pulling it right past the pit of your stomach.

RUNNING SKIP

Rope—twenty-five feet long with a brass honda.

Down the arena of the circus tent comes the colorful cowboy, running at top speed, the flying loop of his lariat zigzagging back and forth as he skips through it, without missing a step or slowing up in the slightest. It is the Running Skip—a headliner in any circus, and a challenge to the toughest and most strenuous of athletes.

This trick is a hard nut to crack, not that it calls for the learning of another difficult roping trick, but that it demands perfect coordination and a sturdy constitution.

It goes without saying that the chief prerequisite is a perfect Skip. Given this, there is nothing to stop one from trying to run with it.

Two steps are taken between skips, that is, the roper takes two running steps, makes the first jump through the loop, and so on. In other words the rope is skipped on every third step. The running must be done in rhythm with the spinning loop. Spin the loop twice and jump through on the third spin. The stepping thus coincides with the spinning, the roper taking one step for each spin and in rhythm with the spin. To be spectacular the running must be fast, and since the feet must keep time with the spinning the steps are typically long and gliding. The third step, on which the jump through takes place, is more of a jump into the air than a step, the roper bringing both feet up high beneath him.

Practice by walking rather than running. By taking short steps and not attempting to cover much ground, the movements can be practiced with fewer breakdowns. Once the movements become habitual the pressure can be applied and the run speeded up.

Perhaps the hardest movement in this trick is spinning the loop on the left side while running. It takes considerable muscular effort to spin the loop while reaching across the body with the right arm at the same time that one is running.

If you ever valued a smooth floor for roping practice, you will appreciate one here. And once you try to do this trick on a polished floor, you will appreciate what the circus cowboy is up against when he must do it over the rough and sometimes muddy ground in a circus tent.

This trick may be done by using either of the methods of doing the Skip described above. The Alternative Method for the Skip (page 173) is perhaps a little more desirable for the Running

Skip than the standard method for the reason that in this method the rope is being spun forward, in the direction of the running, and consequently the motion given the loop in spinning it tends to carry it forward.

Backward Running Skip.—This novelty is exactly like the Running Skip except that the roper moves backward. Needless to say the steps are short and the speed of movement much slower.

VERTICAL RAISE ONTO BODY

Rope—twenty-five feet with a brass honda.

Figure 76 tells the story of this movement rather clearly. It is scarcely classified as a roping trick, but it is a handy movement

FIGURE 76. VERTICAL RAISE ONTO BODY

to know when giving a roping exhibition, in that it is often used as a transition from one trick to another.

Use the twenty-five-foot rope with its brass honda, but allow the end to extend over into the left hand, thus shortening the rope three or four feet. Start a flat loop in front of the body or one that is a cross between a flat and vertical spin, as shown in A, Figure 76. Raise the loop into a vertical spin as in B, and then continue to raise the arm until the loop is spinning over the head in a plane parallel to the floor, as in C. When in this position it will settle down into the Wedding Ring around the body of its own accord.

When the rope is spinning in the vertical plane, remember that the emphasis must be placed on the upward stroke of the arm, rather than on the downward. This not only spins the loop successfully, but tends to prevent it from sagging down toward the floor—it serves to lift the loop. The loop must be raised gradually and the lifting done in this upward stroke of the spoke.

This is, really, a very simple maneuver. In fact, it is often easier for a beginner to let a vertical spin settle down over his head into the Wedding Ring than it is to keep it spinning vertically. For example, in learning the Skip the beginner must take precautions to keep the loop spinning vertically and to prevent it from settling down over the head. That is why the Skip should be learned before the Raise—the Skip forces one to master a clean, vertical spin, which will be easier to accomplish if one has not practiced letting it drop back into a flat spin.

Just how high overhead the loop can be raised depends upon the length of the rope used. If the full length of the Skip rope is let out, it will be difficult to raise it completely over the head; what will happen is that the top of the vertical loop will settle back over the head and down behind, thus forming the Wedding Ring, without the loop flattening out into a flat spin over the top of the head. With a shorter rope, it will be possible to raise the loop higher.

VERTICAL RAISE ONTO ARM

Rope—fourteen feet long with a light metal honda.

Use a fourteen-foot rope equipped with a brass honda weighing three-fourths of an ounce or an ounce—about half the weight of the standard brass honda. This honda is made by grinding down the edges of a standard brass honda.

Spin this rope in a vertical plane, counterclockwise as usual. Raise the arm gradually until the loop is spinning around the spinning arm in a flat spin. The result is a tiny Wedding Ring around the right arm.

RAISE OFF THE BODY OR ARM

When the Raise onto Body has been completed and the loop is spinning around the body in the Wedding Ring, it can be raised off the body by gradually bringing the spinning arm back to its original position. The loop will then be spinning vertically in front of the body.

The Raise Off the Arm is done in the same way.

THE BUTTERFLY

Rope—fourteen feet long with a light honda.

The Butterfly is one of the most beautiful of the lariat tricks. Many regard it as the acme of roping grace. It is a delicate little

FIGURE 77. THE BUTTERFLY

trick, however, and consequently is considered rather difficult by most learners. Small, delicate motions requiring careful balance and timing are always more difficult to perfect than the full, strong movements. Further, the Butterfly does not stand out in a roping exhibition nearly as vividly as the larger loops, and does not give the impression of being as hard as it really is.

In the Butterfly, a small loop is spun vertically in front and to the left of the body, and then is carried across to the right side in front, then back to the left side again, and so on without interruption. The loop thus floats back and forth in a sort of figure-of-eight motion. Figure 77 may help to make it clear. The principle is the same as in the Skip except that the trick is done in front of the body without the jump through.

Use a fourteen-foot rope while learning, holding it with the end in the right hand. Start a vertical loop *clockwise* in front of the left shoulder, using a spoke about one foot long. The loop is spun at right angles to the chest, not parallel to it—study Figure 77. Start the spin at shoulder height and then allow it to drop down to the line of the waist. Try to revolve the loop as slowly as possible.

Here again the question of timing comes up. Just as the honda reaches the bottom of its revolution draw the hand across to the right and a little upward. This will carry the loop across to the right side. Unless the pull across is made just at the right moment, the spoke will be in the way and will hit the loop. If made as directed the spoke will be pulled out of the way.

When the loop reaches the right side, it will be spinning in a counterclockwise direction and the hand must pick up this spin immediately. Again, just as the honda reaches the bottom of its revolution, draw the right hand across to the left and a little upward, thus throwing the loop back to its original position. Continue to carry the loop back and forth in this way. The rule to remember is to make the reverse *when the honda is at the bottom of the loop.*

Although it may be necessary to spin the loop several times on each side while learning, the Butterfly calls for two spins on each side and this rhythm should be picked up just as early in the practice as possible. As a matter of fact, the loop makes one-and-a-half circles on each side and is carried over to the other side on the last half circle. The emphasis in spinning should always be put on the first spin on each side.

This trick is done almost entirely with the wrist. The wrist must be kept very flexible and must flow smoothly back and forth with the rhythm of the loop, without jerks or sudden movements.

Here rests the chief problem in learning the Butterfly. When a small, light loop is being spun vertically, any slight jerk will destroy it. It will take time to train the wrist so that the proper movements will be made evenly and automatically. The right hand follows a figure-of-eight course as it goes back and forth, circling twice with each loop of the eight. The body turns slightly to the left when the loop is on that side, then to the right, with a gentle, swaying motion.

It will be a great help to count as you spin the loop, saying *"One* and, two and, *one* and, two and." The loop is carried over on the second *and*. Emphasizing the *one* helps you to give greater emphasis to the first spin on each side.

The loop spins *clockwise* on the left side, and counterclockwise on the right side. In reality, it is spinning in the same direction throughout, but *in relation to your position* it spins in opposite directions on each side. There is no interruption in the spinning nor any reversal of direction—the loop merely appears to be going in opposite directions as viewed by the roper.

It may help to visualize the proper time to carry the loop across if you think of the spinning loop as the face of a clock. The time to carry the hand across is when the honda reaches *six o'clock*. This applies to both sides.

THE BUTTERFLY—FORWARD AND BACKWARD

Rope—fourteen feet long with a light honda.

In the standard Butterfly the loop is carried back and forth from left to right in front of the body. It can also be done forward and backward.

Start a vertical spin clockwise in front of the right shoulder so that the plane of the loop is parallel to the plane of the chest. The movement is exactly as in the standard Butterfly except that the loop is pulled back past the right side, from which point it is carried forward again. The timing is exactly as in the Butterfly, the loop being reversed when the honda is at the bottom of its revolution, that is, when it is in the six o'clock position.

The same trick can be done at the left side of the body, which latter should be as thoroughly mastered as the right-side motion in that it leads up to and serves as a foundation for the picturesque Arrowhead, the next trick to be learned. Spin the loop clockwise in front of the left shoulder and carry it backward past the left side, then forward again.

Both of these tricks can be learned very quickly once the standard Butterfly is well in hand. They will then involve nothing new in the way of roping.

FIGURE 78. THE ARROWHEAD

THE ARROWHEAD

Rope—fourteen feet long with a light honda.

This is a combination of the standard Butterfly and the Forward-and-Backward Butterfly.

Start the trick as in the Forward-and-Backward Butterfly: spin the loop clockwise in front of the right shoulder and carry it backward past the right side. When it is brought forward again, it is drawn to front and center of the body, and from here it is carried back past the left side. The rope follows the course shown in Figure 78. This course forms an arrowhead, hence the name of the trick. It is sometimes referred to as the Triangular Butterfly.

Any one who can do a good Butterfly will have no trouble in learning this trick.

REVERSING THE BUTTERFLY

Rope—fourteen feet long with a light honda.

The best way to reverse the direction of the loop in the Butterfly is to reverse the direction of the *body*. Spin the standard Butterfly as usual, clockwise on the left side and counterclockwise on the right side. When the loop is on the left side, make a quick about-face to the left, facing in the opposite direction—you will find yourself spinning the loop *clockwise on your right side*, thus forming the first movement of the Reverse Butterfly in front of the body. Practice this about-face until you can spin the rope easily in the clockwise direction on the right side.

Now spin the standard Butterfly and when the loop is on the right side, do a sudden about-face to the right, and you will be spinning *counterclockwise* on the *left* side.

When both of these reverse spins have been learned, it will be easy to put them together into the complete Reverse Butterfly without turning the body.

This reversal of your body position is always a good feature when giving an exhibition of vertical spinning.

Keep in mind the fact that the direction of the spin is not actually reversed in any of these movements. The loop spins in the same direction throughout, but merely appears to be different as viewed from the standpoint of the roper.

THE ROLLING BUTTERFLY

Rope—fourteen feet long with a light honda.

This flourish is a graceful variation of the standard Butterfly. Start the Butterfly back and forth in front of the body, but instead of drawing the hand directly across, draw it upward to the line of the neck, then lower it to the usual level on the other side. The loop will follow the hand and its course will form a sort of figure-of-eight. Care must be taken not to jerk the loop or force it with sudden movements.

THE ZIGZAG

Rope—fourteen feet long with a light honda.

The Zigzag is a Butterfly in which the loop is spun once on each side rather than twice. It is a favorite of the ropers and is much used in spinning exhibitions.

In this trick the loop is not carried back and forth across the body but rather is shifted in similar fashion on either side of the spinning hand which remains directly in front of the body. Thus we have the loop spinning in two parallel planes only a few inches apart, one on the left side of the spinning hand and the other on the right.

There are two methods of spinning the Zigzag, which really constitutes two separate tricks, but they are so nearly alike in effect that none but an expert can detect the difference. Both should be learned, however, and one leads easily to the other.

First, spin it exactly like the Butterfly but with one spin on each side rather than two. Give the loop a clockwise spin on the left side, and just as the honda reaches its lowest point give it a gentle pull upward and to the right which will shift the loop to the right

FIGURE 79. THE
ZIGZAG

side of the hand; then shift it back on its first revolution, making the pull as the honda reaches its lowest point. The arm remains stationary directly in front of the body, the hand turning from side to side by a movement of the waist only. This trick will take an agile and flexible wrist.

The second method differs from this in that the loop is not shifted from one side of the hand to the other, but rather the *hand is shifted* from one side of the loop to the other and the loop remains in practically the same plane throughout. If Figure 79 will be studied carefully, it will give the idea more clearly than words can do. Use a very short spoke. Make a clockwise spin just as in starting the Butterfly but with the loop directly in front of the body. In making this spin the hand is on the right side of the loop. When the spoke reaches the *top* of the loop, turn the hand over to the left and give it the second spin from the left side. Then when the spoke reaches the top again, carry the hand over the top to the right and give it another spin. There is one spin on each side, the hand turning over from one side to the other as indicated in Figure 79. The time to shift in this trick is when the spoke reaches its highest point.

If the first method of doing the Zigzag, the Butterfly method, is practiced conscientiously, you will find yourself drifting into this second method easily and naturally.

The Zigzag is an excellent climax for a series of Butterfly spins. One can go from the Butterfly to the Zigzag and back again at will.

Reverse Zigzag.—To start a Reverse Zigzag, begin by doing the Reverse Butterfly, and from there go into the Zigzag.

THE OCEAN WAVE

Rope—twenty-five feet long with a medium-heavy honda.

No trick in the whole category of roping carries more of brilliance than the Ocean Wave, save only the Skip. And the Skip and Ocean Wave are very similar, in fact, are often combined in the best presentation of the Ocean Wave. The two are frequently referred to as variations of the same trick. Ropers generally have a fondness for the Ocean Wave and at the same time regard it as one of the most difficult of roping tricks.

The Ocean Wave is really an oversized Butterfly that is carried all the way around the body. It is the Skip minus the jumping-through feature, the large loop being carried across in front of the body and then back across in the rear of the body. A clockwise spin about five-and-a-half feet in diameter is started on the right side and is carried over to the left side just as in the Butterfly, from which point it is·carried back behind the left shoulder, then across the back to the right side again.

With this general description let us attack the details of learning the trick.   Use a twenty-five foot rope with a medium-heavy honda.   The ordinary, light honda made by bending the end back and wiring it will not supply weight enough to carry the large loop in the vertical position.   On the other hand, the brass honda on the skip rope is much too heavy.   Add a little weight to the

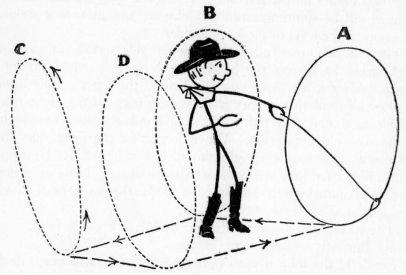

FIGURE 80.   THE OCEAN WAVE, SHOWING THE SERIES OF SPINS

light honda by wrapping it with wire, or use a light aluminum honda.

Prerequisite to the learning of this trick is the mastery of the Butterfly, the Reverse Butterfly, and the Skip.

There are several ways of starting this spin but happily the method approved by tradition for exhibitions is also the easiest for the beginner.   Grip the rope three feet from the end with the right hand, allowing the end to extend over into the left hand. Start the spin just as in the Butterfly with a clockwise spin on the left side, and carry it across to the right side as in the Butterfly, then back to the left side again. At this point do an about-face as in the Reverse Butterfly and the loop will be spinning clockwise on the right side and thus in position to start the Ocean Wave.

The time to pull the loop across to the left side is when the honda is at the top, that is, when it is at the twelve-o'clock position —the time is the same as in drawing the loop from right to left in the Skip. As in the Skip, the right hand must be carried across rather close to the body and must follow an upward slant to raise the loop higher on the left side. When the loop reaches the left side it will be spinning counterclockwise, and its center should be about at the level of the left shoulder.

Give the loop one full spin on the left side and then carry the right hand back over the head, thus drawing the loop straight back. After it has made one spin behind the left shoulder, give it a strong pull that carries it across the back to the right side. The time to make this pull is when the honda is at its lowest point —the six-o'clock position. When it reaches the right side, the loop will be behind the right shoulder, and here it is given one spin and carried forward to the starting position. The loop makes four spins in making the circuit of the body, the positions of which are indicated in Figure 80.

The speed of spinning in the Ocean Wave is much faster than in the Butterfly, at least twice as fast.

Similarly the loop is carried around the body at a much more brisk pace than it is moved in the Butterfly.

In the Ocean Wave the loop floats along with graceful, un-dulating curves. It is this characteristic movement that gives it its name.

OCEAN WAVE WITH SKIP

Rope—twenty-five feet long with a medium-heavy honda.

In this variation of the Ocean Wave, the trick is started just as in the standard Ocean Wave. Give the large loop a clockwise spin on the right side and carry it across in front of the body to the left side. Now, instead of carrying it behind the back, jump through it as in skipping, thus bringing it over to the right side, where the trick is started over. When the loop is on the left side it is spinning counterclockwise and is in exactly the same position for the jump from left to right as in the standard Skip.

FORWARD-AND-BACKWARD OCEAN WAVE

Rope—twenty-five feet long with a medium-heavy honda.

This is the same as the Forward-and-Backward Butterfly except that the rope is carried all the way around the body. Use a loop about five feet in diameter. Start a Forward and Backward Butterfly on the right side. When the loop comes forward carry it straight across to the left, in a plane parallel to the chest. Here give it one spin and then carry it across behind the back in a plane parallel to the back. All movements and timing are as in the Forward-and-Backward Butterfly.

The only difference between this trick and the standard Ocean Wave is in the direction that the loops face. In the Ocean Wave the loop is at right angles to the plane of the chest as it crosses in front, whereas, in this trick, it is parallel to the plane of the chest.

This trick is seldom used and is lacking in popularity as compared to the Ocean Wave.

THE ROLLS

Rope—fourteen feet long with a light honda.

The Rolls are exceedingly difficult tricks. Being intricate and involving a small loop, they do not carry well and possess but little show value. Spectators very seldom realize their difficulty or appreciate the great amount of time required to develop the necessary skill. They receive no applause comparable to the "hand" given the heavy tricks. Consequently many ropers feel that they are not worth the effort required to learn them. Certainly they should not be taken up until after all the standard roping tricks are well in hand, for the reason of their difficulty, their lack of show value, and their inability to provide exercise while practicing.

In the Rolls, the loop is caused to roll over the arm, the back of the neck, the leg, or other parts of the body. In these maneuvers, the loop is not spun from the center as in other tricks, but rather it is given a circular jerk so that it rolls along much like a hoop, the spoke being pulled outside the loop.

There is almost a limitless number of Rolls. Once the principle involved has been mastered, one finds himself originating new varieties constantly. This chapter will discuss a few of the better known ones which will serve to indicate the type. Since a person will be rather expert as a roper before taking up the Rolls, there will be no need to go into minute detail in describing these maneuvers.

Roll Over the Spinning Arm.—The Rolls always develop out of a Butterfly. Start a Forward-and-Backward Butterfly at the right side of the body. When the loop is thrown forward, it will be spinning in a clockwise direction. Carry this clockwise spin across in front of the body parallel to the chest in two revolutions. When it reaches the left side it should be about waist high. Give the loop one more spin and just as the honda reaches its lowest point and is ready to start upward, raise the loop upward sharply. Shove the right hand under the loop, bending the wrist up so that the hand can follow the spoke as the loop rolls over the arm. As it crosses the arm, the honda should be on the top side of the loop. As soon as the loop falls from the arm, the right hand is pulled back and picks up the spin again.

Roll Over the Shoulders.—The start of this Roll is exactly like the Roll Over the Spinning Arm described above. When the loop reaches the left side, it is lifted and pulled back onto the left shoulder. At the same time the roper bends down and the loop is rolled across his back at the line of his shoulders.

Roll Over the Chest.—This is exactly like the Roll Over the Shoulders except that the roper leans well backward and the loop is rolled across his chest.

Roll Over the Left Leg.—In this trick the left leg is extended straight out in front. The trick is started just as in the Roll Over the Spinning Arm. When the clockwise loop is carried to the left it goes under the raised leg. The right hand gives it its momentum to go back over the top of the leg from beneath it. As soon as the right hand tosses the loop up and over the leg, it releases the spoke and catches it when the loop falls on the other side. The Butterfly is then picked up again.

CHAPTER XII

Trick Knots with a Lariat

With a flip of his skillful wrist the circus cowboy throws a knot into his lariat—perhaps a Pretzel, perhaps a Figure-of-eight, or perchance a Slip Knot. And it all happens so quickly as to defy the eye to detect the method. A straight rope, a flash of the wrist—and there it is! Another jerk and it is no longer there but has been transformed into another knot.

This tying of knots in the cowboy fashion takes on the flavor of magic, so deftly and quickly is it done. And with the use of one hand only! The hand is always quicker than the eye—happily so, for if it were not this way, the tying of cowboy knots would lose its glamour. These are simple knots, but when tied in the trick way they intrigue and arouse wonder—they have show value sufficient to hold a spot in any roping act. In stage roping they are sure-fire.

There is no question about the interest these cowboy knots carry for the doer. There are few more fascinating things in roping. Requiring very little muscular effort, they can be practiced during breathing spells while learning the rope-spinning tricks. These knots are well worth all the effort required for the learning. Few do them, even among the expert performers. In fact a number of the knots are original with the author.

Some of these knots belong in a rope-spinning act, being done with a spinning rope, while others fit better into a lariat-throwing exhibition, performed as they are with a catch-rope.

GRADED LIST OF TRICK KNOTS

It is recommended that the trick cowboy knots be learned in the following order:

1. Pretzel
2. Figure-of-eight
3. Overhand
4. Slip
5. Pretzel to Figure-of-eight

6. Figure-of-eight to Pretzel
7. Combinations of Knots
8. Half-hitches
9. Flying Overhand

TRICK KNOTS WITH A SPINNING ROPE

These knots are tied with the end of an ordinary spinning rope made of braided cotton sash cord. A well broken-in rope that is soft, flexible, and free from wiry kinks is required. The skip rope with its brass honda is preferred for these knots in that the weight of the honda is a decided asset. They can be done with any spinning rope, however.

THE PRETZEL

The Pretzel is the most interesting and attractive of all the knots, and since it is no more difficult than the rest, it may as well be tackled first. The fact is that when you have learned the Pretzel you have really learned how to tie two knots, and have mastered the essential features of all of them. The others are all variations of the same movement.

Take hold of your spinning rope with your right hand about three feet from the honda and allow it to hang down by your side as shown in A, Figure 81. Note that the palm of the hand as it holds the rope is up. Now quickly flip the hand over, throwing the rope back over the wrist, forming the loop shown in B. After this movement is made, the palm of the hand is down. Practice this movement many times, without attempting to complete the trick, until you can do it easily and smoothly, making a loop of the same size each time.

This done, we are ready for the second half of the trick. In the same motion with which you turn your wrist over, jerk up the honda and catch it in the loop as indicated by the arrow in B, Figure 81. Shake the loop off your wrist gently and let it fall—you will have the Pretzel shown in C, Figure 81.

Practice this trick until you can do it like a flash. It cheapens the stunt to do it slowly and deliberately. The whole idea here is to flash the knot into the rope so quickly that the eye cannot detect what happens. With practice it can be done just that quickly.

To speed up the process, as soon as you jerk up the honda shove the hand down to meet it, thus catching it in the loop. Instantly jerk the hand up again and the knot is tied.

Keep the left hand far over to the left side so that there can

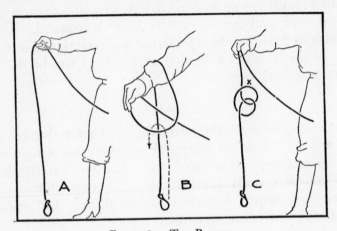

FIGURE 81. THE PRETZEL

be no question about the knot being tied by the right hand alone, entirely without assistance.

You may be surprised to find that even though you follow these instructions to the letter you get not the Pretzel, but the Figure-of-eight. There is no mystery here because the two knots are tied by exactly the same process, and this being the case, the instructions for the Figure-of-eight should be studied while learning the Pretzel.

THE FIGURE-OF-EIGHT

If you have practiced tying the Pretzel you have probably already discovered that the Figure-of-eight results from the process about as often as does the Pretzel. The beginner, therefore, jumps to the conclusion that there is no way to predict just which knot will result. On this point he is not so far wrong in that the method of tying the two knots is precisely the same, and even an expert sometimes starts to tie a Pretzel and finishes with a Figure-of-eight, much to his annoyance.

The difference rests not in the tying but in the shaking of the rope off the arm. Figure 81 shows the process of tying the Figure-of-eight as well as the Pretzel, and the instructions for the Pretzel in the foregoing section all apply. If the knot is given a jerk as it falls from the arm the Figure-of-eight (Figure 82) will result, whereas if it is shaken off gently the Pretzel will appear. If a rope with a brass honda is used, the Figure-of-eight will normally result, the weight of the honda serving to jerk it sufficiently as it falls. An unweighted honda will usually produce a Pretzel. With practice, however, you will be able to tie whichever knot you choose with reasonable consistency, using the same rope for both. Since a brass honda is such a great convenience in tying trick knots, it should always be preferred. In tying the Pretzel with it, lower the hand a little as the rope falls, thus relieving the jerk which the heavy honda produces.

Practice is the whole secret in these trick knots. You do not have a knot learned unless you can do it twenty-five or fifty times in succession without a miss on several successive days. And remember that speed is the goal for which you must aim constantly.

FROM PRETZEL TO FIGURE-OF-EIGHT

This and the trick that follows are two of the cleverest turns that can be given to the tying of trick knots with a lariat. These two tricks are original—I have never seen or heard of them being done by others in the past. Many are the stage artists of roping who tie the Pretzel and the Figure-of-eight, but I have never seen one turn a Pretzel into a Figure-of-eight by a jerk of the rope, or vice versa.

There are three parts to a knot: the knot proper, the end, and the standing part. The end refers to the end of the rope at the honda. The standing part is the section between the hand and the knot.

To get the idea of the trick, use the hand to convert the Pretzel into a Figure-of-eight: tie the Pretzel as described above, then take hold of the upper loop (X in C, Figure 81) with your left hand and turn it downward. The result is a Figure-of-eight.

Now do it in trick fashion: when the Pretzel is tied and held as in C, Figure 81, jerk the hand quickly downward so as to throw the standing part against the upper loop of the knot at X. Note in C that the standing part passes behind the upper loop of the knot. With the knot in this position, the hand would be jerked diagonally forward and downward in order to turn the upper loop downward.

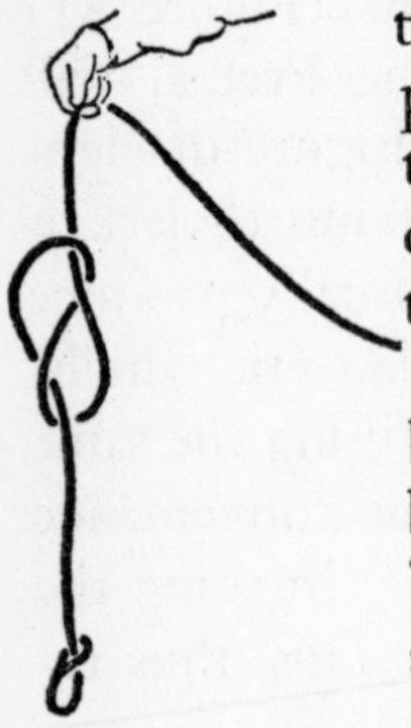

In the actual tying of the knot the Pretzel should be turned so that the upper loop is toward the body and the standing part away from the body. Then the hand is jerked diagonally backward and downward. Only a slight jerk is necessary, the hand moving only about three inches, but it must be a sudden and decisive jerk.

FIGURE 82. THE
FIGURE-OF-EIGHT

This is good stuff. The onlookers will label the performer as a sort of magician. It has just one shortcoming from the standpoint of showmanship—it happens so quickly that the spectators often do not realize what is happening and frequently are not aware that the resulting knot is any different from the original. To overcome this, it is well to call their attention to the change. Having tied the Pretzel, hold it up and say, "The Pretzel!—Now watch it very carefully." Convert it quickly and hold up the Figure-of-eight, saying, "The Figure-of-eight! Now let's do it again—first the Pretzel—now—it's the Figure-of-eight"!

In tying these knots before spectators, it is necessary to tie each two or three times in succession. First tie the Pretzel two or three times, then the Figure-of-eight a time or two. Then tie the Pretzel and convert it into the Figure-of-eight. Having repeated this a time or two, tie the Figure-of-eight and convert it into a Pretzel.

Practice for speed always in making these transfers. If done slowly, there is no stunt value in it.

FROM FIGURE-OF-EIGHT TO PRETZEL

This trick is performed exactly like the above. If the upper loop of the Figure-of-eight is turned downward the knot becomes a Pretzel.

Note in Figure 82 that the standing part passes behind the upper loop of the knot. By jerking the hand diagonally downward and forward, the standing part would turn the upper loop downward and thus convert the Figure-of-eight into a Pretzel. In preparing to perform the trick, it is more convenient if the knot is turned so that the standing part is away from you and the upper loop toward you. Then a slight jerk backward and downward, sharply administered, is all that is necessary.

Remember that speed is the byword always.

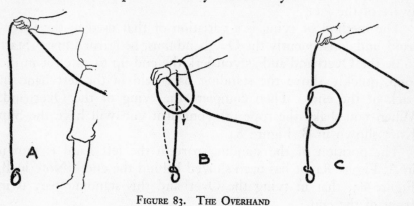

FIGURE 83. THE OVERHAND

THE OVERHAND

Figure 83 tells the story of how the Overhand Knot is done in circus fashion. Hold the rope as in A and turn the hand over, throwing the rope over the wrist as in B—this is exactly the same movement made in starting the Pretzel. At the same time that this is done, jerk up the honda and catch it in the loop as indicated by the arrow in B. When the rope is shaken off the arm, it will contain the Overhand Knot shown in C.

Note that the only respect in which the tying of this knot differs from that of the Pretzel is that the honda is passed through the loop from the opposite side—compare Figure 81 with Figure 83.

In the finished performance that comes with practice, the honda is not tossed upward through the loop as would be supposed from the arrow in B, but rather, it is jerked up only a few inches and then the hand is shot down quickly to catch it in the loop.

Practice until you can do it like a flash.

THE SLIP KNOT

This is the knot to use as the finale for the knot-tying section of a roping exhibition. I have never seen this knot tied by the ropers, and if it has been used by others in the past, I am not aware of the fact.

The method of tying is a variation of that used in the Overhand, and consequently the Overhand must be learned first. Start to tie the Overhand and as you jerk the end up to catch it in the loop, quickly shove the standing part held in the left hand in back of the end. Then complete the tying of the Overhand. When you shake the rope off your arm you will have the Slip Knot shown in B, Figure 84.

The position of the standing part in the left hand is shown in A, Figure 84—it has been shoved behind the end. Note in B, Figure 83, that in tying the Overhand this standing part is in front of the end.

It will be seen that two hands are really used in tying the Slip Knot, but the function of the left hand is so slight that it is seldom noticed. If the left hand is moved quickly the eye will not detect the part it plays. To further cover up this movement, the left hand can be placed in position before the knot is started and the left arm made rigid, then when the time arrives the body

is bent downward slightly so as to give the rigid arm the movement necessary to carry the rope back to the end.   This gives
the impression that the roper is merely intent on making his right-
hand movements correctly.

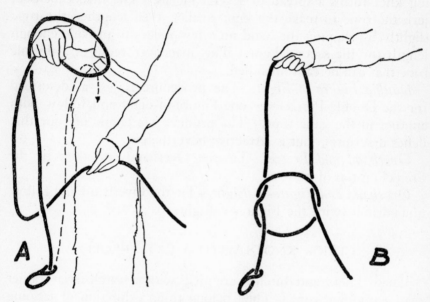

FIGURE 84.   THE SLIP KNOT

COMBINATION OF KNOTS

It is possible to tie one of these knots on top of another and so
produce a knot that is ornate, complicated, and impressive.   In
some case the result is a tangle of rope that defies description but
it is always graceful in lines and the tying is spectacular and gives
the impression of difficulty.

Double Overhand.—Tie an Overhand in the trick fashion described above, then immediately tie another with the same rope.
The second knot forms on top of the first producing a neat and
attractive tie.

Needless to say the second knot is more difficult than the first
because of the presence of the first knot in the rope.   Having

tied the first knot, it is usually necessary for the performer to slip the right hand up a few inches, thus lengthening the rope.

Double Pretzel.—Tie the Pretzel as usual and then immediately follow with another Pretzel tied in the same way. The resulting knot forms a spread of several inches. The first knot tied, jerk the rope to make the knot smaller, then lengthen the rope slightly by slipping the hand up a few inches to provide enough length for the second knot. This maneuver requires a flexible rope that can be easily handled.

Double Figure-of-Eight.—The procedure is just as described for the Double Pretzel—tie one Figure-of-eight and follow with another in the same rope. The product is a tangle of rope that defies description but is attractive nevertheless.

Overhand and Pretzel.—Tie the Overhand and then tie the Pretzel on top of it.

Overhand and Figure-of-Eight.—Tie the Overhand and follow immediately with the Figure-of-Eight.

TRICK KNOTS WITH A CATCH-ROPE

These knots and hitches are tied with a catch-lariat rather than a spinning rope. They belong to an exhibition of lassoing rather than rope spinning. Any flexible catch-rope will serve the purpose.

THE FLYING OVERHAND

This stunt consists of throwing an Overhand Knot into the far end of a lariat twenty or thirty feet long by jerking the end through a loop.

Holding one end of the rope, toss it out on the ground so that it is lying straight and free from kinks. Now jerk the end toward you so that it rises at least a foot from the ground. Instantly after you do this, throw an overhand half-hitch down the rope through which the end should pass if it is still extended up in the air. Allow plenty of slack in the rope for the loop of the half-hitch.

The half-hitch is made by throwing the hand straight forward —this forms a loop which travels down the length of the rope and extends upward from the rope. The loop thus thrown is called an overhand half-hitch, the word *overhand* referring to the fact that the loop extends upward from the rope and is made by an overhand motion of the arm.

If the end of the rope is off the ground this loop should encircle it producing an Overhand Knot. A backward pull will tighten the knot.

This trick is difficult. On the start it will be a pure matter of luck—sometimes you will snare the end with the half-hitch, but more often the loop will miss it. It will take a great deal of practice to catch the end regularly. The feat is of no practical value, and as an exhibition of roping skill, it has less of show value than the other trick knots in this chapter.

THROWING HALF-HITCHES

Here we have a trick that not only has show value but is of great practical importance in the work-a-day life of the cowboys. It is a maneuver that every one who engages in outdoor life will find useful. In steer roping the cowboys frequently find it necessary to throw the animal and tie up his legs, and here it is the half-hitches thrown from the hand end of the lariat that ensnare the legs.

Fasten the noose of your lariat around the top of a post and stand off about ten feet. There should be plenty of slack between your hand and the post. Throw an overhand half-hitch toward the top of the post and almost at the same instant swing the hand diagonally to the left and downward. If correctly done, the half-hitch will encircle the top of the post.

The overhand half-hitch is sent down the rope by throwing the hand straight toward the top of the post as in throwing a ball. A loop will form extending upward from the rope which will roll down the length of the rope to the post. The purpose of the swing of the arm to the left and downward is to throw the loop over the top of the post—were it not for this the loop would hit the top of the post and collapse. This left swing should follow immediately after the hitch is thrown.

When you can perform the stunt at ten feet, move back a little and continue this until you can use the full length of the lariat. The farther back one stands the larger in size the half-hitches must be.

Having learned to half-hitch the top of a post, attach the noose of the lariat around the wrist of a person's arm held horizontally to the side. Throw the half-hitches in the same way, endeavoring to encircle the arm with them. With practice you will be able to rope a person and tie him up with half-hitches so that he cannot move his arms or legs.

The term *overhand* half-hitch refers to one thrown with an overhand motion of the arm—such a throw forms a loop extending upward from the rope as it moves along. The underhand half-hitch is thrown with an underhand motion of the arm and the loop thus formed extends downward from the rope.

CHAPTER XIII

Lariat Throwing

One can scarcely appreciate the intrigue that is coiled up in a good catch-rope until he has handled one long enough to have a feeling of mastery over it. One's rope becomes a sort of pal to him. He likes to have it near him, even though just hanging on the wall in his room, his study, or his office. It is a symbol of a rugged outdoor life, a constant reminder of joyous hours.

The lariat seems to be a sort of extension of one's self. It is a long arm that reaches out and takes hold of an object. It does no damage to its prey; it is silent, accurate, sure. It is the most personal of all the types of weapons.

The art of the catch-rope is in no wise similar to rope spinning —the equipment is not the same, the objective is different, and the movements not at all similar. Skill in one is but little help in learning the other, except for the familiarity with the general handling of ropes that results. Yet, the two arts are closely enough related so that any one who takes up one would want to learn the other.

By comparison with rope spinning, lariat throwing is much the easier to learn. True, it takes years to perfect one's skill so that he can put his rope accurately and dependably on an animal from any angle, whether the thrower is on foot or horseback, and regardless of the speed at which the animal is moving. But even so, rope spinning is unquestionably the more intricate art.

There is one form of roping that combines both rope spinning and lariat throwing—the so-called *trick-and-fancy roping* of the Wild West shows and rodeos. Here there is a preliminary display of rope spinning with the lariat which is followed immediately by a catch; that is, the spinning noose itself is hurled to rope the horse.

In the parlance of the Wild West shows and rodeos, roping is divided into three categories: *rope spinning*, in which no catch is made; *catch-roping*, in which an object is roped but without the use of spinning; and *trick-and-fancy roping*, which combines both rope spinning and catch-roping. This chapter will discuss first the art of ordinary catch-roping, and then the complicated skills of trick-and-fancy roping.

The description of the making of the proper practice rope, and of the various other types of catch-ropes useful for different purposes is recorded in Chapter IX.

HANDLING THE LARIAT

There are two types of throws used in catch-roping, the *Wind-up Throw* and the *Toss*. Before approaching the subject of learning these throws, however, it is necessary that we master the art of coiling the rope and otherwise handling it skillfully. Without this ability much time will be wasted in practicing and much unnecessary confusion encountered.

COILING THE ROPE

There is a knack to coiling a rope quickly and neatly, and even though this coiling has nothing to do with the actual art of roping, it is nevertheless very important. In fact, catch-ropers and rope-spinners both are frequently judged by how neatly their ropes are coiled, both while being used and when hung up or stored away. In lariat throwing, the rope must be so neatly, carefully, and uniformly coiled that it will run out smoothly and evenly when thrown.

Take hold of the honda and toss the remainder of the rope out on the ground so that it lies reasonably straight and is free from kinks. Now form the loop and hold it in the right hand as shown in A, Figure 85. This is the loop that encircles the target when thrown. The loop should be roughly four or five feet long and should be held in the right hand at the level of the waist.

With the loop arranged, coil the remainder of the rope with the left hand as in B, Figure 85, taking the coils in the right hand.

The coils should be in the neighborhood of fifteen inches in diameter. When the rope is all coiled and held in the right hand, transfer the coils to the left hand and keep hold of the big loop only with the right hand. When transferred, the coils should be held in the left hand as illustrated in C, Figure 85—note that the

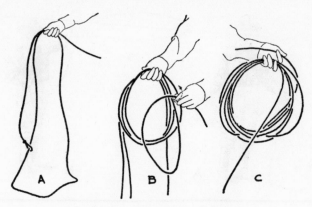

FIGURE 85.   COILING THE LARIAT

end is held between the thumb and forefinger and that the three remaining fingers hold the coils.

It is of course possible and indeed often desirable to begin the coiling with the hand end of the rope rather than with the honda end. In this case, the end is held in the left hand and the coiling done with the right hand.

Ordinary coiling tends to twist the rope with the result that the coils become wiry and stand out akimbo. There is a little trick in coiling, however, which, if followed, will cause the coils to lie flat and smooth in your hand. Holding the loop in your right hand as in B, Figure 85, bring the coil around with your left hand and just as you lay it in your right hand, give it a turn toward you with the fingers of your left hand, as indicated by the arrow in B. If each coil is given this twist in the direction indicated, the twist caused by the coiling will be offset and the loop will lie flat. This should be practiced until the knack becomes so automatic that it is used unconsciously whenever rope is being coiled.

THE WIND-UP THROW

This is the type of throw in which the loop is swung around the head a few times before it is hurled at its target. It is the

FIGURE 86. THE WIND-UP THROW

type of movement that most people think of in connection with throwing a lariat.

Let us suppose that we are to rope a post three or four feet high erected in the backyard, or a chair set up on the gym or clubroom floor. Stand about ten feet from the post, facing it squarely. The proper arrangement of the rope is clearly illustrated in A, Figure 86. The loop held in the right hand is roughly three or four feet long as it hangs by the side. Note that the honda is on the *outside* of the loop, away from the body—this is important —and that it extends a little over half way down the length of the loop. The method of arranging the loop and coiling the rope is described in the preceding section.

The rope all arranged, start swinging the loop around above the head as shown in B, Figure 86. This is the wind-up and serves several purposes: It keeps the loop open constantly and

ready for the throw at any instant. It gets you set for the throw
—steadies your nerves, places your arm in position and readiness,
and improves your control. It is the same sort of thing as a baseball pitcher's wind-up. Furthermore, it lifts the loop up off the
ground and prevents it from touching any object that might de-
flect it, and for this reason the wind-up is an absolute necessity
when roping on horseback.

The direction of the swing is from right to left—that is, as
the loop is passing across in front of the body it is going from
right to left. The movement is made largely with the wrist.
The wrist should be relaxed, kept as flexible as possible, and
you should turn the hand over (palm up) as the rope goes across
behind the head, thus keeping the loop spread open and untwisted
at all times. In actual roping on the range two or three swings
is usually sufficient, but during one's learning days the process
may be continued as long as desired. Keep the wind-up going
until you are all set for the throw.

As you swing the loop overhead, its size can easily be increased.
Open the hand for a fraction of a second with each swing, thus
permitting a few inches of rope to slip out. The loop may be
increased in this way until it feels right in the hand and seems
to have the necessary size and weight to carry to the post. This
ability to judge the size of the loop for a throw of any particular
distance can be acquired only by experience. It will come with
practice.

While winding up keep your eyes constantly on the top of
the post, studying its position and judging the distance. Continue
the wind-up until you are sure you know just where the post is.
Then take a long step toward it with the left foot and throw the
loop directly at it. Throw the whole body forward as you step,
thus giving the rope momentum, using the arm chiefly to guide
the loop. As you hurl the loop, open the left hand and let the
coiled rope run out freely.

The whole process is similar to throwing a ball at the post
with an overhand throw. Hurl the loop forward just as if you
had a ball in your hand. Do not take your eyes off the post

from the time the wind-up starts until the loop has hit or missed. Having released the loop, let the right arm follow through easily and naturally, keeping it up in position until the loop has reached its mark. The whole affair is really very simple, but one thing is certain, the rope will never encircle the post unless it is actually thrown there—keep your eye on the post and *put the rope there*.

If the loop fails to stay open during the wind-up, it is probably due to the fact that the rope is twisted. In this case there is no use attempting to complete the throw. Drop the rope to the ground, untwist it, and coil it up again.

From here on it is a matter of practice. Some will have better control than others, just as do some baseball pitchers. Control is largely a natural asset, but all can improve it with practice.

Count your catches as you practice. How many can you make out of fifty attempts? Do not admit that the trick is learned until you can catch the post fifty times in succession without a miss. Try to defeat your yesterday's record.

When the post can be roped regularly at ten feet, move back to fifteen, then to twenty, and so on. Thirty feet will be about the limit. Some southwestern cow-hands make catches up to forty feet but one who is dependable at thirty feet is doing plenty.

THE TOSS

In the Toss, the rope is hurled without a preliminary wind-up. The loop is merely held to the rear of the body as shown in A, Figure 87, and thrown forward as in B. The Toss is preferred by most ropers when on foot, whereas the Wind-up Throw is used almost exclusively when on horseback. On foot the Toss is as efficient as the Wind-up under all conditions except when great distance is necessary. In handling stock it is absolutely indispensable. Horses have a fear of rope and if they are subjected to roping often, they will clear away pronto at the sight of a lariat. It would be the height of folly for a roper to go into a corral swinging the loop of his lariat overhead in a wind-up—the stock would immediately be put into a frenzy and the catch made exceedingly difficult. The wise stock-hand goes in quietly, dragging the loop behind him, concealing it as much as possible, and when the opportunity presents itself, sending it forth like a flash, using the Toss rather than the Wind-up.

The loop is arranged just as in the Wind-up Throw, except that it is perhaps a little larger, there being no opportunity to enlarge it during a wind-up. Study A, Figure 87, for the details.

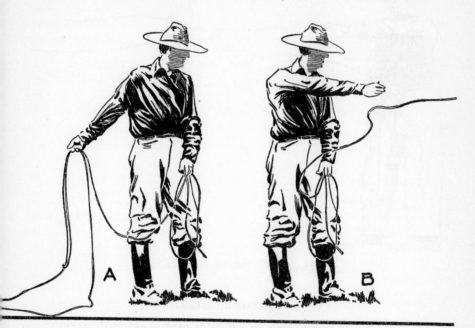

FIGURE 87. PREPARING FOR THE TOSS

With everything arranged swing the arm forward and upward past the side, thus sending the loop forward so that it settles down over the target. It will be noted that the movement is a sort of underhand or side-arm swing, rather than a straight overhand throw. If one is very close to the target the loop may be merely tossed forward with the arm as the roper is doing in B; however, it is usually necessary to take a long step forward with the left foot, thus swinging the body forward to give the rope momentum.

This is an easier throw to master than the Wind-up but should not be taken up until the Wind-up has been learned. Here, as in all roping, the only road to success is in untiring practice.

FIGURE 88. THE TOSS COMPLETED

THE LEFT-TO-RIGHT THROW

The post we have been using as a target extends straight up in the air and consequently can be easily roped by a right-handed person with a natural forward throw of the lariat. The same would be true if the target were a crosspiece nailed to the post so as to extend to the roper's right—a natural throw with the right hand would bring the loop in from the right so that it would easily encircle the crosspiece. This so-called natural throw with the right hand is a right-to-left throw.

The situation becomes different and much more difficult if the crosspiece extends out from the post to the roper's left. Here a backward or left-to-right throw is necessary to catch the target.

The same is true if the target is a pony's head facing to the roper's left—a backward throw would be necessary for a right-handed person, whereas if the pony faced to the roper's right, a natural or right-to-left throw would do the trick. For a left-handed person the situation is of course reversed, but for the sake of convenience we shall discuss the matter from the stand-point of a right-handed roper.

Let us assume that we are to use the Wind-up Throw to rope a target extending horizontally to the roper's left, such as a horse's head. Start the wind-up in the opposite or backward direction, that is, so that the loop, when it passes across in front of the body, is going from left to right. When the loop swings forward over the top of the head, take a long step forward with the left foot and hurl the loop forward toward the target. As it approaches the target the loop will be extending out to the left and should easily settle around it.

To use the Toss for such a catch, hold the rope a little further to the right side of the body than shown in A, Figure 87. Swing the right arm up behind the head, then forward across the top of the head, thus sending the loop forward from the left side of the body.

These Left-to-Right Throws are considerably more difficult to perform accurately and dependably than the standard type, and will take more practice.

ROPING MOVING TARGETS

The real challenge of catch-roping comes in trying to put the loop on a target that is moving. Any one with a little practice can drop the noose over a post or chair—it is easy to find and it stays there awaiting the convenience of the roper. Not so with the living agent, however, which has ideas of its own regarding the rope and the matter of being captured by it. Your steer or pony is here one second and there the next, dodging and changing pace, always heading away from the waiting noose. One has to make up his mind in a flash, and throw from all conceivable angles. It takes much in the way of skillful manipulation to catch up with such a changeable target. The Left-to-Right Throw is as essential as the standard throw, and again, the loop must often be so hurled that it will go past an animal running dead away from you and then turn and open in front of him so as to ensnare his head.

I used to practice on the horse, the cow, the dog, and even the chickens—in fact, on anything in the neighborhood that could run. Perhaps you can so train your dog that he will look upon being roped as a sort of game and enjoy it. Many dogs are like

FIGURE 89

that. Do not attempt to rope him if he does not like it, however, for some dogs have a mortal fear of ropes and under such conditions, to throw at them would be inexcusable cruelty.

The goal of every young roper is to be able to rope a horse, yet few have horses on which to practice. A horse is not a necessity in learning the essential skills of horse catching, however, nor is one a necessity to attain the full joy of catching a running target—a boy will serve the purpose just as well.

If you will recall the horse catching by the cowboys in the circuses and the rodeos, you will note that the most spectacular catches were made by roping the animal's feet. Indeed, most of the catches in trick-and-fancy roping have as their target the legs. Sometimes it is the front legs only, and again it's all four legs. There are a few catches, however, which involve the roping of the head, the rider, or the tail.

In the tricks that follow, a good quality of maguey rope will be a decided asset (see page 116).

ROPING RUNNERS BY THE FEET

The first requirement here is for some one to play the role of the horse and run past you while you attempt to rope his feet. He should start some distance away and run past you at a space of eight or ten feet. All animals are "rope shy" at first exposure to the lariat, and the boy who runs for you will probably be no exception. That is, just as you throw for his legs he will probably shy away from you unintentionally or slow up a little to dodge the loop, thus making a good throw turn out to be a miss. To avoid this, place a stick on the ground ten feet in front of you and instruct the runner to run over it. Also tell him to run fast, pick his feet up high, and keep a constant pace, increasing his speed, if anything, as he nears the stick.

Arrange the rope in your right hand as in the ordinary Toss, but make the loop larger—it should be at least eight feet long for a beginner. Stand so that the runner comes in from your left as illustrated in A, Figure 90. Note in A that the *back* of the hand holding the loop is toward the runner. Now yell to him to come and tell him to come fast! Just as he passes throw the loop over and down toward his feet as in B, Figure 90. In B, *the back of the hand is still toward the runner*. The noose was not swung around parallel to the ground but rather thrown over and down, with the back of the hand kept toward the runner throughout. Herein lies the chief difference between roping the feet and throwing for the head—instead of throwing straight at the feet the loop is turned over and the catch made with the opposite or back side of the loop. If the throw is timed correctly, the loop will be in front of his feet as he passes and he will step into it. Then jerk up quickly and you have him. You see, he really ropes himself—all you do is throw the loop in front of him and he runs into it.

Eagerness to make the catch often tempts one to throw too soon. The time to make the cast is when the runner is directly in front of you. In fact, you can even wait until he is a few feet past you—it is always easier to make a catch when he is a little past than before he has come into line with you. When one throws too soon the loop collapses before the runner reaches it. He may catch his foot in it as it lies on the ground, but a clean roping catch is impossible.

Just as soon as you tighten the rope around his legs, drop the lariat on the ground so as not to trip him. The runner can be a great help to you in learning if he will run fast and pick his feet up high, for the faster the running the easier is the catch.

FIGURE 90. ROPING A RUNNER BY THE FEET

He can cooperate, too, by not shying, changing pace, or attempting to hurdle the noose. He must get the idea that he is not playing a game with you, attempting to prevent you from roping him, but rather, helping you by running as you direct. However, he will not fancy the task if he is tripped and thrown each time he is caught. You must cooperate with him in this respect if you expect him to cooperate with you.

If the runner is coming in from the opposite direction, that is, from your right, the throw is made in exactly the same way. In this case the palm of the rope hand would be toward the runner throughout.

When the catch can be made regularly at ten feet, increase the distance to fifteen.

This stunt of roping by the feet is great sport. It is always fun to do and is a spectacular number in any roping exhibition.

ROPING SEVERAL RUNNERS

The circus cowboy who ropes six horses running abreast in one loop is really performing a very simple feat, for it is no more difficult to rope several runners than it is one, provided they are running in line and close together. The only difference is in the size of the loop. Figure 91 illustrates the trick.

FIGURE 91. ROPING SEVERAL RUNNERS BY THE FEET

Start out by roping two boys with arms locked and running together. Proceed just as if there were only one, following all the instructions given in the preceding section on how to rope a runner by the feet. You will find the stunt in no wise different or more difficult than roping a lone runner. This accomplished, double the number and rope four runners, then six!

The important thing is that the runners lock arms and stay as close together as possible, keeping in step as they run. A line of six will of course require a very large loop—it is better to err on the side of too large a loop than too small a one, since the rope can be jerked up quickly once the runners are in it, thus taking up the slack immediately. When a big loop like this is used, the top of the loop strikes the waist line of the runners as they step into it and they are thus captured around the body instead of the ankles.

Here we have one of the most spectacular of the catch-roping stunts and consequently one that is particularly effective in a roping demonstration.

ROPING HORSES BY THE FRONT LEGS

The circus crowd is quick to acclaim the roper who catches the running horse so spectacularly, but few give a thought to the

FIGURE 92.   CATCHING ALL FOUR LEGS

contribution to the act made by the rider of the horse or that made by the horse himself. The horse must be put past the proper point at the right time, without shying away or changing pace. The roper and the rider constitute a team that has practiced together repeatedly. The horse, too, comes in for consideration because some ponies are too high strung for the job and others are too "rope shy"—all the practice in the world would not make suitable performers of these. The ponies that serve as targets for the ropers' art are carefully selected, being suitable by temperament for the task, and are trained for it by long rehearsal. If the horse were running wild around the arena, the roper would have to be on horseback himself to catch him. Since the roper is expected to stand on one spot and display his skill, the horse must be ridden past him within reach.

It is necessary, therefore, that we have a suitable horse and a rider to handle him for us. If the horse is ridden past just as the boy ran past in the preceding section, it will be no more difficult to catch his front legs than it was to catch the boy, and the procedure is precisely the same. Don't shy from the horse as he comes by—step right up and throw the loop down toward his front feet. Read the preceding section on roping runners for the details. As soon as the horse hits the rope, jerk up quickly and you will have him by the front legs. Then release the lariat at once and let it fall to the ground so as not to trip him. Further, have the rider stop the horse as soon as the catch is made. If you should throw the horse you might not only hurt him and his rider, but would probably develop a fear of the rope on the part of the pony, thus making him rope shy and ruining him for the purpose thereafter. There is no danger of such a result if the lariat is dropped as soon as the legs are caught.

The rider should station himself at least fifty feet from the roper and wait until the roper calls or signals him to come. Then he should ride past at a good fast canter or trot. The catch made, the rider stops the horse and allows the rope to fall off the legs, then immediately rides back and prepares to run for the next catch.

Several horses can be caught in one big loop by following the same procedure used in roping several boys running with locked arms. The horses must be kept abreast and as close together as possible. Each horse must have a rider. Simple as it is for any good roper, this feat always proves to be most dramatic.

CATCHING ALL FOUR LEGS

Shake out a large loop and throw it in front of the approaching horses' feet in the usual way. After the horse hits the rope, hesitate for a second or so, then jerk up the rope—you should have him by all four legs. If you jerk up immediately, the rope will close on his front legs, but by hesitating a second the hind legs will have time to enter the loop. The horse should canter, not trot. Release the rope immediately after the catch has been made.

ROPING THE HORSE'S NECK

The horse should be ridden past the roper in the usual manner at a distance away from him of about fifteen feet. Either the Wind-up Throw or the Toss may be used. The technique of the throw is the same as if a post were being roped. A small loop should be used, three or four feet in diameter. Wait until the horse's head is directly opposite you, then toss the loop straight out and over his neck. Do not throw until the horse is opposite or, if anything, a little past you. If you can rope a post you will find this catch very simple indeed.

ROPING BOTH HORSE AND RIDER

In this stunt the loop of the lariat is caused to encircle both the horse's head and the rider. The throw is made in exactly the same way as when roping a horse by the head, except that a larger loop is used. Throw the loop high enough so that the lower rope catches the horse under the jaw, thus permitting the upper rope of the loop to settle down behind the rider's back. The motion of the running horse aids in carrying the rider into the loop. Jerk up the loop as soon as the catch is made.

CATCHING THE HORSE'S TAIL

Here is a stunt that brings a laugh always. It is a favorite of the circus clowns who mimic the feats of the cowboys while they are roping, although it is often used by the ropers themselves.

The horse should be stationed to your right and ridden past you in the usual way. Use a very small loop, not more than two feet in diameter. Step up close to the horse as he approaches, and just after he has passed you, slap the loop up sharply onto his rump and around his tail. The rider should ride right on after the catch, dragging the lariat after him. Let out rope after the catch until the limit has been reached, then hang on to the end and run along after the horse, pulling on the rope in an apparent effort to stop him.

ROPING WHILE STANDING ON YOUR HEAD

This spectacular feat is done by a few of the better stunt-ropers and is occasionally seen in the rodeos. It consists of roping a horse by the feet while standing on your head. For a gymnasium exhibition, a boy will serve as well as a horse. The two prerequisites are, first, the ability to catch a horse or runner by the feet, and second, the ability to stand on your head steadily with the aid of the left hand only.

Draw a line on the ground on which you are to do the head stand. Arrange a large loop and lay it out carefully on the ground behind the line, with the part to be held by the hand extending up to the line. The right hand is to hold the loop at this point while you are standing on your head. Lay the coils of the lariat in front of the line at the point where the left hand is to be, keeping the end only in the left hand. Now stand on your head, facing away from the spot the horse is to cross, taking the weight on your head and left hand. As soon as you have everything under control, yell to the rider to come. Just as the horse passes, throw the loop forward toward his feet, with the right hand, thus causing the horse to step into it. Since the rope is lying on the ground it will uncoil of its own accord.

Since you are facing away from the horse it is impossible to see him at the time of the throw. From rehearsal with the rider, however, you know the distance away from you that the horse will pass. You can tell from the sound of his hoofs when he is passing you, but it will be better to have the rider yell when the proper second arrives for the throw.

At best this stunt will take much practice and long rehearsal with the rider.

THROWING THE LARIAT WITH THE FOOT

In this trick the loop is hurled forward with the right foot instead of the hand. The object is to catch the runner around the head. Shake out a large loop as for the Toss and lay it on the ground. Let go of it with the right hand and place the toe of the right foot under the point where the hand was. Place the left foot well forward. As the runner approaches kick the right foot forward and upward vigorously, thus causing the loop to open up and fly forward in the same way as if it were thrown by the hand.

TRICK-AND-FANCY ROPING

The expression "trick-and-fancy roping" refers to a combination of rope spinning and catch-roping; it involves a preliminary display of rope spinning while the horse is approaching which is terminated by a catch of the horse as he passes. Such roping always involves a catch at the end, otherwise it would be merely rope spinning. Without the preliminary display of spinning, the stunt would be called ordinary catch-roping.

While any of the rope-spinning tricks may be used in the preliminary flourish of spinning, yet almost invariably the choice of the ropers is the Ocean Wave. Trick-and-fancy roping, therefore, really refers to an Ocean Wave which terminates with a catch. Since it involves the best of rope-spinning ability (the Ocean Wave being one of the hardest of the tricks) and the best of catch-roping skill, trick-and-fancy roping represents the acme of roping performance.

Although some show cowboys do a trick-and-fancy roping turn while sitting on horseback, practically all such roping is done on foot. A thoroughly skilled and dependable rider is necessary to bring the horse past at precisely the right second in order that he will be within reach when the spinning rope is in the proper position.

Before one can attempt this feat he must be a thorough master of the intricacies of the Ocean Wave.

A good quality of maguey rope of the proper size and weight to suit the roper is required (see page 116). It is well to use this rope in practicing the Ocean Wave in order to lay the proper foundation for the trick catching.

THE OCEAN-WAVE CATCH

Mark out the path down which the rider is to canter the horse. Stand about ten feet from this path with your right side toward it and facing in the direction from which the horse is coming. Start the Ocean Wave as usual and when the loop passes your back let it go right on over to the right until it crosses the path. A great deal of practice of this movement will be necessary before one is ready to practice with the horse and rider.

This much learned, it is a case of perfect coöperation and timing between the rope and the rider. Long practice will determine just how far away the horse must be to reach the roper at the proper second, and also how many times the Ocean Wave must be carried around the body while the horse is covering a certain distance and coming within roping range.

As the horse comes up, carry the Ocean Wave around the body, pull the loop across the back briskly and let it continue on over in front of the horse. As the loop approaches the horse's path, pull back slightly on the rope in order to turn the loop at right angles to the path so that the horse can step into it.

Any of the standard catches described earlier in this chapter may be made in this way: catching the front feet, all four legs, the horse's head, and both horse and rider.

Many variations in the use of the Ocean Wave in this connection may be worked out. For example, the roper may wait until the horse almost reaches him, then start the Ocean Wave in front, carry it around behind and then on over for the catch. Or he may carry the Ocean Wave around him three or four times before throwing for the catch. Again he may insert one or more

Skips in the series. Each one of these tricks must be worked out with the rider to insure the proper timing.

THE ROLLING CATCH

In this trick the loop is rolled like a hoop along the ground into the horse's path. In its simplest form, the loop is arranged as for a Flat Spin except that it is held at the right side of the body. The hand is carried over and forward, thus rolling the loop along the ground. More frequently the trick starts with an enlarged Butterfly. When the loop reaches the right side of the body, going counterclockwise, it is carried forward and down to the ground, where it is rolled into the horse's path.

Rolls of this sort are often seen in connection with the Ocean-Wave catches.

CHAPTER XIV

Roping Exhibitions and Contests

Every one who learns to rope wants to display his ability to others. He hopes some day to be able to do a complete and finished roping act of the type performed by the artists of the stage. Organizations using roping as an activity usually feature it in demonstrations, field days, shows, parents' nights, and so forth. In fact, one of the most appealing aspects of roping is its show value—folks like to watch it. It is unique, different, colorful; its symbolism stirs imagination; it is graceful, esthetic, pleasing to the eye.

This chapter presents the routines for individual roping acts and for mass demonstrations. It describes certain special stunts that add color to roping shows.

When roping is used in organizations such as clubs, camps, playgrounds, and gymnasiums, the ropers welcome contests which test ability and determine champions. The last half of this chapter is devoted to such roping championships and contests, and to games involving roping.

ROPING DEMONSTRATIONS

There is a traditional type of roping act in which the roper talks along as he ropes, getting off a quaint humor that smacks of the ranch house and a homely philosophy that reminds one of the old Westerner who finds himself, boots, hat, and all, on Fifth Avenue in New York. Good ropers use such comedy in a quiet, casual sort of way, if at all, merely to add a little sparkle to their roping, but they rely chiefly on the roping itself to "get across." Some actors who are better comedians than ropers, use the roping solely as a screen for their comedy.

There are other ropers who do their roping turn as best they can, going at it in business-like fashion, and say nothing at all during the course of the act. Such is the characteristic way of real, honest-to-goodness, ranch-raised ropers who work in the rodeos. This is by all means the course to follow unless one has marked talent as a comedian. There will be sufficient glamour and appeal in the roping to insure success for a short, fast, rope-spinning act without resorting to the addition of comedy. This proves to be the case in rodeos, circuses, and the like, the talking type of act being limited to the theater stage. In a gymnasium exhibition, a playground demonstration, or a camp circus, to attempt to talk would be a mistake—the thing to do is to concentrate on good roping. The same would apply to a stage roping act put on by any one who is not most gifted in comedy.

In roping before an audience the emphasis should always be on graceful, rhythmic movement. One's desire to impress often leads to speeding up the spinning in an effort to make it appear more spectacular. Invariably the resulting effect is the very opposite of that desired. The charm of rope spinning rests in the beauty of the graceful, floating curves of the rope. When one gets down to the finale with its Big Loops, Hurdles, and Skips, then is the time for speed and strenuous effort, but not so with the lighter tricks which constitute the body of the act.

ONE-MAN ROPE-SPINNING ACT

Much depends on the order in which the various tricks are presented in a roping act. It is a fundamental principle of showmanship that the least difficult and impressive stunts should be used at the start and the series should gradually build up to the stronger ones, closing always with the most spectacular.

While the following order of tricks is presented with this principle of showmanship in mind, it should be remembered that it is suggestive merely, and could be nothing more than such, since roping tricks vary in spectacular qualities as different ropers do them. One will find from experience which of his tricks are the most striking. On one point there will be no dispute, however—the large, heavy-rope tricks are more colorful than the light-rope ones. For example, a good roping act can be put on without even including the delicate and difficult Butterflies and Rolls, provided it makes skillful use of the less intricate but heavier tricks. This being the case, the flashy Skips and Hurdles should always be used as concluding features. It is not the difficulty of the trick that determines its spot in the act, but rather its spectacular qualities.

The following recommended order of tricks assumes that one can do all of the tricks in these chapters. Such a complete array is, of course, not necessary for a good demonstration. The general order will apply, however, regardless of how many tricks are to be included.

The tricks should be presented in approximately the following order:

1. *Trick Knots*

   Overhand
   Pretzel
   Figure-of-eight
   Pretzel to Figure-of-eight
   Figure-of-eight to Pretzel
   Double Overhand
   Slip Knot

2. *Flat Spins with Twenty-Foot Rope*

   Wedding Ring
   Hand-shaking
   Juggle
   Lying down

3. *Flat Spins with Sixteen-Foot Rope*

   Flat Spin
   Merry-go-round
   Two-handed Merry-go-round
   Jumping into Flat Loop
   Jumping Out
   Up and Over

Juggling Up and Over
Lift onto Body
Skyrocket
Tapping In and Out

4. *Vertical Spins with Sixteen-Foot Rope*

Butterfly
Forward-and-backward Butterfly
Arrowhead
Vertical Raise onto Arm
Rolling Butterfly
Zigzag

5. *Flat Spins with Twenty-five-Foot Rope, Brass Honda*

Hand-shaking around One Leg
Hand-shaking around Alternate Legs
Hurdling

6. *Flat Spin with Seventy-five-Foot Rope, Very Heavy Honda*

Big Loop

7. *Vertical Spins with Twenty-five-Foot Rope*

Ocean Wave

8. *Vertical Spins with Twenty-five-Foot Rope, Brass Honda*

Skip
Skip and Turn

It will be noted that the demonstration is broken up into units, each unit consisting of a series of tricks which calls for a different rope than the preceding. Some ropers have argued that the mark of good roping is the ability to do practically all tricks with the same rope. Suffice it to say that such ropers do not do a wide variety of tricks since it would be absolutely impossible to perform all the tricks listed above with the same rope. More than anything else, the thing that makes the difference in ropes is the weight of the hondas. Sections 2, 3, and 4 in the above list might be done with the same rope, but even here the chances are that the roper will have a special rope for each of these series which he will prefer to use. It would be stupid not to use the rope best suited for each trick. When the series of tricks with one rope is finished, that rope should be coiled up and placed aside as the next rope is picked up.

The series of tricks using the same rope should be done continuously, without hesitation between the tricks. That is, the roper should go from one trick to another without allowing the spinning loop to stop. This will not always be possible but it will be in many cases.

Five to six minutes is a good length for a roping act. It requires a whale of a good act, no matter what it consists of, to carry longer than six minutes.

PARTNERS IN ROPING

An effective roping act may be presented by two people roping together, each sharing the spot equally. This is frequently done by a boy and a girl. In presenting the simpler tricks, both may be roping at the same time, standing side by side, the purpose being to present a spectacle of gracefully floating ropes. In handling the more spectacular tricks, however, the ropers should take turns.

There are a few tricks in which both may work in the same rope. For example, the two may stand close together while one spins a Wedding Ring around them both. After a few spins the other may take the spoke without stopping the spin and continue it. The spoke may thus be passed back and forth frequently. The Wedding Ring may then be turned into a Juggle and this followed by Hand-shaking. In the latter trick the roper on the right, spinning the rope with his right hand, drops the loop to the floor, and the one on the left takes the end in his left hand and carries it around behind, where the first roper takes it in his right hand and brings it around in front again, and so on.

One of the best of the partner tricks is the Skip. The two stand one behind the other, as close together as possible, the one doing the roping standing in front. The Skip is performed in the usual fashion with the partners jumping together and thus both skipping the rope. This requires long practice.

Occasionally a man will present his roping act with a lady assisting him by handing up the various ropes as he needs them. When the finale is reached with its Skip, the girl joins the roper in the partner trick and both skip together.

MASS ROPING EXHIBITIONS

No more beautiful sight can be presented in a gymnasium than fifty ropers, spaced uniformly about the floor, all spinning their ropes at the same time. This eclipses completely any of the traditional mass demonstrations of gymnastic exercises. So, too, on the playground, or the campus of the summer camp—mass roping, wherever staged, has excellent show value. Furthermore, as a gym or playground demonstration feature it has the valuable asset of presenting all the individuals who are able to rope, not merely the few star performers.

The main requirement for a successful mass demonstration is that all ropers perform the same trick at the same time. It is not necessary that all arms and ropes move in unison—that would be scarcely possible nor would it be desirable—but all should be doing the same trick. This means that the possibilities are limited to a few simple tricks that all can do perfectly. The picture is destroyed if a few of the ropes are breaking down constantly, which would be the case if difficult tricks were being attempted.

This necessity of using simple tricks in no wise detracts from the effectiveness of the exhibition, for the reason that it is gracefully floating ropes that create the desired mass picture, and here there is nothing more satisfying than the Wedding Ring. No more could be asked for than a floor covered with beautiful, smooth, rhythmic Wedding Rings. A slow Juggle is another good trick, provided all are able to do it well, which, unfortunately, will seldom be the case. The Merry-go-round has no superior for mass use. In short, the Wedding Ring and the Merry-go-round are the two ideal tricks and it is unwise to attempt to go farther than these. Indeed, the Merry-go-round may be eliminated if need be, thus letting the Wedding Ring stand alone.

It should be emphasized to the ropers that the objective is a mass picture, and consequently all individual frills and flourishes should be eliminated.

If it is desired to present as many ropers as possible and at the same time as many different tricks as possible, all in one number, the procedure to follow is to form a mass chorus of ropers across the floor, all doing the Wedding Ring, and place a star performer in front on one side, facing the stands, which latter does the complete series of roping tricks. If the crowd is on both sides of the arena or floor, a star performer may be placed on each side. All the time the ropers occupying these spots are performing, the chorus ropers continue to do a steady, rhythmic Wedding Ring.

AN AMATEUR CATCH-ROPING ACT

Horses suitable for roping will scarcely be available in the field days and exhibitions put on by physical-education departments, camps, clubs, and playgrounds, and neither will the persons in such demonstrations be familiar with such roping, with the result that the usual pattern for a catch-roping act cannot be followed. This fact, however, will not prevent the inclusion of a good lariat-throwing act in such a program whether it be staged in a gymnasium or out-of-doors.

A stationary object can be placed in the center of the arena or floor to serve as a target. A gym horse makes a very acceptable object for the reason that when one faces its side there is an extension both at the right end and left end, thus making possible both right-to-left and left-to-right throws. Minus such a horse, a chair, box or any similar object may be used.

A boy may be used as a running target with catches made around both his head and feet. Six or eight boys with arms locked will make possible the big catches. A boy riding a bicycle will supply a fast-moving target.

Each catch should be demonstrated three times in succession before taking up the next one.

The order of events may be as follows:

Stationary Target

Wind-up Throw
Toss
Backward (Left-to-right) Wind-up Throw
Backward (Left-to-right) Toss
Half-hitches

Running Target

Toss for Head
Wind-up Throw for Head
Throw for feet
Catching Two Runners at Once
Catching Eight Runners at Once

Bicycle Target

Toss for Rider from Standing Position
Wind-up Throw for Rider from Standing Position
Wind-up Throw for Rider while Riding Bicycle

A HORSE-ROPING ACT

A horse trained for roping and an expert rider will be necessary for a standard catch-roping exhibition. The following tricks should be included in such an act:

Toss for Horse's Head
Wind-up Throw for Horse's Head
Throw for Front Feet
Throw for All Four Legs
Throw for Both Horse and Rider
Throw for Horse's Tail

GYMNASIUM ROPING EXHIBITION

These suggestions for a roping exhibition in a gymnasium or similar inclosed area apply to physical-education demonstrations,

Boy Scout rallies, Y.M.C.A. open houses, and all similar events in which roping may fit into the program.

The traditional physical-education exhibition with its more or less formal presentation of exercises, tumbling, acrobatics, and dancing is giving way to a pageant-like approach with much emphasis on color. The ideal procedure here is to assume a theme and then use the traditional activities, giving them the color suggested by the theme. A few special activities growing out of the theme will be used also. Such a demonstration not only presents all the usual activities but sets them forth in such a way that they carry a romantic touch and thus appeal strongly to imagination. This is simply good showmanship—good showmanship for the type of activities the physical-education department is sponsoring.

A theme may be selected that is appropriate to the section of the country in which the city is located, using the color characteristic of the area, although this is not at all necessary, and is difficult to do, year in and year out, and still be original. There are many excellent themes, offering remarkable opportunities for color, that are always appealing wherever they may be staged —and the old-time West is one of these.

Entirely aside from its use in such demonstrations based on Western atmosphere, roping will make a colorful spot in any exhibition or rally.

The roping may all be thrown into one number or it may be divided into the following several acts, each carrying punch enough to stand alone:

> Catch-Roping of Stationary Targets
> Mass Rope Spinning
> Catch-Roping of Running Boys
> Catch-Roping of Bicycle Riders
> Rope-Spinning Act (by two or three stars)
> Whip Cracking

SPECIAL DEMONSTRATION STUNTS

Here are a few special stunts—frills, if you please—which may be used to add a colorful and dramatic touch to a roping demonstration.

COLORED STREAMERS

Hold a strip of red, yellow, or blue silk of very light weight, two to three feet long, in the left hand. Spin the Wedding Ring as usual, and when it is going nicely, throw the strip of cloth

FIGURE 93.   WAVING THE FLAG

against the spoke as it comes around in front. The streamer will float out behind the spoke as it encircles the body.

Two or three streamers of different colors may be kept in the pocket and pulled out and thrown on one at a time, thus placing two or three floating colors on the spoke. They should be spaced equally, one above the other. It is more effective if the streamers are of unequal length.

Another method equally as effective is to tie a number of streamers to the rope at distances apart of two feet, this being done before the spinning starts. By handling the rope carefully, this will not interfere in any way with starting the spin.

WAVING THE FLAG

Attach a small American flag about a foot in length to the spoke of a twenty-foot rope and proceed to spin the Wedding Ring—the flag will float beautifully behind the spoke as it swings around the body. Figure 93 shows it. For the best effect, the flag should be attached so that the bottom is about a foot above the point where the honda rests in spinning.

A special rope that is not needed in the other stunts should be used for this feature. The flag should be attached before the exhibition starts and the rope coiled up in the usual way. It can then be picked up and spun without hesitation when the time arrives.

LIGHTED ROPES

Attach a small electric light bulb just below the honda of a twenty-foot rope and run the wire along the rope to the battery held in the hand at the rope's end. Start to spin the Wedding Ring as usual and after a moment of spinning have all lights turned off, leaving the place in darkness. After a few seconds of darkness, light the bulb on the rope. The effect is vivid and beautiful.

Three bulbs may be attached instead of one—one at the honda, one across the loop from the honda, and one midway between the honda and the hand.

A still more colorful effect can be produced by using bulbs of varying colors resembling a string of Christmas-tree lights.

LUMINOUS ROPES

Another delightful feature on a darkened stage is produced by painting the ropes with luminous paint. This creates an entirely different scene from that produced by electric bulbs attached to the rope. The painted rope flickers softly and beautifully.

In staging this scene it is well to have two or three ropers with luminous ropes standing on the lighted stage. The orchestra should play softly and slowly some old-time western tune. After a moment of spinning on the lighted stage, the lights should be faded out slowly into complete blackness, leaving visible only the flickering ropes.

DANCING IN A ROPE

Such a trick as the Wedding Ring leaves the entire body free and unencumbered for dancing, and practically every movement in the usual tap-dancing routine can be done without the rope interfering with the dancing. With practice most of the flat spins and such light verticals as the Butterflies can be done while dancing. The most effective maneuvers, however, are those in which the dancer is inside of the spinning loop most of the time. It is possible to step in and out of a flat spin without breaking the rhythm of the dancing.

A good finale to a combined dancing and roping act is the trick called Tapping In and Out, described on page 154.

I know of one stunt enthusiast who dances, spins the Wedding Ring with his left hand, and plays a trumpet with his right, all at the same time.

ROPING CHAMPIONSHIPS

In organizations for girls and boys in which roping is featured, the roping championships are always enjoyed and looked forward to with much anticipation. The rope-spinning championship of a summer camp is always a much-sought-after honor. Likewise on a playground or in a Scout troop. Perhaps the most definite means of stimulating the ropers to perfect and polish their skills is the knowledge that they will soon match skills with the others in the championship contest.

ROPE-SPINNING CONTEST

Because of the nature of the activity there is no way to conduct a rope-spinning championship contest other than to base the rating of the contestants upon the opinions of a group of judges. Appoint a panel of three judges, one at least being a person familiar with all the intricacies of good roping. The ropers should be called upon to display their skill in two series of tricks, one the flat spins and the other the vertical spins. Prepare two lists of tricks, one containing the flat tricks such as those listed on page 122, and the other the verticals recorded on page 165. Place these lists in the hands of both the contestants and the judges some time before the event.

The ropers need not present their tricks in the order on the list, the list merely serving to indicate to them the events the judges will anticipate and which they will consider as an indication of complete performance.

The names of the contestants should be thrown into a hat and then pulled one at a time to determine the order in which the ropers will compete. Each roper in turn performs all the tricks on the list that he is able to do and any others not on the list. The judges watch the demonstrations and grade each roper on each trick.

The selection of the winners is based upon the following items in good roping: (1) number of tricks performed, (2) technical correctness of the tricks, (3) grace of movement, (4) rhythm, (5) showmanship. The most satisfactory procedure is to grade each trick on the basis of these items and then total the grades for the contestant's score. In a contest made up of ropers of average skill, such as would be the case in a camp, club, or playground, greater weight should be given the vertical spins as compared to the average run of flat spins. The usual procedure is to double the ordinary rating in order to obtain the score for the vertical spins and for the more difficult flat spins such as the Lift onto Body and the Skyrocket. The scores made in the other flat spins are added to these doubled scores to determine the contestant's total rating.

As an added precaution, it is well for the judges to select the three contestants with the highest rating and have them compete a second time in order better to rate them as first, second, and third. In this second performance the judges can give more careful attention to rhythm, grace, and showmanship.

LARIAT-THROWING CONTEST—STATIONARY TARGET

The contestants may use any type of lariat they choose. Since they take turns in competing, the same rope may be passed around if necessary.

One or more of four types of contest may be used here: (1) *Most Consecutive Throws, Number 1;* (2) *Most Consecutive Throws, Number 2;* (3) *Throwing Half-hitches;* (4) *Longest Throw.* The first of these is the one most commonly used.

Most Consecutive Throws, Number 1.—Place a post, chair, or other object to serve as a target fifteen to twenty feet from a throwing line, the exact distance depending on the skill of the contestants. The players take turns in competing. Each makes twenty-five throws from behind the throwing line and is credited with one point each time the loop of the lariat completely encircles the target. Either the Wind-Up Throw or the Toss may be used as the contestant prefers. The contestant wins that makes the highest score.

Most Consecutive Throws, Number 2.—The target consists of a post five feet high on the top of which a six-foot bar has been nailed so that it extends three feet out to each side. The throwing line should be fifteen to twenty feet distant, parallel to the crossbar. The contestants take turns in competing, each making ten throws of the standard type with a right-to-left swing of the arm (for a right-handed player), and ten more throws of the opposite or left-to-right type. Each successful catch scores one point. The one with the highest score wins.

Throwing Half-hitches.—The target is the same as in the preceding contest, and the throwing line is ten to fifteen feet distant. The contestants take turns in competing. The contestant throws and catches the crossbar and then makes five attempts to throw a half-hitch around the bar. He makes five of these throws, each being followed by five attempts at half-hitches. One point is scored for each successful half-hitch. The one with the highest score wins.

Target Throw.—Mark a series of throwing lines ten, fifteen, twenty, twenty-five, and thirty feet out from the target. Each contestant makes three throws from the ten-foot mark, three from the fifteen-foot mark, and so on. He scores one point for each successful throw from the ten-foot line, two points for each from the fifteen-point line, three from the twenty-foot line, four from the twenty-five foot line, and five from the thirty-foot line. The player with the highest score wins.

LARIAT-THROWING CONTEST—MOVING TARGET

Mark a throwing line on the ground and ten feet from it and parallel to it, another line known as the target line. The moving target may be either a running boy, a boy riding a bicycle, or a horse.

Running-Boy Target.—The runner stands fifty feet from the roper. At the roper's signal, he runs down the target line and the roper attempts to rope him as he passes. He has ten attempts and scores one point for each successful catch. If, in the judges' estimation, the runner changes pace or dodges away from the rope, the attempt is played over. The contestant with the highest score wins.

Two contests are possible here—roping the runner by the feet and roping him by the head. The first is preferable.

Bicycle Target.—This contest is the same as the above except that the target consists of a person riding a bicycle and the aim is to rope him over the head.

Running-Horse Target.—This event is conducted in the same way as roping the running boy. There must be a rider for the horse who puts him past the roper at the proper time and distance. The rider must control the horse so as to give each roper a fair chance in each attempt; otherwise the attempt is repeated.

Two contests are possible—roping the horse by the head and by the feet. The latter is always more popular and should be preferred.

LARIAT-THROWING CONTEST WHILE MOUNTED

Most organizations will not possess horses trained for roping but that need not rule out the event—the roper may ride a bicycle. This makes an excellent contest for a playground or a gymnasium.

Erect a post or other object for a target and mark a throwing line ten to fifteen feet away, the distance depending on the skill of the contestants.

Roping from a Bicycle.—The roper rides down the throwing line and attempts to rope the post as he passes. The contestants take turns in competing. It will usually require twenty-five throws to determine a winner, in that if fewer throws are required there will be many ties. One point is scored for each successful catch and the person with the highest score wins.

Roping from a Horse.—The conditions are the same as in roping from a bicycle except that a horse is ridden.

ROPING GAMES AND CONTESTS

Here are a few roping games and contests that will be much enjoyed by boys and girls for informal sport around a club, camp, playground, or gymnasium. Since most of these call for no more in the way of roping skill than the Wedding Ring, or a simple throw with a lariat, a beginner has as much chance as the expert and all enjoy them equally.

ROPE-SPINNING DUEL

This is a dual contest and is an excellent council-ring event.* The two ropers, standing a few feet apart, start to spin the Wedding Ring, and at the starting signal attack each other with intent to stop the opponent's rope from spinning. The one wins who stops his opponent's rope provided his own rope is still spinning. All tactics are fair.

* For a detailed description of how a council-ring program of dual contests is conducted, and a description of many suitable events, see Bernard S. Mason and E. D. Mitchell, *Social Games for Recreation*, pages 223 to 292. New York: A. S. Barnes & Company, 1935.

As soon as one of the pair is defeated, some one challenges the winner, and this continues until all have competed and the champion has thus been determined.

Variation.—Same as the above except that the Flat Loop is spun instead of the Wedding Ring.

MASS ROPING FIGHT

This event is similar to the Rope-spinning Duel except that several players are competing at once. All start to spin the Wedding Ring and at the signal all attempt to stop the others' ropes from spinning. The one wins whose rope is spinning after all the others' have been stopped. An area should be marked out beyond the boundaries of which the ropers cannot retreat. Stepping over the boundary eliminates the offender.

CATCH-ROPING DUEL

While scarcely usable in the confines of a council ring, this dual contest is interesting to boys on the campus, playground, and gym floor. Mark out an area about fifty feet square within which the two players must remain. Each player has a catch-rope. At the signal both try to rope the other and at the same time to avoid being roped. The one wins who first closes the noose of his rope tightly on the other. Some one challenges the winner and so the contest continues until a champion is determined.

FREE-FOR-ALL CATCH-ROPING

This is the same as the Catch-roping Duel except that several are competing at once, each trying to rope the others and to avoid being roped. As soon as a player is roped he is eliminated and withdraws. The one wins who remains when all others have been roped. An area should be marked out within which the players must remain.

WEDDING-RING RACE

The distance is fifty yards. Each holding his spinning rope, the contestants line up behind the starting line, so spread out that there are at least eight feet between the individual players. All start to spin the Wedding Ring and when all have it going, the starting signal is given. The contestants run down the course while spinning the rope and the one wins who finishes first provided his rope is still spinning. A contestant is eliminated the moment his rope ceases to spin.

Flat-Loop Race.—This is like the Wedding-ring Race except that the Flat Loop is spun and the distance is twenty-five yards.

WEDDING-RING BICYCLE RACE

This event is the same as the Wedding-ring Race except that the contestants ride bicycles. The distance is one hundred yards. Each contestant places one leg over the bicycle preparatory to mounting, and while in this position starts the Wedding Ring. The starting signal is given when all ropes are spinning.

LARIAT RACE

Establish a starting line and parallel to it mark four other lines, all lines being fifteen feet apart. Mark a spot on the starting line for each contestant, these spots being ten feet apart. Out from each of these spots on each fifteen-foot stripe, drive a stake two feet high into the ground. Thus there is a row of four stakes in front of each contestant as he stands on the starting line, these stakes being fifteen feet apart. Each contestant has a catch-rope.

At the signal each player tries to rope the nearest stake. He is not permitted to step over the starting line until the stake is "caught." Once the stake is roped, he runs to it, removes the lariat, and tries to rope the next stake. This continues until the last stake is roped, whereupon the contestant runs to it to finish. The one finishing first wins.

SKIPPING RACE

This difficult event is suitable only for expert ropers. The distance is twenty-five yards. The racers go down the distance with the Running Skip (see page 174). The one finishing first wins.

CALF-ROPING CONTEST

This is a standard event of the western rodeos and while it can scarcely be used by amateurs in other settings, it will be of interest to all ropers nevertheless.

The calf is enclosed in a pen and the roper, mounted on his horse, is stationed behind a line about twenty-five feet in back of the gate to the pen. The gate is opened and when the calf runs out the referee blows his whistle and the roper dashes in pursuit. He ropes the calf with his catch-rope, leaps from his horse and runs up to him, touching him with his hand. The timers record the time with a stop-watch from the whistle until the hand is placed on the calf. Then the next contestant tries, using another calf. The one with the best time wins.

Sometimes this event is conducted by requiring the roper to place a rubber band around the calf's lower jaw. Having done this he throws up his hands as the signal to the timers.

BULLDOGGING

The colorful event to which western tradition has attached the name of Bulldogging involves no roping at all, and certainly it is no pastime for amateurs, being a dangerous and daring undertaking when attempted by even the most experienced and hardened of professionals. On two counts, therefore, it does not fall within the strict scope of this chapter. However, every one concerned with learning to rope will be interested in knowing the events associated with roping in the rodeos and the rules governing them. Certainly he will want to be able to talk the language of the rodeos and "Bulldogging" is an important word in that language.

Rather than roping his steer with his lariat, the bulldogger seizes him by the horns with his hands and wrestles him to the ground. He chases the steer on his horse and when near enough, dives down grasping the horns with his hands, stops the steer's progress by bracing the feet of his stiffened legs against the ground, then throws the steer by wrenching his horns. Needless to say it is a strenuous and rugged sport, replete with hazard at every turn.

The procedure in conducting the event is to station the competitor behind the starting line which is about twenty-five feet back from the gate of the pen. As the gate is opened and the steer dashes out, the referee sounds his whistle and the bulldogger spurs his pony forward. The steer having been stopped, the event is concluded in one of two ways, depending on the rules in use in the particular rodeo: the contestant may throw the steer and sit on his head at which second the timers stop their stopwatches, or he may force the steer's head to the ground and slip a rubber band over his lower jaw, this being the signal for the timers. The latter method is preferred by many on the grounds that it is more humane and less liable to injure the steer. The contestant wins who finishes in the shortest time.

CHAPTER XV

Whip Cracking

Out over the backs of the six-mule team floats the long black-snake lash—*bang!*—the flies that were pestering the ears of the left front mule are sent scurrying to safer quarters! And the peaceful plodding mule was never touched! Yes, the old mule-driver could handle his whip. So, too, with the cowboys on the western range, the drovers in far-off Australia, the stockmen wherever they are found in the open country around this old globe.

Down the arena of the circus drifts the cracker of the eighty-foot whip—*bang!*—the paper in the cowgirl's hand goes floating downward! and her fingers are as safe and sound as ever! Up into the drops of the vaudeville stage a paper sack is thrown, and after it darts the stinging end of the plaited lash—*bang!*—downward floats a shower of confetti! Across in front of the footlights the western showman sends his leather "finger" seeking the trigger of the six-shooter in the hand of his partner—*bang!* says the whip, *BANG!* answers the six-shooter.

Around the gymnasium the boys are standing, across the campus the campers are scattered, in the meeting room the Scouts are gathered—all would-be cowboys of the plains and drovers of the herds. *Bang!* say their whips—*bang! bang!* answer the echoes.

I like whips. (And where is there a man or boy who does not?) I like their rugged appearance, the robust life they seem to symbolize. They speak loudly of far-reaching plains and of distant misty horizons, of saddles and boots, sombreros and chaps, of lanky cowboys and rugged mule-whackers. They tell of lusty life, of violent days, of turbulent surroundings. They carry the odor of cattle, of mules, and horses. They are masculine, and appeal to men.

I like to handle whips, to throw them, to make them speak

241

violently, to send them to their target with the precision that only a whip can attain. As the whip bangs forth its arresting report there is a thrill that strikes deep. Here is a sport that somehow rings true. It not only is rugged and full of vigorous exercise, it not only is noisy and turbulent, but withal it has an accuracy about it, an exactness, a precision that smacks of the rifle. And to me, no arrow or bullet that finds the bull's-eye can quite cause the thrill of satisfaction that comes when a whip in my hand reaches the tiny target cleanly and truly. Whip cracking combines noise and vigor with marksmanship.

What of the danger involved? There isn t any, if the whip is used with a little discretion. Certainly the person handling the whip is entirely safe, and common sense should prevent him from throwing his whip promiscuously at others—the instruments used in any sport or game may become dangerous if thrown recklessly at people.

PLACE IN THE EDUCATIONAL AND RECREATIONAL PROGRAM

The fact that the whip brings the joy indicated in the preceding paragraphs is recommendation enough of recreational worth. It is another of those colorful pastimes that appeals strongly to the imagination at the same time that it furnishes excellent exercise. It fits admirably into the program of the Scout troops, the camp, and the club. Furthermore, it has much to offer to the school's physical-education program.

Although a novelty, whip cracking has every bit as much to offer in the way of exercise as many of the traditional activities of the gymnasium—and it goes beyond these in one priceless contribution, that of *picturesqueness*, of appeal to *imagination*. Boys take to it as ducks take to water. And it is of particular interest in the corrective work of physical education. It deserves a place in any program designed to educate in hobby skills for leisure.

Physical-education departments and recreational organizations today are thinking in terms of exhibitions and demonstrations that are built around certain colorful themes, thus avoiding the stereotyped displays of yesterday in favor of romantic appeal. Here is a glamorous activity that will add spectacle to any performance, and at the same time will give the participants the benefits of vigorous and compelling exercise.

WHIPS THE WORLD AROUND

Wherever around this old world there are stockmen who handle large herds of cattle or drive long teams of mules, whips aplenty are sure to be found. And as one goes from country to country he finds that while the whips may vary in detail, they all fall under two general types: the *American style* with its short handle, and the *Australian type* with its long handle. A knowledge of the differences in construction of these two patterns and the strong and weak points of each is essential to every one desiring to become proficient in the art of the whip. Before whips can be intelligently discussed, however, we must be familiar with the parts of the whip.

PARTS OF A WHIP

A whip consists of four parts—*handle*, *lash*, *fall*, and *cracker*. The *lash* refers to the whip proper, the long plaited section. The *fall* is the straight unplaited strip of leather attached to the end of the Australian style, and which constitutes an extension of the lash. For reasons discussed later in this chapter, it is advisable to attach a fall to every whip, whether Australian or American. The *cracker* is the piece of string, braided cotton, or silk attached to the end of the fall—it is this cracker that makes the noise when the whip is cracked. American stock whips are made with a leather thong to serve as a cracker, but this soon breaks off and must be replaced with another. And the usual procedure is to replace it with braided crochet cotton or string.

The lash or whip proper consists of a center core or filling over which the leather is plaited. Buckshot, rattan, or rawhide may be used for the core. The best whips are filled with rawhide, those of medium quality of rattan, and the cheaper and inferior ones with buckshot.

The *handle* will be discussed in the following sections.

WHIPS OF THE AMERICAN STYLE

The whip of the American West is one with a short handle—it is the type with which every American is familiar, and being traditional in this country, it is what comes to the American's mind when the word *whip* is mentioned. Figure 94 illustrates its familiar lines. It is commonly called a "bull whip" or a "black-snake whip."

The handle is about six inches long. It is usually made of steel and covered with a single piece of leather sewed up the side, al-

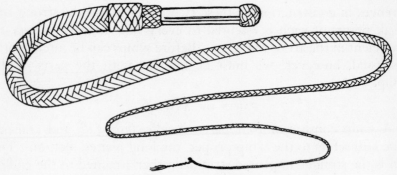

FIGURE 94. THE TYPICAL AMERICAN STOCK WHIP

though some of the cheaper styles have uncovered wooden handles. Most of the American whips have revolving handles, that is, handles that are fitted into a socket so that they will turn around. The whip proper is attached to the handle, which is just long enough to accommodate the hand, and consequently there is no stiffness or rigidity to the whip beyond the hand that holds it. The cracker is usually attached directly to the whip proper, there being no "fall" or leather extension between the lash and cracker as on the Australian whip.

There are numberless special styles of American whips, each carrying a special type name or trade name, but these variations are minor and practically all whips made in this country correspond to the same general pattern. Of these special types, the so-called California style will probably serve the purpose a little better than the others.

The standard lengths of American whips range from eight feet to twenty feet over all. Long whips up to eighty feet in length are frequently seen in circuses but these are made specially for the show business and have no practical importance. American-style whips in these long lengths are extremely hard to handle.

In appearance the American whip is a rugged and colorful weapon, and it lets go with a bang when it is cracked, but aside from its excellent capacity as a noise maker, it must take second place to the Australian style. By comparison, it seems coarse and clumsy, and cannot be thrown at a target with the accuracy of an average Australian lash. Although American cowboy performers prefer it by tradition and use it rather exclusively in the Wild West shows, it is scarcely comparable for careful whip cracking to its Australian counterpart. This is not due to any inferiority in workmanship in producing the American whips but rather to the difference in style between the two models. The American whip serves well the purpose for which it was designed in handling stock, but the precision which results from the long handle makes the Australian type preferable for expert performance.

WHIPS OF THE AUSTRALIAN STYLE

The stockmen of far-off Australia will have none of the short-handled bull whips which have played such a colorful part in the tradition of the western plains of America. Theirs is a whip with a long straight handle, onto which is attached the plaited lash by interlocking loops of leather. Figure 95 shows the traditional Australian pattern.

The handles vary in length from eighteen to twenty-two inches, the longer handles being on the shorter lashes. The handles are usually of steel over which leather is plaited, frequently in intricate and beautiful designs. The handles are often made with a finer plait than the whip itself and consequently set off the whip with a delightful effect. Occasionally one sees the owner's name plaited in such a handle. The cheaper whips, however, have an uncovered wooden handle. At the end of the handle is a leather loop to which the loop at the end of the lash is attached, these loops of leather permitting considerable play and producing much the same effect as the revolving handle on the American style of whip.

While the cheaper Australian whips are made of calfskin, the better ones are plaited with leather from the belly of the kangaroo.

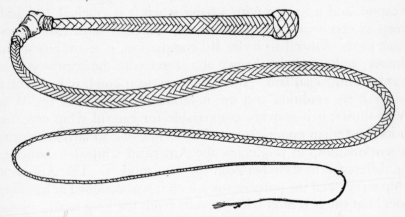

FIGURE 95. THE AUSTRALIAN WHIP

This is unusually strong leather and makes the world's finest whips. Such lashes are frequently referred to as "plaited belly whips." As contrasted to the six, eight or twelve plait of the typical American whips, the better Australian whips range from twelve to twenty-four plait. This fine plaiting combined with the incomparable quality of the kangaroo hide makes whips of rare perfection.*

On the end of the whip is attached a "fall," or unplaited strip of leather about three feet long, to the end of which is attached the cotton cracker. This fall is not typical of the American style.

The length of an Australian whip refers to the length of the whip proper, not including the handle or "fall." Thus an eight-

---

* Excellent Australian whips of the type and quality described may be obtained from T. Henderson & Company, Sydney, Australia.

foot whip, equipped with a two-foot handle and three-foot fall, would measure thirteen feet over all.

It is possible to handle with ease a much longer whip of the Australian style than of the American. However, the usual lengths range from six to twelve feet, which means that the length over all would range from eleven to seventeen feet.

ON BUYING A WHIP

First off, let us assume that the whip is being purchased for a beginner who merely wants to learn to crack it and do the simple stunts that novices can hope to accomplish. The selection of whips for experts will be discussed later (see page 261).

In the hands of a beginner, a standard American drover's whip of the California style, ten feet in length, will answer every purpose. Longer lengths are sure to defeat him and shorter lengths are frequently harder to crack than the ten-foot one. A finely plaited whip will be no easier to handle than a coarse one—secure an inexpensive eight-plait lash. You will be wise, however, to obtain the type of whip that has a leather-covered metal handle rather than one of the wooden-handled kinds which almost always are shoddy and poorly-balanced, and consequently are difficult to manage.* Ten-foot whips with metal handles usually range in price from two to eight dollars, depending on the quality of leather and amount of ornamentation. The cheaper ones should be used while learning.

Schools, camps, scout troops, and clubs taking up whip cracking can do no better than to secure a few of these inexpensive ten-foot whips with metal handles.

It is not to be inferred that the American style of whip is easier for the beginner to manage than the Australian with its long handle—in fact the opposite is the truth. But Australian-style whips are not manufactured in this country and so are harder to obtain, and furthermore, the American style is the one that most

---

* American-style stock whips may be secured by mail from any of the western saddlery and leather-supply companies and cowboy outfitters. The large mail-order houses also handle good whips for the beginner. Wooden-handled whips may frequently be picked up in any city at harness shops.

beginners in this country would want to handle. It has a ruggedness and "Wild West" atmosphere about it and in general fits the American picture better. Any one who learns to throw an American whip can certainly handle an Australian. However, a person seriously taking up the art of the whip as a hobby will want both an American and an Australian whip. The proper length of the Australian for the beginner is seven-and-one-half feet, which means that including the handle and fall the whip will measure about twelve feet over all.

MAKING THE FALL

The fall is an extension of straight unplaited leather at the end of the whip. American whips are not made with a fall but it is usually needed and can easily be added. First try out the whip as it comes from the factory and if it is perfectly balanced and cracks easily, leave it as it is, merely attaching the cracker to the end. The chances are, however, that it will work much better if a fall is added.

The typical American whip is coarse and heavy near the end and needs to be narrowed down. The fall serves this purpose. Most American whip-crackers plait on an extension to the whip, thus narrowing it down to the desired thickness, but this is unnecessary labor—the adding of the fall does just as well. Furthermore, when the end of the plaited whip hits a hard object, damage to the slender plaited strips of leather may result, whereas the straight unplaited fall is less susceptible to such injury. The fall serves as a protection to the whip.

While you can make the fall yourself, you must buy the leather from a harness shop, and so it is easier to have them cut it to the proper dimensions. It is thirty-six inches long, one-fourth-inch wide at the widest end, and tapers down to one-eighth inch at the narrow end. The leather should be one-fourth inch thick. It should be made of the very finest and toughest leather obtainable in that it will be subjected to more wear and tear than any other part of the whip. A three-fourth-inch slit through which the small end is passed, is cut near the wide end. To attach to the whip, merely slip the loop thus formed over the end of the whip and pull tight.   Attach the cracker to the end of the fall.

MAKING THE CRACKER

Crackers are made of string, silk thread, or crochet cotton. Every one will have to make his own since suitable ones are not on the market, the usual buggy-whip crackers not being usable on these heavy stock whips.

A six-inch piece of heavy cotton string tied on the end of the whip will make as loud a bang as any one could desire, but it will only stand a few cracks before becoming frayed out or broken. The few minutes required to make a good one from crochet cotton is time saved in the end.

Secure a ball of medium-sized white crochet cotton.   Some whip artists prefer silk but cotton is every bit as serviceable and louder if anything in its report.   Drive a nail in a board, and holding your finger about nine inches from it as in A, Figure 96, wind the string around the finger and nail *thirteen times*—there are thus twenty-six strands of thread.   Cut the end of the loop farthest from the nail (B, Figure 96). Grip each group of threads between the thumb and forefinger about a half inch from the nail, and twist them with a movement of the thumb and finger from left to right, as indicated in B.   Having twisted, lay the *right over the left* and take the threads that were in the right hand in the left, and those that were in the left in the right (C, Figure 96).   Then twist again in the same way and lay the right over the left as before.   Continue until the twisted section is four inches long. Now divide the threads in the left hand into two parts, and with one of these parts tie a half-hitch around the end of the twisted section as shown in D.   Pull the half-hitch tight and the cracker is finished.   As you go along, twist very tightly, and pull hard on the threads each time you lay the right section over the left. The twisted part should be four inches long and the spread end five inches long (E, Figure 96).

Remove the cracker from the nail and tuck the end through the hole where the nail was, pulling it through until a loop has been formed at the end. Tie a knot in the end of the fall, and slip this noose over the knot and tighten, as indicated in F, Figure 96.

Such a cracker will make a loud report and stand plenty of wear. With use, however, it will become frayed out and must be

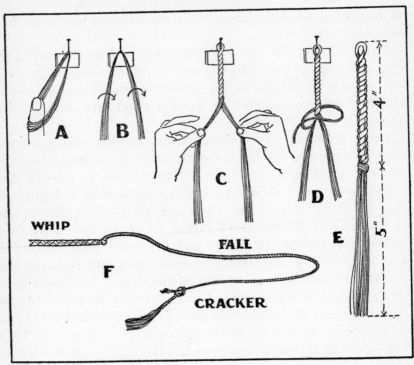

FIGURE 96. MAKING THE COTTON CRACKER FOR THE WHIP

replaced. Make a half dozen crackers and keep them handy to replace the worn-out ones.

A HOME-MADE WHIP

A person really intent on learning to handle a whip should if possible purchase an inexpensive stock whip, but for those who desire to improvise their own, the following suggestions will be helpful. To attempt to make a good plaited whip will be a little too much of an undertaking for the average person, but a service-able practice lash can be fashioned without plaiting.

Let us make the whip after the Australian pattern. A broom-stick will furnish the handle; cut off a twenty-inch length and taper it slightly by drawing it down with a draw-knife (A, Figure 97). Cut an eight-inch strip of pliable but strong leather, one-and-one-half inches wide, and lay it over the small end of the

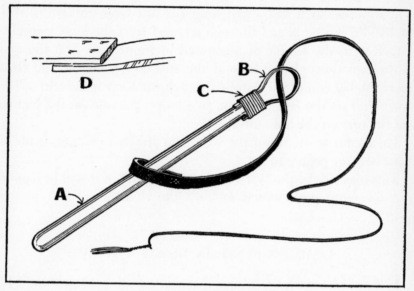

FIGURE 97. PLANS FOR THE HOME-MADE WHIP

handle, forming a loop one-and-one-half inches long, as illustrated in B. Drive a few brads through the leather into the handle, and then wrap tightly with cord as illustrated. Give the cord a coat of shellac to set it.

The whip proper consists of a straight strip of leather eight, ten, or twelve feet long, to suit your taste. Better make it ten feet. If you can locate a worn-out and discarded machine belt, you will be fortunate indeed for it will supply you with the leather in one straight piece without the necessity of splicing. Cut a strip from the belt three-fourths of an inch wide for the handle end, tapering it down to three-eighths of an inch wide at the tip. If the leather is sufficiently strong it may even be tapered down to one-fourth inch. Failing to find a machine belt, the whip may be made in sections from pieces cut from old harness reins, or even from a couple of your old leather belts. Overlap the sections about three-fourths of an inch and fasten with two or three hollow rivets obtainable from any hardware store, as illustrated in D, Figure 97.

To complete the lash, double the handle end back, forming a loop about an inch and a half long (or just large enough so that the handle can be passed through it), and rivet the loop securely. Attach it to the handle as illustrated in Figure 97: Slip the end of the lash through the loop at the end of the handle and then insert the big end of the handle through the loop at the end of the lash. Pull on the lash until the two loops, the one on the handle and the one on the lash, interlock.

Tie a knot at the tip of the whip and attach a cracker, made as described on page 249.

This may not be the best whip in the world but it will be a good practice whip with which to learn the elements of this joyous sport.

COMMON SENSE IN USING A WHIP

It should go without saying that the use of a whip should be tempered with a considerable amount of common sense. There is no danger of one hurting himself with a whip, nor need there be any danger of his hurting any one else or any living creature. It should be made a hard and fast rule never to throw the whip in the direction of another person, or at a dog or other animal. If the cracker should hit a person it would not only inflict pain but might do much more serious damage. Dogs and other animals have a thorough-going fear of a whip, and they should neither be struck with it nor teased or threatened with it. If the rule of never throwing the whip at or around a living creature, man or beast, is always adhered to, the whip will never get you into trouble and you will not have to sacrifice the joy that this rugged western sport can give you.

Perhaps you have seen a whip artist on the stage or at a circus or rodeo crack his whip with skill around his lady partner, taking paper out of her hand, cigarettes from her mouth, and so forth. Needless to say, these stunts are not for the beginner nor have they any place in the recreational use of the whip. There is plenty that can be done with a whip without attempting these dangerous stunts. Swimming is dangerous unless we use discretion; the same is true of archery, horseback riding, and countless other sports. Used with the same discretion, the whip can be a harmless plaything and a constant source of joy.

HOW TO CRACK THE WHIP

Most of the sport of handling a whip centers around making it crack. All whip crackers, young and old, find intrigue in banging the whip, and in the hands of a good whip cracker, it can be made to let go like a young-sized cannon. A whip sounds doubly loud when cracked in a gymnasium or hall.

There are several methods of cracking a whip, each of which will be described in turn.

THE FORWARD THROW

Hold the whip in the right hand and allow it to trail out behind you. Throw it straight forward and as it straightens out—*bang*. Perhaps not the first time, for a whip has a way of tangling up and refusing to straighten out when in the hands of a novice, but all this is relieved by practice.

There are two important points which must be remembered in this forward throw: At the beginning of the throw your hand should be directly in front of your shoulder and almost touching it. To make the throw, *punch your fist straight forward at the level of the shoulder*—at no time is it above or below the shoulder level. Every beginner wants to swing his forearm forward and down so that his hand follows a semicircular course. The result

of this is that the whip also swings in a semicircular course overhead, is straightened out throughout the swing, and since it has no
slack, it cannot crack. If the hand is properly punched forward

FIGURE 98. CRACKING THE WHIP BY MEANS OF THE FORWARD THROW

from the shoulder the whip will trail past the body at the level
of the shoulder and will straighten out in front with a rifle-like
report. This hand movement may be a little difficult to acquire

but it is the first and most fundamental rule of whip cracking.

The process is shown in Figure 98: In A, the right hand is in proper position in front of the right shoulder. This hand is then punched straight forward as in B and straightened out at shoulder level, throwing the whip forward for the crack, as in C.

The second rule has to do with the movement of the wrist: *As the whip straightens out in front, turn the wrist sharply downward.* More than anything else, it is this downward turn of the wrist that makes the whip crack. It serves to send the cracker down against the air with a bang. If needed to give additional momentum, the wrist may be turned down sharply and at the same time jerked back a little.

If these two movements are mastered, you will have no trouble making the whip crack: punch your hand straight forward from the shoulder, and as the whip straightens, turn your wrist sharply downward.

When you can crack the whip from a start of trailing out behind you, try picking it up from the floor in front of you and cracking it. Straighten it out on the floor directly in front of your right shoulder, holding the handle in your right hand with arm extended at full length in front. Pick up the whip by raising the hand high over the level of the head, then swing it back behind the right shoulder by bringing the hand back to its position just in front of the shoulder (A, Figure 98). Give the whip plenty of time to settle down behind you, then punch the handle forward, sending the whip out in front of you for the crack (B, Figure 98). You will probably rush the process so much at the start as to cause failure—throw the whip back behind you slowly and gently, and give it time to settle down and almost reach the floor before sending it forward.

THE CIRCULAR THROW

Hold the whip in your right hand. Swing the hand slowly in a circle over the head, thus causing the whip to swing around the body parallel to the floor at about the level of the shoulders. The direction of the swing is from right to left, that is, as the whip passes in front of the body it is going from right to left. Practice making this swing a few times until the whip can be controlled in this position. Now to crack it: As the hand comes around in front, hesitate a second and then reverse the direction, jerking your hand sharply back to the right and downward. A louder bang will result than can be produced by any other method of cracking. Two factors cause difficulty for beginners in mastering this feat:

First, there is usually a tendency to rush the movement. If the whip is swung around over the head too rapidly, it straightens out and does not have the slack needed to make possible the crack. The swing is made slowly, with just enough momentum to keep the whip under control and elevated to approximately the height of the shoulders. As it nears the front, the whip is thrown up above the level of the head. Here the hand hesitates long enough to let the whip drop a little and accumulate slack. Then the handle is jerked sharply and forcefully back in the opposite direction, that is, to the right and a little downward. With experience the feel of the whip in your hand will tell you the proper time to make the crack without the necessity of watching it and studying the position. The secret in this trick is largely one of timing.

The *second* factor offering an obstacle is the fear that the whip will strike the face. The beginner flinches and closes his eyes, and encounters difficulty in pulling his hand back forcefully enough. This fear is entirely unfounded. It is scarcely conceivable that the whip could hit the man who is handling it in this trick. In fact, the reverse movement that cracks the whip throws the cracker away from the body, not toward it. A little practice will relieve all such fear and from then on progress will come rapidly.

OTHER METHODS OF CRACKING

In addition to the cracking of the whip in front of you and at the side, as described in the two foregoing sections, it is possible to crack it in almost any position in relation to the body. The essential requirement is that there be plenty of slack in the whip.

Regardless of where it is, if it is relaxed and not extended to its full length, all that is needed to crack it is simply to jerk the handle and straighten the whip out suddenly. It may be behind the back, off to one side, high or low, over the head, or in any conceivable position. You will have no difficulty cracking it in all positions once you are completely at home with a whip in your hand.

DOUBLE CRACKS

There are several ways by which the whip can be cracked twice in rapid succession. The circular swing described above may easily be utilized for a double crack, or in fact, for a rapid-fire succession of bangs. Swing the whip around overhead from right to left and as it swings around in front and nears the left side, crack it as described in the discussion of the circular swing. This throws the whip to the right and downward. Immediately swing it upward to the right so that it is off in front of the right shoulder, and then jerk the handle sharply to the *left* and downward. A second bang will thus result about two seconds after the first. Then immediately swing it up to the left so that it is off in front of the left shoulder and crack it again. You can thus continue the rapid cracking as long as you desire.

There is another effective way of cracking the whip twice, very similar to the above: Swing it around overhead and crack it as described above, and as the whip swings down and to the right after the crack, let it float around past your right side, and then throw it straight forward forcefully for the second crack. Then immediately throw it up to left and start the series of two cracks over again. In throwing the whip forward for the second crack, the hand is held sidewise, thumb-side up, and the whip is thrown with a sideward motion, this motion continuing after the crack in order to elevate the whip above the level of the head to the left, thus placing it in position to start the series over.

The forward throw may also be used for a double crack. With the whip lying on the floor in front of the right shoulder, pick it up and toss it straight back behind you slowly, bringing your hand up close to and directly in front of your right shoulder. Here hesitate a second or so, allowing slack to gather in the whip, then snap it sharply forward, thus making it crack behind your back. Then continue the swing forward and crack it in front as usual. In making the crack behind you, be sure to punch your hand directly forward from your shoulder and not to swing it upward in a semi-circular motion—to do the latter may crack the whip behind you just as effectively but it will make impossible the crack in front.

HITTING A TARGET WITH A WHIP

First off, let it be repeated that a whip should never be thrown at or near a person or animal. Plenty of targets may be found on which to practice your skill without attempting to take papers or other objects out of a person's hands—these stunts are for experts, not beginners.

A whip can be thrown with amazing accuracy. It is probably true that, given a good whip, an expert can hit a smaller target consistently than can be hit with any other instrument save only a gun. Of course much depends on the whip—a coarse, poorly balanced lash can not be expected to cut down the tiny targets that the thin and finely plaited whips will reach. But regardless of the quality, a whip can be depended upon to go where it is thrown with startling accuracy.

For target work, an Australian-style whip is preferable from every standpoint to the American style. Its long handle permits a preciseness of control that is impossible with the short-handled and limber stock whip of the western plains. However, reasonably accurate work can be done with the latter model and both are handled in the same way. Precise target work calls for a whip ten feet in length or shorter.

Let us suppose that we are going to clip a leaf off a bush about three feet above the ground, using a ten-foot whip. Stand about eight feet away from the leaf, thus making it possible to throw the end of the whip beyond the leaf and hit it with the fall rather than the cracker. While learning, do not attempt to crack the whip but merely to throw it forward and hit the leaf. Lay the whip on the ground directly under the leaf, pick it up and toss it behind you, then throw it forward and down on the leaf. Since the aim is not to crack the whip, the hand is not punched straight forward from the shoulder as is usual but thrown forward and down with a semicircular motion.

Keep your eye focused on the leaf—set yourself, study the location of the leaf, and throw straight at it. If you are able to handle a whip, it is pretty hard to miss.

Now to crack it: When you can hit the leaf regularly without cracking the whip, try hitting it by the regular forward throw described on page 253. The whip should hit the leaf simultaneously with its crack. Given a good eye and steady nerves, all that is needed to make the leaves go floating downward with monotonous regularity is plenty of practice.

There is one important point to remember here: *never attempt to hit the target with the cracker*. The cracker should always be thrown beyond the target, the aim being to hit the target with the fall a foot or so from the cracker. This is the chief purpose of the fall. If the whip has no fall, the slender plaited end of the whip must hit the target, and hard targets frequently cut and ruin the delicate plaiting. Furthermore, the cracker hits with tremendous force and may do serious damage to any object it hits, whereas the fall or plaited end of the whip is relatively harmless.

STUNTS FOR THE BEGINNER

Here are some stunts with a whip which not only supply the best of practice in accuracy but are excellent exhibition stunts when incorporated in pageants and demonstrations. The long whips never fail to appeal and the spectators marvel at the accuracy with which the cracker seems to find its mark.

In all of these stunts, the forward throw is used and the whip is caused to crack as it hits the target.

Catching the Stick.—Place two small packing boxes of the same height on the ground five inches apart, and lay an eight-inch stick between them near the front side. Stand the proper distance away, throw the whip, and attempt to hit the stick. When this can be done regularly, try to hit the stick in such a way as to cause it to fly toward you so that you can catch it. To do this, you will have to stand close enough so that the tip of the fall can wrap around the stick. Just as the whip hits it, jerk the stick toward you and into your hands.

Hitting a Paper.—Tear out a piece of newspaper a foot long and four or five inches wide, and crumple it into a slender strip a foot long. Insert one end of this in a crevice of a board or other object so that it sticks out in a horizontal position about four feet from the ground. As you face the paper it should extend to your right. Crack the whip at the end of the paper, attempting to clip off an inch or so of the end. Continue until the paper has all been cut away.

Putting Out Candles.—Set up a lighted candle on the ground and crack it out. The technique here is to crack the whip so that the cracker bangs just above the flame, thus blowing it out. Of course the whip can be cracked so as to hit the flame but that will doubtless upset the candle, thus making the stunt look cheap.

In giving an exhibition, set up a half dozen candles in a semi-circle, and crack them out in rapid succession without stepping from your position.

Breaking Balloons.—This is a colorful and noisy stunt with a whip, the bursting balloons adding their pops to the cracking of the whip. The balloons may be on the floor or suspended any place within reach of the whip. It makes a good show to set the stage with a dozen balloons placed in different positions and at different heights, then to pop them out one after the other in rapid succession.

To burst the balloon, it is usually necessary to hit it with the cracker—fragile as they are, the balloons have a way of bouncing off to one side and remaining intact when hit by the fall of the whip.

Paper in the Hand.—There are several ways in which paper may be cracked out of one's hand—the expert can hold the paper in any position one can name and crack it out with a ten-foot whip. Most of these stunts are dangerous in the hazard they present to one's fingers. There is one, however, that is both harmless and spectacular. Hold the piece of paper in the left hand behind your back so that it extends out to the right of the body, the hand holding it touching the small of your back as far to the right as possible. Holding the whip in your right hand, lay it out in front, pick it up and toss it behind the back, giving it plenty of time to settle down, then throw it forward just as in doing the standard forward throw. As it goes forward it will pass the right side of the body and clip off the paper, cracking as usual far out in front. It all happens so quickly that the average spectator will think that it was cracked off with the cracker.

STUNTS FOR THE EXPERT

A person attempting to develop a finished whip act will need a variety of whips. He should have an American-style whip ten feet long to use as a noise maker, and in addition, should possess the following range of Australian-style whips:

Handle	Lash	Fall	Total Length
22 inches	6 feet	26 inches	10 feet
20 inches	7 feet	30 inches	11 feet 2 inches
20 inches	8 feet	36 inches	12 feet 8 inches
20 inches	10 feet	36 inches	14 feet 8 inches
18 inches	12 feet	36 inches	16 feet 6 inches

Most whip-crackers attempt to use whips that are longer than necessary for any particular stunt, thinking that the use of the larger whip will make the stunt more spectacular. It is better to forget this angle and aim to select the whip that is best in length and balance to perform the stunt accurately and dependably. The shorter lengths are easier to handle, safer, and in the long run, will make the performer appear to better advantage.

Since the stunts comprising a whip-cracking act as a professional would do it on the stage are of the more daring type that beginners should not attempt, the stunts will not be described in detail but merely listed. By the time the beginner has mastered enough skill to consider them, he will have discovered for himself how they should be performed. Unless it is stated that the performer holds the object in his own hand, there is another person holding the object to be hit in each of these stunts:

Papers from hand held in front
Paper from hand held between legs
Paper from *own* hand
Cigarettes from *own* hand
Breaking a carrot
Breaking a pencil
Splitting an apple
Extinguishing a candle

Cigarette from hand
Paper from mouth
Cigar from mouth
Lighting match on match box
Jerking feet from under person
Knocking cork from bottle of beer
Shooting off revolver
Finale of twelve papers from hand
   in rapid succession

By throwing the whip so that the cracker goes three feet beyond the person, it is possible to wrap the whip around a person's arm or around his neck without any danger of injury. These stunts should be avoided in that they cheapen the act. Never touch the person with the whip—much of the effectiveness of the act depends upon the fear of the audience that the person may be hit, and if he is deliberately hit without injury resulting, the impression is given that there is nothing dangerous about the act. An exception is found in knocking a person's feet from under him by wrapping the whip around the ankles and jerking. This serves admirably in that it seems obvious that the whip must hit with great force, enough, in fact, to knock his feet from under him.

CHAPTER XVI

Spinning the Serpentine

The stage is set with bright and vivid colors. The ladies and gentlemen of the chorus, resplendent with gorgeous tones, are moving gently and rather inconspicuously to the music of the orchestra. To the front and center there is a large white spiral spinning vividly, floating gracefully, alert with life and motion. The audience sits entranced before the magic of this spinning serpentine, scarcely conscious of the splendor of people and color that form the background to it.

The scene shifts from stage show to recreational exhibition: The members of the pageant, dressed in quaint folk-dancing costumes, are massed upon the gym floor or playground. In front are a half-dozen serpentines, their colored spirals whirling vivaciously. Few things could add more novelty, glamour, and intrigue to such a setting.

What is the serpentine? Nothing more than a very long strip of tissue paper which is twirled in the air. When spinning it forms a whirling spiral similar to that shown in Figure 99. There is no denying the eye-magic of these living spirals. And there is no mystery in this appeal, for both psychologists and practical advertisers know full well that a circle or a spiral catches the eye more quickly and holds it longer than any other formation. The serpentine not only presents a spiral but it adds the further appeal of motion.

In a playground or gymnasium pageant or exhibition, the serpentine is of particular appropriateness and interest. It supplies a touch of novelty. It adds spectacle. It is showy, colorful. It seems to fit such occasions. And curiously enough, as we shift the setting from the ruggedness of such a pageant to the delicacy of the finale of a musical show, we find the serpentine blending just as effectively and beautifully into the general atmosphere. Whether in children's physical exhibition or adult amateur musical comedy, the serpentine is within the capacity of the average person.

Spinning the serpentine does not involve the use of a rope, but

FIGURE 99. SPINNING THE SERPENTINE

the art seems somehow to be of peculiar interest to ropers, and its skills are quickly mastered by hands familiar with spinning a rope. Certainly the serpentine will be appealing to readers of a book dealing with the types of subjects that comprise this volume, and its similarity to rope spinning is the justification for its inclusion in this particular section.

MAKING THE SERPENTINE

The ideal material from which to make the serpentine is Japanese tissue paper. This paper is several times stronger than our American-made tissue, is less inclined to tear, and is more cloth-like in texture. A serpentine made of it is light, strong, durable, and possessed of unusual floating quality. However, such Japanese tissue is extremely hard to obtain in this country and the average person will usually be forced to rely upon ordinary tissue paper, which latter will answer the purpose adequately if handled carefully.

Cut the Japanese tissue into strips five inches wide, or the American tissue into strips six inches wide. Fold the strips over and paste the edges, making a double thickness. Thus we have strips two-and-one-half inches wide if the Japanese paper is used or three inches wide in the American tissue. Paste these strips end to end into one long strip. The length of the serpentine depends on the height and skill of the individual using it. It will vary between twenty-five and forty feet. The longer the serpentine, the more spirals it will make and the more effective will be the picture. The beginner will be wise to start with a length of twenty-five feet and add on additional sections as he develops the knack of handling it.

Now it will be necessary to add a handle of wood. Although a little heavy, a two-foot section of a broom handle will answer the purpose. A two-foot stick of cedar, rounded, and tapered a little toward the end, is ideal. Cover the end with glue for a distance of four inches and then wrap the end of the serpentine around the glued area so that the stick serves as an extension of the tissue strip. Wrap this four-inch area tightly with light string and the serpentine is finished.

A serpentine of white tissue will stand out more vividly than one of any other color. If only one is to be used, certainly it should be of white. In a pageant or gym exhibition, in which numbers of serpentines are to be used at once, several colors may be used, so arranged as to blend into a balanced whole. On a stage it is possible to use three serpentines, a large white one in the center and a smaller one on either side, the side ones being red and blue.

SPINNING THE SERPENTINE

Hold the handle of the stick in the right hand and allow the serpentine to rest on the floor off to the right side. Swing the stick in a large circle in front of the body, the direction being from right to left as the stick crosses at the top. In other words, the direction is counterclockwise for a righthanded person. The serpentine will follow the stick and will trail out into the spiral shown in Figure 99.

In swinging the stick the emphasis must be on the upward motion, which tends to lift the serpentine with each spin and prevent it from sagging down and touching the floor. The serpentine should spin in a vertical plane, as nearly perpendicular to the floor as possible. If the stick is whirled in such a vertical plane, the tissue trailer tends to float out and away from the performer. To prevent this, the stick should be shoved out at arm's length as it crosses the top of the circle, and pulled in a little at the bottom.

The spinning will of course twist the strip of tissue near the handle, and unless precautions are taken, the paper will soon break or become so knotted as to cause the serpentine to get out of control. To overcome this, the handle should be turned in the hand once every time the serpentine is whirled. This turning of the handle is usually done as the stick crosses the lower part of its circle, the hand tightening on the upward stroke so as to give the stick an emphatic upward swing.

Perfect rhythm is important in producing a beautiful spiral. Do not rush the spinning, but rather time it just fast enough to keep the serpentine under control and floating lightly and beautifully. The speed must be determined by practice for each individual serpentine. A long serpentine must move a little more rapidly than a small short one.

The intrigue of the spinning serpentine is in the magic of the floating spiral. The performer should fade out as much as possible behind the spiral, doing nothing to attract attention to himself but being content to allow the spiral to hold the spot. And the

spiral is well able to do this without the assistance of other attractions.

Music from the orchestra is appropriate when the serpentine
is being spun. A waltz rhythm should permit the performer to
whirl the stick gracefully in time with the tune.

The appeal of the serpentine is so great that it will hold the
attention of the spectators for a full two minutes. Most amateur
stunt performers are inclined to drag their acts out and thus
defeat them, but here is one stunt that is usually cut too short by
the beginner. Even though the performer may have the feeling
that he is doing nothing very spectacular, he should keep right
on whirling the tissue, confident in the knowledge that the spiral
has a rare capacity to entrance.

Part III

THE WOODSMAN'S SECTION

Blowguns, Darts, Tomahawk Throwing, Log Rolling

CHAPTER XVII

Tomahawk Throwing

In the colorful pageant of American pioneer days, few things loom in larger proportion than the hatchet. No instrument except perhaps the rifle is so indelibly and inseparably a part of that glamorous picture—the tomahawk of the Indian, the Hudson's Bay ax of the northern halfbreed, the belt ax of the pioneer, the double-bit of the woodsman—yes, axes are part and parcel of American tradition. And while they may belong to the seven thousand years of yesterday as an absolute essential of everyday existence for the most of us, axes will never leave the American picture—they will live forever in the fancy of boys, in the imagination of penned-up city dwellers—they will live forever in the recreation of outdoor-minded folk, young and old, throughout this rugged and vigorous land.

Whether a gray-haired camper or a boy playing Indian, the little camp ax brings to mind the Indian's tomahawk—and as he hurls it at a dead tree or a stump, his imagination tells him he is a red warrior sending his tomahawk crashing out at his enemy, or a pioneer using his belt ax Indian-fashion against the Redskins.

Certain it is that the glorious background of this picturesque sport has much to do with its appeal to all men and boys who know it. It smacks of Indians, of pioneers, of woodsmen, of mountaineers—of the rough, hard life of yesterday. Imagination colors it with a glamour that is irresistible.

But ax-throwing carries more of a punch than mere imagination. Delightful and important as the imaginative aspect is in any really worth-while recreation, the activity must have some intrinsic worth. The sturdy, vigorous nature of ax-throwing makes it a sport for men and boys—it is truly and exclusively masculine. And men find that it somehow rings true. A strong-armed throw—the ax flashes through the air—thud! it quivers in the tree! And a thrill of deep-rooted satisfaction quivers up the back of the thrower. A chip is placed on the log—thud! and the chip drops in halves! Forty feet from the tree stands the thrower—one, two, three, four summersaults the ax turns as it zips through the air—thud! It finds the target! No object thrown at a target can cause a greater thrill! It is somehow the thud of the ax as it cuts deep and true into the log and remains motionless, that grips. There is no bouncing off the log or no feeling of make-believe about this missile—when it hits it sinks deep in business-like fashion. And it awakens something deep within—it is as if it stirs an age-old racial memory.

AXES AND TARGETS

AXES TO USE

The ideal ax for throwing is the common Scout or camp ax. Experiments indicate that of the various makes of these, the best model for the purpose is the official Scout ax of the Boy Scouts of America—it is ideal in weight and balance. However, there are many makes of scout and camp axes on the market, any one of which is reasonably acceptable.

The scout or camp axes made for boys are knock-about axes that will not keep a sharp edge and are inefficient for fast chopping, but they are excellent for the rough usage that throwing necessarily involves. No really fine camp ax should be subjected to such abuse. A finely-made ax that will keep a keen chopping edge is necessarily more brittle than those of lesser worth, and such axes are apt to chip if thrown. They are not made for such purposes and no one who appreciates a good ax will use them in this way or subject them to any kind of unnecessarily rough usage. A good camper respects his chopping ax, protects it, and will not allow any one to use it except himself. Secure an ordinary scout ax for throwing—it can stand it and will not chip. In ordinary camping, it is always advisable to have one of these knock-about axes in addition to a good chopping ax, in that there is always rough work to do, to which no good ax should be subjected.

The handle of the throwing ax should be taped throughout its entire length in order to give it greater strength. The jolt caused by the ax hitting the log frequently splits the handle lengthwise. Further, an untaped handle of an ax sticking in the log will, if hit when another ax is thrown, be shattered and ruined, whereas if the handle were taped, it may be only cut and can easily be repaired by adding more tape. After the tape has been applied, rub the handle with sand to remove the stickiness.

THE AX-THROWING LOG

Any standing *dead* tree may be used as a target for ax-throwing when one or two fellows are out hiking in the woods. However, in camps and on playgrounds where the activity will be indulged in regularly, a log should be set up especially for the purpose.

Never throw an ax at a living tree. Plenty of dead trees and stumps may be found without abusing living trees and inflicting injuries and permanent scars that will be eyesores as long as the tree lives. Any boy old enough to have the strength to throw an ax should have better judgment than to strike any living tree unnecessarily with the blade of an ax. And furthermore, *beware of telephone poles:* Although a little narrow, they are ideal otherwise and are always a temptation. Their use may place you in the same predicament as the boys that thoughtlessly made a target of a telephone pole until it was well-nigh chipped in half, whereat they found themselves in the office of the telephone company discussing ways and means of finding the money to pay for a new pole. And one cannot blame the telephone company! Find a stump in the woods or an old dead tree that is still standing—there are no better targets and the use of them causes injury to no living thing or to no valuable property.

To set up a log for the purpose, find a solid dead log eighteen inches or more in diameter. The kind of wood is not particularly

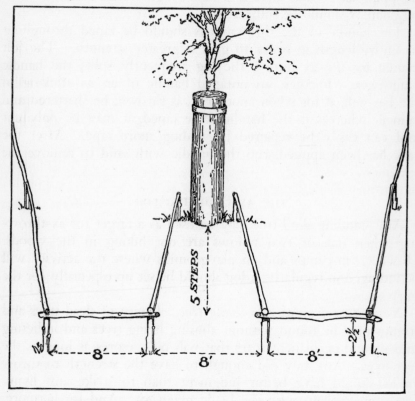

FIGURE 100. THE AX-THROWING LOG WITH GUARD RAILS

important except that the softer woods chip away more rapidly and have to be replaced sooner. I had a beech log that stood up for three seasons of hard usage in a summer camp for boys, and I also obtained two seasons of constant use from a hemlock log. Select the largest log that can be found regardless of kind. Saw off six or eight feet of the butt end and haul to the location. Set up the log in front of a sapling and wire the top to the sapling—this is all the support that is needed.

In an organized camp or playground the log should be erected at a spot a little off the beaten path so that there will not be too many interruptions caused by people passing within range behind the log, and yet not so far away but that the log will be seen regularly and thus constantly offer its invitation to come and throw.

Rails should be erected in front of the log and along the sides, as illustrated in Figure 100, to keep people from inadvertently walking within range of the axes. The front rails should be about twenty feet in front of the log, and the outer side rails should be about thirty feet away from the log. If the log is so located that people may wander in back of it without being noticed, a rail should also be erected there. This rail should be fifty feet in back of the log, which distance is much farther than an ax would travel when thrown in such a way as to make it strike in the log.

AX-THROWING BOARDS

Instead of using a log, a board may be constructed in which to stick the ax. Such a board would scarcely be advisable for everyday use by the rank and file of ax-throwers around a summer camp or playground, because the planks will not stand much abuse nor be as durable as a log. Furthermore, there would be no purpose in using a board in preference to a log for such ax-throwers. However, boards are definitely preferable for use by expert ax-throwers who are interested in careful target practice. When one has the flat surface of a board before him, he can throw several axes in succession, aiming to so place them as to create designs on the board. A board certainly is desirable in ax-throwing exhibitions and demonstrations.

The ax-throwers working together may make all sorts of interesting designs on a board, and do feats of accuracy with an ax that would be impossible on a log. I have used a movable board on a stage, placing it at the rear of the stage and throwing the axes at it from near the footlights. An ax-throwing act, using a board, is an excellent number in a camp or outdoor circus, particularly if the throwers are costumed as Indians and the act billed as a demonstration of Indian tomahawk throwing. When

used on a stage or indoors, the floor immediately surrounding the
board should be covered with old canvas.

To make the board, secure solid, clear planks, two inches thick.
The board should be six feet high and three feet wide, supported
behind by a frame of two-by-four-inch material. The board
should stand perpendicular to the ground, and should be so constructed that it can be picked up and moved.

Boards are less inclined to split under the barrage of axes if
they are water-soaked. Before using the board it is well to
thrown a few buckets of water on it.

TARGETS

There are two types of targets ideal for ax-throwing: the
Cross and the *Bull's-eye*.

The Cross Target.—Down the center of the ax-throwing
board, made as described above, paint a two-inch stripe midway
between the edges, and also paint a similar stripe crosswise of
the board midway between the ends, as illustrated in Figure 101.
Then paint the other lines as illustrated, making them one-half
inch wide, thus creating squares nine inches in size.

Such a target is scarcely usable for contests but it is excellent
for careful target practice, and makes an ideal board on which
to train in preparation for an ax-throwing exhibition. The heavy
center lines provide perfect targets at which to aim and their
presence leaves no question in the mind of the ax-thrower as to
where the center of the board lies. The other lines block out
the board into areas at which to aim when several axes are being
thrown in an effort to create designs on a board.

Bull's-eye Target.—On an ax-throwing board made as described in the preceding section, paint a bull's-eye consisting of
five concentric circles as illustrated in Figure 101. The center
circle is seven inches in diameter, and each of the others three-
and-one-half inches wide. Number the circles from the center
out 9, 7, 5, 3, and 1. This target is excellent for use in ax-
throwing contests between two or more people to determine

who can throw with greatest accuracy and make the highest score. It is not as useful as the cross target for exhibition work.

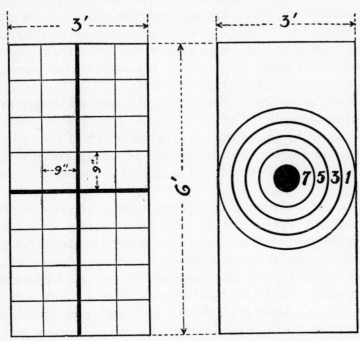

FIGURE 101. TWO TYPES OF TARGETS FOR AX-THROWING BOARDS

AVOIDING ACCIDENTS

To many the very word ax-throwing brings to mind dark forebodings and prophecies of dire results. Obviously enough there is some element of danger in promiscuous ax-throwing, but the danger can be practically eliminated if the few simple precautions that common sense would dictate are taken. Precautions against injury are necessary in every sport, and certain it is that they are necessary here, but the element of danger is not nearly so great in ax-throwing as the name of the sport seems to imply to the popular mind. Given the precautionary measures that any boy would reason out as necessary, this glorious sport can be indulged in freely and safely.

Many organized camps have made extensive use of the sport of tomahawk throwing for years with nothing approaching an accident. It has long been a favorite sport of the Boy Scouts and experience has proven it to be safe and most gripping in its appeal. The danger in ax-throwing is no greater than in riflery and archery, yet there is no opposition to the use of these sports on the grounds of safety by the many organizations for youth that feature them with competent supervision.

First off, it is obvious that there is absoluely no danger to the ax-thrower himself. The only possible hazard is in some one else being in the line of the ax, or within reach of the ax should it glance off the log. And since the ax cannot possibly travel very far, a small restricted area is all that is necessary to insure safety.

When one is throwing an ax alone, there is no cause whatever for concern. When two or more are throwing, there is just one requirement, and this should be made a hard-and-fast rule: *never throw the ax when a person is in front of the throwing line or within the possible range of the ax.* And conversely: *never step in front of the throwing line when a person is preparing to throw.* Make it a rule that after each man throws he is to go at once to the log, withdraw his ax, and return; and the next thrower is not to step to the throwing line until the preceding man is behind it. Of course, the policy may be followed of having every one throw before any one goes to the log to retrieve his ax—this is even more satisfactory from the safety standpoint, but such a procedure often results in the splitting of ax handles. The handle of an ax in the log often is shattered by an ax thrown later. If care is taken in aiming, this splitting of handles can be quite consistently avoided, but many object to the possible danger to the handles and want to withdraw the axes immediately after throwing. Whichever policy is followed, the important thing is that *every one understands thoroughly when he is permitted to step in front of the throwing line.*

In summer camps and other organizations where a feature is made of ax-throwing in the program, it is well to set up a log for the purpose and limit all throwing to this log. Rails may then be erected to keep spectators from inadvertently wandering too close, as described on page 274. In such organizations it is also well to make it a hard-and-fast rule that no ax-throwing is to be permitted unless a counselor or adult supervisor is present.

With such rules in force, this challenging and glamorous sport may be indulged in with all safety.

THROWING THE AX

Almost every one has attempted at some time or other to throw his scout ax at a tree, only to find that even though the ax hits the tree the blade does not strike and consequently the ax does not stick—the ax seems to strike on the handle, the end, the back side, and in every position except on the blade. What these throwers fail to appreciate is that the ax revolves as it passes through the air, and one must stand at just the right distance from the tree or the blade will not be in the proper position to hit.

Here rests the primary secret in ax-throwing: *stand just the right distance from the log.* After this proper distance is found, the rest is easy. Put your back to the tree and walk away five steps—not five paces but *five ordinary steps.* Mark this spot on the ground for it should be about the right distance from which to throw. Try it and see. If not, move backward or forward a few inches until the exact spot has been located. Too close or too far and the blade of the ax will not come around in time. No two persons require exactly the same distance, and each will have to discover for himself the distance best suited for him. But five steps, taken by the individual himself, will not miss it very far.

At five steps the ax will revolve once and stick. And of course, if this distance is doubled or tripled, the ax will revolve two or three times and stick. Most ax-throwing is done at the one-revolution distance.

The above suggestions are for the straight overhand method of throwing the ax. There are several other ways of throwing described in detail in the following pages, some of which require different distances. The following table indicates the distance for each type of throw:

Straight Overhand Throw	5, 10, 15 steps
Straight Underhand Throw	5, 10, 15 steps
Backward Underhand Throw	5, 10 steps
Sitting Throw	5, 10 steps
Lying Throw	5, 10 steps
Reverse Overhand Throw	7½, 12½, 17½ steps
Reverse Underhand Throw	7½, 12½, 17½ steps
Between the Legs Throw	2½, 7½, 12½ steps

THE OVERHAND THROW

Distance—five steps from the log.

There is of course no magic in ax-throwing: One must stand at the proper distance, hold the ax in the proper way, and throw it in such a way as to cause it to stick—unless these details are all correctly performed one cannot hope for success. If the ax misses regularly, it is obvious that there is something awry with the thrower's form.

Grip the ax firmly in your fist as near the end of the handle as possible. Perhaps you may prefer to curl your little finger under the end of the handle—or perhaps not—that is a matter of choice.

Having measured off your five steps, dig a little hole in the ground at the proper distance, in which your right toe is to rest. Take your position facing the log, standing with your feet squarely on the ground, the left foot a little in front of the right, and the right toe in the little hole, as shown in Figure 102. Hold the ax in front of you with your right hand and steady it by placing your left hand on the handle, as shown in Figure 102. Note in Figure 103 and in A, 104 that the ax is straight up and down—in a vertical line to the ground. This is important: the blade must not be tipped one way or the other or the ax will go wabbling through the air, strike crosswise to the grain of the log, and fail to stick.

Hold the ax steadily in this position for a moment while you get set and size up the target, then draw it back without tilting or turning it (B, Figure 104) and throw it at the log with a *downward motion of the forearm,* at the same time stepping forward with your left foot. Do not throw your arm straight out and allow it to follow through as in throwing a ball, but

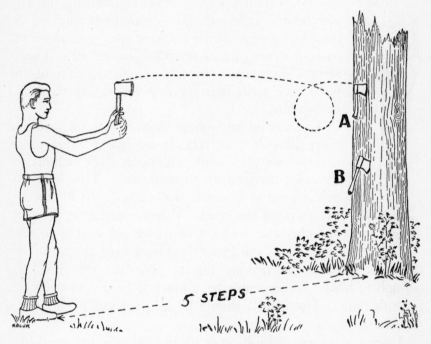

5 STEPS

FIGURE 102. READY FOR THE OVERHAND THROW

rather swing your arm forward and sharply downward as you let the ax go, your hand being considerably below the level of the shoulder after the ax is released. It is much more of an arm than a shoulder motion. This choppy downward motion of the arm releases the ax when the handle is vertical to the ground (C, Figure 104), whereas if the arm is thrown straight out the handle will be nearly parallel to the ground.

When properly thrown the ax should stick in the log with

the full width of the blade, the handle perpendicular to the ground, or nearly so, and parallel to the log in which it sticks. The ax shown in A, Figure 102, is properly stuck, whereas that in B rests at too much of an angle.

There are two pitfalls into which one may very easily stumble in throwing an ax, without being aware of the fact. The first has to do with a wrist motion in releasing the ax—just before letting the ax go, some people are inclined to give it a little forward spin with the wrist to help it turn its summersault in the air. This is always disastrous. Beware of any motion of the wrist: *the wrist must be kept absolutely rigid and immovable.*

FIGURE 103

The second stumbling block is less obvious and more difficult to correct: It consists in tilting the ax a little sideways while pulling it back behind the shoulder preparatory to throwing. This sends the ax forward at an angle that causes it to hit the log crosswise of the grain. When it strikes in this way, an otherwise well thrown ax is apt to fail to stick and fall to the ground—even a hard throw of this type has difficulty in making the ax penetrate the wood far enough to hold. Some people have much difficulty in overcoming this fault. The handle should be in a vertical plane as it is thrown forward.

Always pick out a definite spot on the log at which to throw, and do not be satisfied with your aim until you can come within at least a foot of it each time. While this spot can be any place on the log, it is a little easier to stick the ax accurately and consistently at the lower levels, say between a foot and a half and three feet from the ground.

Having learned these movements, nothing remains for the thrower but to practice. Once the form has been mastered, one can stick ax after ax without a miss—fifty or a hundred in a run will be every-day occurrences. In attempting these long runs, the main thing is to get set for each throw, steady your nerves, and throw very deliberately each time.

While the greatest joy in ax-throwing will always result from throwing at five steps, the long throws offer a challenge that appeals strongly to all ax-throwers.

FIGURE 104. HOW THE OVERHAND THROW IS DONE

Mastering the Long Throws.—It is useless to attempt these long throws until the proper form in ax-throwing has been perfectly mastered and the ax can be thrown accurately, easily, and rhythmically at five steps. Measure off ten steps from the log, the distance at which the ax will make two revolutions before reaching the log. Proceed exactly as at five steps away, except to aim a trifle higher and·throw a little harder. This is not too hard a throw for any reasonably strong boy. Faults in form become very obvious here: if the ax is tilted very slightly when released, it will accumulate more tilt as it travels this longer distance than if it were thrown at five steps. Furthermore, when one tries to throw the ax hard, he is inclined to straighten out his arm as in throwing a ball, rather than to use the choppy downward motion characteristic of ax-throwing.

The next distance to try is fifteen steps, then twenty steps. While there are records of throws at twenty-five steps, twenty steps will be all that a very strong person can hope to handle. It is extremely difficult to throw the ax hard enough at these very long distances and still maintain the proper movement of arm and stiffness of wrist.

FIGURE 105. POSITION OF THE AX IN THE UNDERHAND THROW

THE UNDERHAND THROW

Distance—five steps from the log.

In this throw the ax is tossed at the log with an underhand motion. It is an interesting stunt and is useful in exhibitions but is not so popular as the Overhand Throw, nor is it such a good exercise.

Facing the log at a distance of five steps, grip the end of the ax handle between the thumb and forefinger of the right hand and hold it down beside the leg, as shown in Figure 105, steadying it there with the left hand. Hold it motionless for a second or two while you look at the target, draw it back, and toss it straight forward. The ax will turn a backward flip in the air and stick with the handle up. Take a good full swing with the arm but be sure to release the ax before the arm swings up in front—that is, release it just after the ax has passed the body and when it is at the lowest point of the swing.

The same two points must be remembered here as in all ax-throwing: First, keep the wrist absolutely stiff—throw straight at the tree and do not try to aid the ax in turning its flip by tossing it with the wrist. In fact, the whole arm is kept stiff and permitted to swing only at the shoulder. And second, be sure to keep the blade in a perpendicular plane to the ground throughout the entire swing, that is, do not tilt the ax to one side or the other.

The ax can also be thrown at ten steps by this method, and occasionally at fifteen steps.

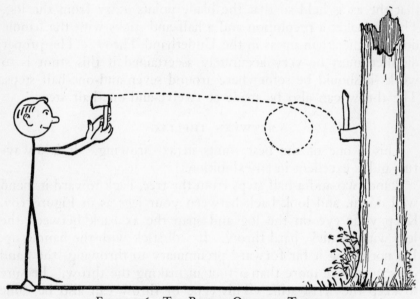

FIGURE 106. THE REVERSE OVERHAND THROW

REVERSE OVERHAND THROW

Distance—seven-and-one-half steps from the log.

This method of throwing the ax is second in popularity only to the Overhand Throw. It is an Overhand Throw in which the ax is held backward, as illustrated in Figure 106. Stand seven-and-one-half steps away from the log, facing it, and throw with exactly the same movements as in doing the Overhand Throw. The ax makes a revolution and a half and sticks with the handle *up*. The distance from the log has to be more precisely correct in this throw than in any other, but further than this, it is no more difficult to perform. The longer distances at which the ax can be thrown by this method are twelve-and-one-half steps and seventeen-and-one-half steps.

REVERSE UNDERHAND THROW

Distance—seven-and-one-half steps from the log.

This is performed just as in the Underhand Throw except that the ax is held so that the blade points *away* from the log. The ax makes a revolution and a half and sticks with the handle down, rather than up as in the Underhand Throw. The proper distance must be very accurately ascertained if this stunt is to work—it should be somewhere around seven-and-one-half steps. The throw can also be made at twelve-and-one-half steps.

BETWEEN THE LEGS

This is one of the best stunts in ax-throwing. It is always fun and is excellent in an exhibition.

Stand two-and-a-half steps from the tree, back toward it, bend well down, and look back between your legs as in Figure 107. Keep your eye on the log and snap the ax back between the legs with a quick, hard throw. It will stick with the handle up. Do not swing it far forward preliminary to throwing—the hand does not move more than a foot in making the throw. Be sure to keep the wrist stiff. This type of throw can also be done at seven-and-one-half steps.

With practice it is possible to throw six or eight axes in succession in this way. having them all stick side by side in the log.

FIGURE 107. THROWING BETWEEN THE LEGS

REVERSE THROW BETWEEN THE LEGS

Distance—five steps from the log.

Take the same position as described for the Between-the-Legs Throw (Figure 107), standing five steps from the log, and holding the ax so that the blade points away from the log. Swing it back between the legs in the same way—it will make a half revolution and stick with the handle down.

THROWING BACKWARD

Distance—five steps from the log.

Ax-throwers always enjoy trying to find out how many different ways they can throw the ax and make it stick. Facing

away from the log and tossing the ax backward is an oddity that
appeals to these stunt enthusiasts, and furnishes an excellent item
in an ax-throwing exhibition.

Stand five steps away from the log, back toward it, and hold
the ax in the right hand down beside the thigh. The blade is
toward the log. Looking back over the right shoulder, swing
the ax forward, then throw it straight back. Be sure to keep
the arm and wrist rigid throughout the throw. To one who has
mastered the Underhand Throw, this stunt should be easy to
learn.

THROWING WHILE SITTING DOWN

FIGURE 108. THROWING
WHILE SITTING DOWN

Distance—five steps from the log.

Sit on the ground at a point five steps
from the log, and spread the legs
widely apart, as shown in Figure 108.
Throw just as in the regular Overhand
Throw. This is an easy stunt that any
one can master, and it is particularly
effective when used in an exhibition of
ax-throwing.

By sitting seven-and-a-half steps
from the log, the Reverse Overhand
Throw may also be used.

THROWING WHILE LYING ON BACK

Distance—five steps from the log.

This is a novel method of ax-throwing that appeals to boys
and adds color to a demonstration of the various ways an ax
can be thrown. Lie on the back so that the shoulders are over
the five-step mark, raise the legs and spread them widely apart
as in Figure 109. Throw between the legs as in the regular
Overhand Throw.

The Reverse Overhand Throw may be used by moving back so that the shoulders are seven-and-a-half steps from the log.

FIGURE 109. THROWING THE AX WHILE LYING ON BACK

FANCY STUNTS IN AX-THROWING

There are fancy stunts aplenty described in the preceding pages on methods in throwing an ax. In ordinary ax-throwing the Overhand Throw is used the great majority of the time, with the Reverse Overhand Throw resorted to occasionally for variety's sake. The use of any of the other stunts will prove to be an innovation and when well-mastered, will always appear as colorful feats that the average ax-thrower will be unable to do. It is possible, however, in addition to a demonstration of the various types of throws, to work up a number of special features in ax-throwing—these will now be described.

AX-THROWING EXHIBITIONS

In presenting an ax-throwing exhibition before a group of spectators, either a log or an ax-throwing board may be used, but the finished performer will prefer a board. The thrower should have at least four axes which he can throw, one after the other, before going to the board to withdraw them. An exhibition should begin with ordinary ax-throwing using the Overhand Throw and the Reverse Overhand Throw. Then the more unusual types of throws should be brought in one after the other, such as the Underhand Throw, throwing between the legs, throwing while sitting, and throwing while lying down. After demonstrating all of these methods of throwing, the axes should be thrown so as to create designs on the board: they can be thrown so as to stick in a horizontal row across the board, in a vertical row up and down the board, in a diagonal line from one corner to the other, or so as to form a square in the center of the board. Creating designs with axes calls for finished ability, steady nerves, and an accuracy of aim that all spectators will readily appreciate.

To conclude the demonstration, two or three colorful feats of accuracy may be staged: strips of tissue paper may be fastened across the board and the ax thrown so as to cut them. An apple may be attached to the board and split in two with an ax. For the finale, an American flag may be rolled and tied at the top of the board, the rope that holds it being stretched across the board; as the ax cuts the rope, the flag immediately drops down, covering the front of the board.

TWO-MAN EXHIBITIONS

Ax-throwing exhibitions are at their best when two men work as partners and throw alternately. In this case each man should have four to six axes, the handles of one man's axes being taped with black tape, and those of the other man with white tape. With the two men throwing alternately, a rapid-fire act is possible that could not be accomplished with one man throwing alone. While one throws the other is getting set and winding up for his throw. Designs aplenty can be made on the board with the twelve axes thrown by the two men. All of the features suggested in the preceding section may be used in a two-man act much more effectively than if only one man is working.

THROWING EVERYTHING

One of the most delightful ax-throwing acts is one that involves the throwing of other implements in addition to the axes.

The use of these other implements is not recommended for beginners, or for any one other than experts who are attempting to work up a stage or circus act. Consequently the details of handling these implements will not be described fully. They have no place in a recreational program.

Such an act could involve, in addition to the usual ax-throwing events, the throwing of darning needles, ice-picks, scissors, files, knives, and a full-sized, long-handled chopping ax. To throw the darning needle, thread it with four feet of yarn, the yarn being doubled, thus creating a two-foot length. Hold on to the end of the yarn, swing the needle overhead, and throw it at the board. The scissors are grasped by the point and thrown, and since the blades separate while in the air, there is no way to anticipate just how they will stick in the board—both blades may stick and again only one may stick.

A discussion of knife-throwing would be a long story. It is a sport that is not to be recommended to boys nor for general recreational use. Suffice it to say that ordinary knives such as hunting knives and kitchen knives, or in fact any knives made for the purpose for which knives are ordinarily used, are not desirable in knife-throwing. Knife-throwing acts as staged by the experts call for knives made of very soft steel, and while they may look like knives, they are not sharpened at all nor could they be, in that the steel is so soft that it can be bent with the hand. They are entirely blunt on the sides and the point is not even sharpened. A dozen of these can be cut out in a few minutes by a blacksmith. Some are trowel-shaped and heavy, with a wooden handle attached, and are thrown by the handle. Others have no handle and are thrown by the point.

AX-THROWING CONTESTS

Here is a number of contests designed to determine ax-throwing championships that are particularly interesting in the programs of summer camps, playgrounds, and Scout troops.

STANDARD AX-THROWING CONTESTS

Each contestant is given twenty-five throws at the log from the five-step mark, and is credited with one point for each ax that sticks in the log. The throws are taken in succession, each player completing his twenty-five throws before the next man throws. The five men with the highest scores then take twenty-five more throws. Each is credited with the best record whether in the first series or the second.

While the Overhand Throw is used in this contest, a similar contest may be staged for any one of the methods of throwing an ax described earlier in the chapter.

Boy Scout Ax-Throwing Contests.—In the official Boy Scout contest, two horizontal lines are painted around the log, the lower one two feet from the ground, and the upper one two feet above the lower. To score, an ax must stick between these lines; those on the lines are considered as in.

The throws must be taken in turn, not in succession. Each contestant takes five throws from the one-revolution line, and five throws from the two-revolution line. In case a contestant fails to stick his ax between the lines on the log, he drops out of the contest.

MOST CONSECUTIVE THROWS

There is no more popular contest among ax-throwers than the one to determine who can make the most consecutive throws without a miss. Each contestant throws until he misses and is credited with the number of consecutive throws he succeeds in making. The one who makes the most consecutive hits wins the contest. The Overhand Throw must be used in this event.

In summer camps it is wise to continue this contest all summer, permitting any camper to attempt to break the record at any time he chooses, the only requirement being that he have an adult present to count the throws. Each time the record is broken the fact should be publicized and the winner's name posted, to be replaced by another when the record is supplanted. Handled in this way, some remarkable ax-throwing records will be established.*

AX-THROWING FOR DISTANCE

Good ax-throwers enjoy a contest to see who can stick the ax from the greatest distance. The contestants throw first from the one-revolution line, then from the two-revolution line, then from the three-revolution line, etc. Each contestant is given three throws from each distance. If he succeeds in sticking one of the three axes, he is permitted to move back to the next more distant line. Each contestant continues to move back until he misses and thus eliminates himself from the contest. The throwers take turns in throwing at each distance, that is, no one moves back to the two-revolution line until all have thrown from the one-revolution line.

ACCURACY CONTEST

This contest calls for the use of an ax-throwing board with a bull's-eye painted on it as described on page 277. Each contestant is given twenty-five throws, each throw scoring the number of points indicated by the ring in which it sticks. Those sticking on a line are credited with the higher score. The contestants take turns in throwing rather than throwing all twenty-five axes in succession.

* At Camp Fairwood, a private camp for boys in Northern Michigan, such contests have been conducted each year for many years. The all-time record in this camp is held by Richard Thies, who in 1934 threw 447 consecutive throws without a miss and without rest. An unofficial record, made without an approved adult scorer, of 540 consecutive good throws was also established by Thies in 1934.

STRING-CUTTING CONTEST

Tie a string around the log three feet from the ground. The contestants take turns in throwing, the one winning who succeeds in cutting the string.

CANDY DROPPING CONTEST

Drive two nails in the log six inches apart and side by side, three feet above the ground. Tie the ends of a three-foot string to a box of candy thus forming a loop which is hung over the nails. This gives a six-inch strip of string at which the contestants aim, between the nails and parallel to the ground. They take turns in throwing, the one winning the candy who succeeds in cutting the string and dropping the candy to the ground.

In order to safeguard the box of candy against being hit by the ax, a block of wood may be wrapped to represent the candy, the actual box of candy being held back to give to the winner.

APPLE-SPLITTING CONTEST

Drive a nail in the log three feet from the ground and stick an apple on the nail. The contestants take turns in throwing, and the one wins who succeeds in splitting the apple.

CHAPTER XVIII

Log Rolling

The big spring drive of the lumbering season is on. The huge piles of winter-cut logs that bank the river go thundering down into the current and out on the swirling stream of timber go the calk-shoed lumberjacks, pike poles in hand, steering and straightening the logs. An eddy sends some logs toward a snag at the shore—a lumberjack sets his log to burling and it carries him to the strays, which he promptly pulls back into line again. Ahead, a possible log jam looms and over the floating timber the jacks go running, leaping courageously and skillfully from pole to pole, the calks on their shoes sinking deep into the wood at every jump for they know full well that a misstep would send them beneath into the churning black water. All day long the loggers ply their hazardous trade out over the treacherous river, with nary a drop of water above their boot tops.

The logging rodeo is in full gait. The applauding crowds pack the bleachers on the river bank. Out on the whirling log two men with flying feet are in frantic struggle to send each other sprawling into the water. The water churns high and sprays, so fast do they spin the log. The pike poles swing high in the air and slap down on the water with a resounding splash, as first one and then the other momentarily loses his balance. The log drifts farther and farther out from the shore. Suddenly one leaps into the air, whirls about like a flash, and starts the log rolling in the opposite direction—but not quickly enough! for his opponent senses the move and almost simultaneously he too leaps and reverses his direction. Back toward the shore the burling log comes—faster and faster it spins as the men put on the pressure —the end must be soon for such a pace cannot go on for long. Abruptly one sinks the calks of his boots deep into the log on the up-coming side, and so suddenly does the whirling log stop that the other totters backward, his pike pole swinging wildly and his calked boots climbing high as he strains to regain the top of the log again. Whereat his opponent commands the log with a sharp spin that sends sprawling into the river the conquered one. And the champion, raising high his pike pole, turns to receive the acclaim of the crowd, and then burls his log quietly to shore and dry land.

The summer camp is having its annual aquatic meet as the season nears its end. Parents and guests are comfortably seated far up and down the shore. The swimming events are over, likewise the canoeing races and the canoe tilting, and now the two finalists in the log-rolling championship hold the spot. On the log they're standing, pike poles in hand—the gun cracks and they're off! No, the perfection and grace of the lumberjacks are not there (but no jack burling for a championship ever experienced greater thrill) and it's quickly all over—faster spins the log and faster, whereupon one of the lads fails to withdraw his calks in time and down the back of the log he slides, while applause acclaims the champion.

Yes, among the Bushmen it's boomerang throwing, among the cowboys it's rope spinning and whip cracking, among the Indians, tomahawk throwing and blow gun shooting, but among the lumberjacks it's *log rolling*.

Part and parcel of the logger's work-a-day life is this log riding and burling, and conspicuous, too, in his recreation. For when the jacks are gathered in holiday spirit, the burling championship is always a major feature. And amazing is the skill of these cruisers of the log drives. None other than Paul Bunyan, himself, mythical hero of all the logging camps, was the greatest of all the log-rollers, in fact, was the inventor of the sport. For at his camp on the Big Onion at the fork of the Little Garlic in that year of the Blue Snow, Paul burled a log so fast that it spun right out from under him,—there was no catastrophe, however, because the water was churned up to such an extent that Paul was able to walk ashore on the bubbles. At least, so say the loggers, and loggers are truthful men.

The romantic color of logging days and the glamour of lumber-jacks is certainly in the background of the appeal of log rolling to the boys of today. When mounted on the log, imagination dictates to them that they are jacks of the mighty forests. But minus such picturesque ancestry, the sport would continue to thrive and this because of the joy inherent in the activity itself. It is difficult enough to be challenging to any one, yet not so difficult that any one of average athletic ability cannot hope to become reasonably proficient. And in addition to the challenge it offers to one's athletic ability, burling grips because it contains so many thrills, so many exciting moments, so many unexpected hazards. Tipsy indeed is the log, and the burler knows well that failure to anticipate each of its temperamental movements means a ducking in the lake. And even though clothed in a bathing suit, this hazard of being surreptitiously splashed into the water is sufficient to add that gaming quality that invariably enhances the intrigue of any sport. It is a feat in balance, in lightness and quickness of foot, and in judgment. It is a water sport, and added to its own peculiar charms are those that go with swimming and bathing. It is another of those masculine sports that appeal to men and boys as belonging to their realm and theirs alone (which point is open to some controversy, however, because women of late have tried their feet at the stunt, and most successfully, too).

One wonders why so fine a sport is so little used in recreation today. The reasons are close at hand: Its skill and techniques are little known—those familiar enough with it to teach it are few in number. It has had no popular champions to sponsor and to popularize it. It calls for calks for shoes and a log of the proper type to roll—things often a little hard to obtain.

But the most of these difficulties are insignificant. The pages that follow tell the simple story of how the skills can be quickly mastered—with this information any play leader or camp counselor can give the instruction. The log is no more difficult to obtain than the implements used regularly in many sports, and certainly is not as expensive as most sport equipment. The calks can be secured for a few pennies and adjusted as described in the following section.

Here is an ideal sport for a summer camp—certainly by tradition and by nature, it belongs to the camp program. Camping at its best concentrates on woodland activities, and here is a backwoods sport supreme. It is almost equally desirable for any supervised swimming beach.

EQUIPMENT

THE LOG

When the big log drives are on, there is little chance for the lumberjack to choose the log he wishes to ride—it is often a case of leaping onto any log that comes within his path, provided it is large enough to float under his weight. But when it comes to burling or rolling a log for the sport of it, just any log that happens to be lying around will not fill the bill. It is one thing just to stand on a log and float down stream on it, but it is a very different thing to burl it. In riding, it makes no difference if the log is of heavy, green wood that sinks a few inches below the surface when you stand on it, but for burling the top of the log must float well above the surface of the water, even with two men on it. An irregular log with knobs or bulges, or one that is lop-sided, will roll so jerkily and unevenly as to take the joy out of the sport. Too "fast" a log will defeat all but the experts, whereas too "slow" a one will not offer excitement enough for any one.

The management of summer camps and bathing beaches, where a feature is to be made of log rolling, will do well to take pains to locate the just-right kind and size of log.

The first requirement is that the log be of light, soft wood. While a log of very light wood may be used when green, it is always better to seek a dry and well seasoned one. White pine and spruce are good, and hemlock is usable if the log is dry. I once attempted to use a freshly cut hemlock but it was so heavy that it sank two or three inches below the surface under the weight of a man. The best log is a white cedar if you can find one large enough for the purpose—there is no other usable wood that floats so buoyantly. I have used the same white-cedar log for six summers in a camp for boys and it is as serviceable today as when first put into the water; it is rolled upon the shore at the close of each season. Get white cedar if possible, otherwise take the following, listed in order of preference: white pine, spruce, or hemlock. In the western area, lodge pole pine will be found excellent.

The log should be sixteen to twenty inches in diameter, the larger the better. Cut off a twelve- to sixteen-foot length that is as nearly uniform in width throughout as possible. The log should be round and smooth—if it is lop-sided, as many logs are, it will revolve in the water in wobbly fashion and with irregular timing. Remove all knobs and projections very carefully with an ax. If the log is for the use of beginners, as is usually the case in camps and on swimming beaches, the bark should be left on. This tends to "slow up" the log enough so that the amateurs can hope to ride it. A stripped log, if it is round and smooth, is so very "fast" that it will prove bewildering and discouraging. Before the season is over, the bark will peel off from constant use, but by that time the burlers will be at home on the log and will welcome the faster spinning.

Anchor the log out from the swimming beach in water about waist deep. When in use the log can be released entirely, or one end of it may be left attached to prevent it from moving to deeper waters while the burlers are on it. If the latter plan is to be followed, a rope at least twenty feet in length should hold the log to the anchor, and the rope should be attached to the end of the log by means of a swivel to prevent the rope from twisting.

THE BALANCING POLE

The lumberjacks frequently use an ordinary peavey in the hand while engaged in log-rolling competition, and when the log is spinning rapidly they sink it into the log to stop it suddenly and thus send the opponent splashing into the water. A peavey, however, would be useless in the hands of any one but a most expert performer on the log. More commonly the jacks use an ordinary pike pole to assist in keeping their balance on the log. This would be acceptable for beginners were it not for the spikes on the end— the awkward falls of amateurs could conceivably involve injury from the spikes. It is better to cut a long slender pole approximating the dimensions of the pike pole. The function the pole fills will be described later in this chapter.

Cut a long slender sapling of light, strong wood, preferably white cedar. It should be thirteen to sixteen feet long, and three to four inches wide at the butt end, tapering down to one-and-one-half inches at the tip. Remove the bark and smooth up carefully so that there is no chance of splinters or slivers. The more slender the pole is, the better it will serve the burler in maintaining his balance. When held by the small end parallel to the ground, the pole should bend somewhat, and when moved should have considerable whip. Too thin a pole, however, will break as it is lashed back and forth in the water. If made of white cedar, a thin pole will prove to be remarkably light and strong. Three or four of these poles should be prepared, from which the contestants can make a selection.

SHOES AND CALKS

Log rolling is impossible without shoes which have calks in the soles and heels. This fact more than anything else has militated against the wider use of the sport. However, the expense involved in calks is insignificant. For the use of campers in a summer camp, I secured four old pairs of working shoes, had them half-soled, and calks applied. These were placed near the swimming beach and any one wanting to roll the log could help himself. It makes no difference if the shoes are a little too large. Since only two can roll the log at once, the four pairs can be passed around so that all who desire can have access to the sport. The total expense to the camp was insignificant as compared to the cost of most other activities. Of course some of the more enthusiastic log-rollers in the camp secured their own shoes.

Any pair of shoes will answer the purpose provided they extend above the ankle and have very heavy solid soles.

The calks are short spikes about one-fourth inch long which are driven into the soles. These can usually be obtained from hardware stores in the backwoods country that is used for camping, or failing here, from the large mail-order houses. Two rows of calks are placed around the outer edge of the sole. The outer row is as near the edge as possible and the inner row about a half

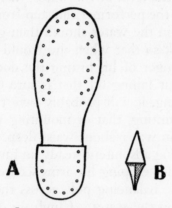

FIGURE 110. LOG-ROLLING SHOES HAVE CALKS IN THE SOLES

inch in from the outer row, as illustrated in Figure 110. Some log-rollers prefer the entire sole covered with calks, but this is unnecessary and if anything is a hindrance. The heel has one row of calks around the outer edge.

Calks of various lengths are used by the log cruisers, depending on the nature of the work they are doing. The slender, sharply pointed types, about three-eighths inch in length, sink too deeply into the log and slow up one's feet so much that successful spinning is impossible—they should be avoided by beginners. Likewise those shorter than one-fourth inch do not grip the slippery log sufficiently. For ordinary log-rolling under average conditions, a calk one-fourth inch long is just right.

HOW TO ROLL THE LOG

MOUNTING THE LOG

Getting onto the log is always a problem for a beginner because he cannot balance himself on the unsteady perch, and before he really gets his bearings he often falls off. There are two methods that may be used in mounting the log: If there is a dock that is not too high above the level of the water, the log may be floated up alongside so that the performer can step from the dock onto it. Some one standing in the water should then gently push the log away from the dock so that when the would-be burler falls off, there will be no danger of his hitting the dock. However, because of the constant falling off that is sure to take place when beginners are learning, it will probably save time to use the second method of mounting, that of mounting while in the water. The log should be in water about waist deep. Have one man in the water hold the log absolutely steady and motionless by facing one of the ends and wrapping his arms securely around it. Lay the small end of the balancing pole across the log, allowing the other end to float on the water. Climb up on the log with the knees and then carefully come up to the standing position, picking up the balancing pole as you do so and getting it in position. When all is ready, tell the man holding the log to release it.

ROLLING THE LOG

The first few times one is up on the log, his footing seems so uncertain and the log so unstable that he develops a feeling of dizziness and utter lack of confidence. To overcome this, do not make any effort to roll the log but merely stand on it as long as possible. This standing on the log, more than anything else, develops self-assurance, confidence, and a feeling of at-homeness.

But even just standing on the log may be baffling enough on the start, and the help of the balancing pole will be necessary. Face sideways to the log, and hold on to the small end of the pole with the hands placed comfortably far apart, the pole ex-

tending at right angles to the log, as shown in Figure 111. Allow
the far end of the pole to sink about three feet below the surface
of the water and hold it firmly at this angle. When you lose
your balance and lean backward, the natural tendency is to pull
up on the pole—the resistance of the water against the pole is
sufficient to give the pole much greater stability than one might
imagine, and one can be quite completely unbalanced and pull

FIGURE 111. ROLLING THE LOG

himself back into position in this way. Similarly, if one starts
to fall forward, his normal reaction is to push downward on the
pole, and being in the water as it is, the pole moves very slowly
under the pressure and offers support enough to enable the
burler to regain his upright position.

The first step in learning to roll the log, then, is merely to
stand on the log in various positions, and learn to handle the pike
pole. When you begin to feel at home and at ease on the log,
can stand there relaxed and unworried, and know how to handle
the pole to regain your balance, then is the time to begin to think
about rolling it.

Standing in the middle of the log and facing sideways, start the log to rolling by lifting one foot off the log and pulling backward with the other—the calks, gripping the log as they do, start it turning very easily. As soon as the foot on the log passes the center of the log, and starts going down on the back side, spring in the air and place the other foot as far forward as possible on the up-coming side. Then just keep it going. The movement is very similar to running in place on the ground.

There are two things to keep in mind constantly while learning: Keep on the top of the log and a little forward, that is, a little toward the up-coming side of the log—if you let your foot go too far down on the back side you will slip back into the water before you know it. And second, tread the log lightly, springing up into the air at each step and touching the log just long enough to make the next spring. In this way you have command of the log, and are not controlled by it as is the case if you sink your calks deeply at each step and keep your feet on it as long as possible. Try to stay up and away from it.

Start the log spinning slowly and keep it going slowly. The log tends to gain momentum at each spin, with the result that in a few seconds it is whirling so fast as to require great skill to stay on it. This is due to faulty timing in treading it. When it is going slowly, keep your eye on it and keep time with it. With practice you will be able to determine the speed at which you want the log to roll and can speed it up or slow it down at will. The controlling of the speed is essential when it comes to competing to put another man off the log, since the main device one has to rely upon is a sudden and unexpected change of speed. At best, however, log-rolling will involve fast and clever foot work—to succeed, you must keep your feet dancing to the rhythm of the log, and it is often mighty fast rhythm.

To all but an expert, success or failure hinges on skillful handling of the balancing pole. Keep the pole in position constantly so that it can be utilized at a second's notice. Since the slender pole bends under pressure, it frequently happens that before the bend can be removed so that the pole grips the water, the burler has gone off. To guard against this, it is well to keep whipping the pole up and down with a slight movement of not over six inches—the pole is thus kept bent constantly and is always in position for instantaneous use.

If you lose your balance, *do not give up*. That is the commonest fault that serves to defeat beginners. Once they feel themselves going, they are as good as in the water. Keep fighting it out and do not admit defeat until you are in the water. When you start to totter, use the balancing pole vigorously, and if it comes out of the water, swing it overhead if need be to pull yourself back. Unless you are hampered by another man on the log, you will find that you can save many and many a ducking if you take a fighting attitude, use your pole, and keep struggling to regain the top of the log.

STOPPING THE LOG

Certain it is that unless you can stop the log once it is rolling, it is only a matter of time before it will put you off. So, after you have learned to make the log revolve under you, the next important step is to learn to stop it.

When the log is rolling, jump in the air, place both feet together, point the toes downward, and sink the calks into the forward or up-coming side of the log. Under average conditions, this will stop the log completely and suddenly, and will not unbalance you. If the log is big and burling rapidly, however, it may only slow it down considerably, and in that case you will have to be ready to repeat the process quickly or be carried over the back of the log and into the water.

If you wish merely to slow the log down rather than stop it, perform the same motions, only gently and without much muscle, repeating until the desired speed has been accomplished.

The second method is more spectacular but not necessarily more difficult. As the log is rolling you are of course facing sideways to the log, with the trunk of the body toward the balancing pole which is held at right angles to the log, as shown in Figure 111. Spring up from the log, turn around in the air, and land on the log facing the opposite side. As soon as you hit the log start to roll it as usual. This will stop the log and start it spinning in the opposite direction. In doing the about face the balancing pale remains in its original position, the arms holding it remaining stationary and only the body turning. Before the about-face, the pole is extended out in front of you, but afterward, it extends out in back of you. It is equally easy to handle it in either position.

In learning to reverse directions, it is better to practice on a stationary log. Merely stand on the log holding the balancing pole in the proper position, jump up and turn, landing on the log with the feet in the opposite direction. You will find that you will do this easily and, after a little practice, will be able to tackle this colorful maneuver on the burling log.

TRAVELING ON THE LOG

Of all the ways of traveling over the water, rolling a log is the slowest and the least efficient, yet it is the most satisfying in the feeling of rare accomplishment that it produces. Sailboats carry a perennial appeal in their calmness and serenity, their delicacy, the closeness that they take you to that world of sky and wind and water. Motorboats thrill in their speed. The canoe has a grace and buoyancy, a familiarity about it that makes it seem a part of one's own personality. And the slowest of these is speedy indeed as compared to the burling log. Yet, when one treads away at the log and slowly carries himself across the river, there wells within his breast a feeling of unusual achievement and of manly vigor that none of the easier and more orthodox methods can produce.

When one can roll a log successfully, he can travel on it—there is nothing more to transporting oneself on the log than merely rolling it. Face sideways on the log and start to roll it, and you will find yourself moving backward, that is, away from the direction in which you are facing. When the object is to travel, spin the log slowly and evenly, just fast enough so that you are working at a comfortable rate of speed. To spin it too rapidly will tire you too soon and at the same time increase the hazard of falling off.

Never attempt to roll the log over deep or rough water. But in case you should slip off into water over your head, remember that the same rule applies as in case of a canoe upset—*stay with the log*. It will support you and you can drift with it, or swim ashore with it. If you are very far from shore, never desert the log.

SPECIAL STUNTS

The greatest sport in log-rolling is competing with another man in an effort to put him off the log before you yourself are forced into the water. But before one can enjoy such a stunt as this he must be a pretty good log-roller, and able to handle the log with confidence and skill when on it alone. A beginner who is wobbly and uncertain of himself on the log will find the odds so heavily against him in competition that he will be off the log before the contest starts; unsteady as the log is when one man is on it alone, it is many times more so when another is on the other end, particularly when he is trying to handle it in such a way as to put you off. So, postpone any ideas of competition until you have practiced long enough to feel that the log is entirely under your control, no matter what turns up.

The two competitors should stand at opposite ends of the log, each about three feet from the end and facing the same direction. Some one should steady the log until both burlers are set and ready, with their balancing poles properly placed. At the signal, the log is released and the contest is on.

There are several tactics which may be used to put the other man off. For the first moment or two just try him out on his ability to spin the log. Start the log to rolling as rapidly as you yourself can handle it and still be sure of staying on. Unless he is an accomplished log-roller, the rapid spinning of the log may be all that is required to dislodge him. Again, if you spin it slowly and then increase the motion suddenly, he may not be able to catch up with you in time to save himself. Remember that in order to win you yourself must be standing on the log when he hits the water.

If, however, your opponent spins the log right along with you, you will have to resort to other tactics. The best of these is suddenly to stop the log when it is rolling. Either of the two methods of stopping the log described in the preceding section may be used. When the log is rolling rapidly, place your feet together and drive the calks of both shoes into the log on the forward or up-coming side. This stops the log abruptly and if he is not alert and has not anticipated your move, he will be sure to go off. Again, when the log is spinning, jump up in the air, turn around, and start the log going in the opposite direction as described on page 305. In this case, your opponent will have to detect your move quickly enough to reverse his direction in time, or a fall on his part is inevitable.

Still another method consists of suddenly starting the stationary log to rolling in a way that your opponent does not anticipate. When your opponent is standing on the log and waiting for you to start rolling it, suddenly jump up in the air, turn in the opposite direction, and immediately start to roll it. Very frequently this will take him by surprise and before he can get himself turned around he will be in the water.

It must be remembered that while you are using these tactics to confuse him, he at the same time is using similar tactics to outmaneuver you. The result is that you must keep your eye not only on the log but on your opponent, and be alert to sense every move that he makes. By watching his feet (which constitute his only means of influencing the log) you have him covered adequately and, at the same time, can see the log. While it is possible with experience to keep your eyes fixed on the log and anticipate somewhat your opponent's movement from the action of the log, it is nevertheless necessary for every one, even an expert, to keep the opponent covered by the corner of the eye. Given good log-rolling ability on the part of both contestants, a great deal of strategy will be necessary for victory, and the honors in the long run will go to the one who not only is able to use his feet, but who is the more alert mentally and utilizes the better strategy. So keep watching your opponent's feet, try to anticipate his movements, and never be caught napping. At the same time try to study his weaknesses and to keep him confused and uncertain as to your intended moves.

Never resort to touching your opponent with your balancing pole, or to striking his balancing pole with yours. It goes without saying that such tactics are unsportsmanlike, and by using them you admit your inability to master him with legitimate tricks.

RIDING A BALL

This is one of the most colorful stunts in connection with the art of log rolling, and constitutes an excellent exhibition number for an aquatic meet or water carnival.

From the end of a log thirty to thirty-six inches in diameter, saw off a section as long as the diameter of the log. Then with an ax round it off into a ball as nearly spherical as possible.

To mount the ball, bring it up beside the dock and step from the dock onto it. The method of rolling is the same as on a log with the balancing pole handled in the same way. Once you are able to roll a log well, this stunt is not as forbidding as it appears, and you will be able to stay on the ball for a long period, much to the amazement of the spectators.

RIDING A STUMP

Riding a stump is an extremely difficult feat which will be of interest only to those who have developed outstanding skill in log rolling. It is sure to be defeating to beginners, but when the necessary skill on a log has been developed, there is no better exhibition feat than this for a water carnival.

From the end of a log about twenty inches in diameter, saw off a section thirty to thirty-two inches long—it should be a few inches longer than it is wide. A stump is not spun sidewise as is a log, but rather end over end. Stand on the side of the stump facing one of the ends, tip the front end up, reach over the end with your foot, and by means of the calks pull the end toward you. As the stump turns, quickly step over on the other side. Keep it going by turning it end over end in this way. When you have mastered this, you may rest assured that you have a feat that very few people will be able to duplicate.

HANDSPRINGS ON THE LOG

Here is a special stunt that will appeal to expert log-rollers who are looking for novel stunts to use in the log-rolling exhibition. Stand on the log facing one end without using a balancing pole. Taking plenty of time to get yourself set, and to make sure that the log is not in motion, bend down slowly and place the hands on the log, then throw the feet up and turn over in a handspring, driving the calks deeply into the log as they come down. Needless to say, this is a difficult feat and will take an endless amount of practice.

ROPE SKIPPING ON A LOG

When you have developed enough efficiency on the log so that you can roll it without the use of a balancing pole it will be possible for you to skip a rope while you roll it. Use an ordinary rope-skipping rope. Proceed to roll the log as usual, and at the same time to jump the rope just as you would do on land. If the rope is swung with the same rhythm with which the log is rolled, this stunt is not as difficult as it may sound.

LOG-ROLLING CONTESTS

There are two traditional contests in log rolling, the first involving putting another man off, and the other rolling the log for distance.

STANDARD LOG-ROLLING CONTEST

A line should be painted around the center of the log dividing it into two halves. The contestants toss for the choice of the end of the log. Each contestant mounts his end of the log and

holds his balancing pole in the usual position. Someone steadies
the log by wrapping his arms around it. At the signal the log is
released and the contest is on. The man wins who is on the log
when the other hits the water. In case both go off simultaneously,
it is ruled a tie and is played over. A match consists of two out
of three falls.

There are three fouls, the committing of any one of which

FIGURE 112. THE LOG-ROLLING CONTEST—FAVORITE SPORT OF THE LUMBERJACKS

counts as a fall for the offender: (1) stepping across the center
line onto the other man's half of the log; (2) touching the opponent with your balancing pole; (3) touching your opponent's
balancing pole with your pole.

LOG-ROLLING FOR DISTANCE

There are two ways that a contest of this sort may be conducted,
depending upon the amount of skill the contestants possess. Of
course, a good log-roller can roll a log for hours at a time without
falling off, and consequently a contest for such contestants must
be conducted in a different way than one for beginners.

For boys with average log-rolling ability, the contest is to see who can roll the log the farthest without falling off. Place the log against the dock or other stationary object until the contestant mounts. At the signal he begins to roll the log and continues to travel with it until he falls off. His distance is measured and the next contestant competes. The one wins who is able to ride the log the farthest distance.

For those of greater log-rolling ability, a stake should be driven fifty yards or so from the dock. The contestant mounts the log at the dock. A stopwatch is used to take the time he consumes in traveling from the dock to the stake. The one wins who travels the course on the log in the shortest time.

CHAPTER XIX

Blowguns

The gray squirrels heard the coming of the old Cherokee and let loose with their usual noisy scolding. Foolish of them, for it led the hunter straightway to their tree-home. A moment of study of the branches and the crafty old Redman raised a long bamboo pole to his mouth— *Spat!* and down came Mr. Squirrel. *Spat!* and reeling earthward came Number 2. *Spat!* and his mate quickly followed. Three hardened old gray squirrels at the hunter's feet! Center shots all; for a wiry old gray squirrel must be taken through the heart or hit so hard elsewhere as to knock him off the branch, or he will promptly bite in two the slender arrow and yank it out.

Scarcely a sound did the dart make as it brought down the first squirrel—no bang to send the other squirrels scurrying to safer quarters. The blowgun has one precious quality over other hunting weapons of equal accuracy—it is *silent*.

The campers are gathered at the archery range. No bows in sight, for long ten-foot shafts are spitting slender darts at the bull's-eye—the championship blowgun tournament is on. Yesterday's archery tournament was a sorry exhibition of finding the gold, as compared to the regularity with which these zipping darts pierce true. They sink deep into the straw—deep they penetrate, too, into the spirit of the shooter! A careful observer can see that there is more here than the superficial joy of engaging in an athletic sport, more than the joy of physical effort, the satisfaction of creditably displaying one's skill. There is something about puffing these slender lances to their goal that quenches a deep-seated thirst—in common with so many of the sports in this book, there is a romantic something involved, an imaginative gripping

313

that highlights the activity, and adds glamour to mere physical expression.

Blowing games and contests, always peculiarly enjoyable, find their pinnacle in blowgun shooting, both from the standpoint of joy and of healthful exercise. Here is a physical exercise of an unusual type. No other sport exercises so deliberately and so strenuously the lungs and their controlling muscles. The force and distance one can achieve in shooting the arrows is increased remarkably with practice.

The Cherokees are the only Indian tribes in North America to use the blowgun. There are a few thorough-going masters of the art among the old Cherokees today, and while an occasional young man may be found who performs well, yet needless to say, the skills of the moderns bear faint resemblance to those of yesterday. This is partly due to the fact that suitable material for good blowguns is scarce in the Cherokee country. Partly, too, it is due to the fact that the old Indian culture, colorful and challenging, is fast giving way to that of the white man. The blowgun has gone the way of all things Indian—it has been buried in the graves of the feeble old men, to be replaced with the inevitable rifle and shotgun. This is unfortunate. Recently the Indian fairs and exhibitions have corralled the few remaining blowgun artists and presented them in competition. But this bears meager fruit in accomplishing the desired revival. The government schools, long intent on teaching geometry, history, algebra, etc., to the destruction of the old Indian culture, could do much to revive this interesting skill, along with other valuable customs, and preserve it for posterity. A shipment of good bamboo poles into the reservation would make the materials available. We need what the Indian has to offer us, and unless we take positive steps at once to preserve the few things that have survived the avalanche of the white man, it will soon be too late.

While the Cherokees alone claim the blowgun in North America, many are the tribes of natives farther south that are still dependent upon it for food. In the Orinoco and the Amazon regions, in the Philippines and in the Malay Archipelago, blowguns are every-day weapons. The phenomenal accuracy of the Guiana Indians with the blowgun has long been a source of amazement among travelers to their homeland.

Walter E. Roth is authority for the statement that the Guiana hunters can set up a knife blade and hit it more or less consistently with an arrow puffed from a blowgun at a distance of twelve or fourteen feet.* H. H. Furness, while visiting the Dyak headhunters, sought to test their skill with the blowgun by placing a potato an inch-and-a-half in diameter on a stick and setting it up at a distance of fifty yards. At this range a headhunter pierced the potato with six of his ten arrows. Could the best of rifle shots under similar circumstances do any better?

Most of these natives of the far south poison the tips of their arrows with a type of poison that suffocates the animal. In this way blowguns are effective weapons both in warfare and hunting, the poison being as fatal to men as to animals. The Cherokees, however, do not and never did poison arrows so far as any available records indicate, and consequently in their hands the blowguns found use only in hunting birds and smaller animals.

Blowguns have much to recommend them for recreational use. They classify along with archery and rifle shooting, and are as valuable recreationally as either of these, and doubtless possess more romantic appeal than either. Given the same supervision as these sports, blowgun shooting is a safe and enjoyable activity for camps, clubs, playgrounds, and gymnasiums.

MAKING THE BLOWGUN EQUIPMENT

Once commonplace weapons among the Cherokee tribe, Indian blowguns are rare items today. Good guns are exceedingly hard to find, and indeed those of any quality are so scarce as to make the search for them discouragingly unprofitable. This does not mean that they are nonexistent, for they can occasionally be

---

* For a detailed description of the Guiana blowguns and their use, see "An Introductory Study of the Arts, Crafts and Customs of the Guiana Indians," by Walter E. Roth. *38th Annual Report* (1916-1917) Bureau of American Ethnology. Paragraph 117 *ff*. Washington: Government Printing Office, 1919.

obtained if one has the right connections on the Cherokee reservations. But certainly they are few and far between.

Not only are they hard to obtain, but an authentic gun is so difficult to make that the average person will find his attempts unrewarding. Happily, however, there are ready-made materials which serve the purpose for recreational use just as efficiently as the best of the Indian weapons, and these can be picked up in almost any community. There will be some, however, who will prefer to attempt to make an authentic gun, and certainly all who use any kind of a blowgun should know the Redman's method of fashioning them.

HOW THE INDIANS MAKE BLOWGUNS AND ARROWS

The Indians made their blowguns from long reeds and bamboo, or from long strips of light wood which they split, hollowed out, and glued together again. I have an excellent Cherokee blowgun made of reed resembling bamboo, light and accurate, measuring eight feet in length with an opening five-eighths of an inch in diameter.

In making these bamboo blowguns, the Cherokee selects a straight piece of reed or bamboo about seven-eighths inch or one inch in diameter and having very little taper, being as nearly uniform in diameter throughout as possible. The average length is eight to twelve feet, although occasionally one extends up to sixteen feet. Until ready to be worked, the pole is hung up by a string attached to one end, so as not to take any chance of its bending or warping. If any bends or curves are found in the pole, the Indian straightens it by heating it while green and bending it at the joints by placing it over his knee and applying pressure.

How the Cherokee gets the partitions at the joints out of these long bamboo poles is a mystery to many people. Certainly no boring tool could be used to remove them. The method becomes simple when we consult an old Indian, however, who removes them with typical Indian woodcraft technique: He *burns* them out. He secures a piece of iron rod about six inches long and

slightly smaller than the bore he desires. He heats the iron red
hot and drops it down inside the bamboo held vertically, thus
burning out the joints. The partitions all removed, he secures a
straight stick a little over half the length of the blowgun and tapers
it a little on one end. Around this tapered end he wraps a piece
of tin through which holes have been punched, thus producing a
tool somewhat like a kitchen grater in principle. This he reams
down the shaft from each end, rasping off the joints to a uniform
bore. Then he removes the tin from the stick and replaces it
with sandpaper wrapped around the stick, and with this he pro-

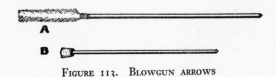

FIGURE 113. BLOWGUN ARROWS

ceeds to sand the hole down to perfect smoothness. In the old
days when sandpaper was not available, he would glue sand on
to the stick instead. The diameter of the bore usually is one-half
or five-eighths inch.

The making of such a blowgun would be an interesting feat
but would take much time and a world of patience, and is scarcely
recommended for the average person since there are other materials that answer the purpose quite well and require no preparation
whatever.

The type of gun that is made from a long piece of wood cut
in two, hollowed out and glued together again, is typical of the
Guiana Indians of South America. These can be made easily
enough by the use of modern wood-working machinery and tools,
but here again the method is not recommended. It is difficult to
obtain a perfect job and there is always the danger of the gun
warping after it is made, thus rendering it useless. If such a blowgun is attempted, the length should not be less than eight feet
and the diameter of the hole one-half to five-eighths inch.

The Indians made their arrows out of very thin strips of hardwood, preferably hickory. Some were short, nine to ten inches

in length, and others as long as thirty inches. The Cherokee arrow shown in A, Figure 113, is twenty-three inches long, this being the most typical length. These darts are rounded and sanded perfectly smooth. Some Cherokees used a dart as thick as a lead pencil but these are not at all common, the usual thickness being three-sixteenths to one-fourth inch. They are uniform in width except for the point. At the butt end the Indians attached tufts of thistle-down thus making a wad a little larger than the hole in the gun. Thistle-down is so smooth and flexible that it slips through the bore of the blowgun very readily, even though it extends out to a diameter a little larger than that of the bore. The wadding on the arrow in A, Figure 113 is five inches long and is made of ten tufts of down, each bound to the shaft with thread so that it overlaps the next. Sometimes the Indians merely glued a small wad of cotton at the butt end. A wadding of some type is necessary in that it fills the bore of the gun and thus catches the air when the shooter blows into the gun's mouth.

MAKING A MODERN BLOWGUN

A person skillful in handling tools may be able to fashion a very satisfactory blowgun after the type of the Indian guns described above, but for recreational purposes, a long glass tube will make as fine a gun as one would hope to secure. In fact there are no better blowguns then those of ordinary glass tubing. No smoother inside surface can be found in any blowgun. And happily, these require no work at all—when one secures a tube of the proper dimensions he has a completed blowgun.

The supply department in any large chemistry laboratory such as those located in universities and large high schools, will have glass tubing excellent for the purpose. Secure a heavy tube with an opening one-half inch in diameter or as near this size as possible. Have the mouth end rounded off. For perfect precision the tube ought to be eight feet long, but it will seldom be possible to obtain straight glass tubing longer than six feet. Since glass tubing is frequently warped, each tube should be carefully studied and those selected that are absolutely straight. Chemistry laboratories supply two qualities of tubing, the glass in one being much stronger and harder than in the other—secure the stronger type. Such tubing will cost only a few cents.

If the glass tube is wrapped throughout its entire length with surgeon's adhesive tape, there will be little danger of breaking the tube. With careful use, however, an unwrapped tube will last a long time under ordinary circumstances.

MAKING A PEA-SHOOTER

A glass tube of the same thickness as that recommended for the blowgun, but shorter, say four feet long, makes an excellent and accurate gun for shooting pebbles. Children enjoy these almost as much as the bigger guns that shoot arrows.

MAKING THE ARROWS

Arrows for the blowgun cannot be picked up as readily as the blowgun itself. They can be made from any hard, strong wood, although hickory is preferred by tradition. Ten to twelve inches is a good length and the diameter should be one-eighth inch. They should be as near uniform in width as possible, except that the tip is sharpened to a point. If one needs only a half dozen darts for his own use, they can be whittled out with a jackknife and sanded. However, such organizations as camps, playgrounds, and gymnasiums needing a large supply will do well to go to a cabinet-making mill and have the sticks turned out. They can then be cut up into lengths and pointed. The arrows are somewhat fragile and a large supply will be needed if the guns are to be used much.

The best and quickest method of putting the "wad" on the end is to stick the end into a cork, as shown in B, Figure 113. The cork should fit the hole in the blowgun quite closely but not so snugly as to prevent it slipping very easily. If there is too much play between the cork and the sides of the tube, so much air will escape that the dart cannot be expelled forcefully enough to carry very far. The use of corks makes it possible to equip a large number of arrows in a few minutes. If the corks are colored yellow and blue they can be found in the grass more easily.

If one is merely preparing a few arrows for personal use, it may prove more satisfactory to glue a wad of ordinary cotton to the end. The cotton can be pressed with the fingers until it slides easily in the tube of the gun.

For a quiver in which to carry the arrows, the Cherokees use the blowgun itself. They slip the arrows into the gun one after the other. When they prepare to shoot they point the gun toward the ground and blow, thus sending the arrows into the ground where they will be sticking up in convenient position when needed.

Boys get much sport from using pebbles in the blowgun rather than arrows. With a good, long blowgun, these pebbles can be projected with startling accuracy. This is good sport and saves the grief of making arrows.

MAKING THE TARGET

For outdoor use a standard archery target makes the ideal blowgun target, particularly if the players are experienced enough with the blowgun to be able to propel the arrows some distance. For boys and girls who are not able to shoot long distances, a smaller target will be preferable. The archery target would be too large if one were to stand only a few feet from it. A small target may be used either indoors or out.

Since the slender shafts of the arrows are easily broken, they should never be shot against a hard surface. The ideal small target is made of corrugated paper. Heavy cardboard, beaverboard, and the like are unsatisfactory because the wooden point on the arrow will not penetrate them unless hurled with such force as to risk destroying the dart. Ordinary corrugated paper, however, does not offer this difficulty.

Secure a piece of corrugated paper two feet square and in its center paint five concentric circles, measuring eighteen inches over all. The bull's-eye is two inches in diameter, and each succeeding circle is two inches wide. Number the circles from the center out, 9, 7, 5, 3, and 1.

If possible the target should be hung up in front of a canvas or curtain so that the stray arrows will not be broken on any hard surface.

SHOOTING THE BLOWGUN

Slip the arrow into the gun so that the cork or wadded butt end is toward the mouth end of the gun. The butt of the arrow should be about one-half inch from the end. Take a deep breath, place the gun to the mouth, and expel the air suddenly. Do not blow

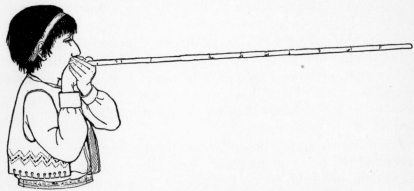

FIGURE 114. HOW THE CHEROKEE INDIAN HELD HIS BLOWGUN

steadily into the gun, but rather expel quickly with a sudden puff.

The Cherokee Indian's method of holding the blowgun is a surprise to most white men, in that one would normally expect him to extend his left arm along under the barrel as in holding a rifle. Not so with the Cherokee, however, who grasps it with both hands as near to the mouth end as possible. He seizes the very end of the gun with his right thumb and forefinger, palm toward his chin, thus forming a cup or sort of mouth piece into which he presses his mouth. Similarly the left thumb and forefinger grasp the gun in such a way that the palm of the left hand is pressed against the back of the right. Figure 114 shows the arrangement.

This method of holding the gun has its advantages. If the left arm were extended under the gun as in holding a rifle, the forceful puff necessary to propel the arrow would be certain to jerk the arm and thus throw the gun off the target. But held in Cherokee fashion, the hands are braced against the mouth with the result that the effects of the bodily movements in shooting are minimized. This method of handling the gun will prove awkward for most beginners, who will prefer to support the barrel in typical rifle fashion. In this case, extreme caution must be exercised in the matter of jerking the arms. Of course one must take a deep breath and hold it preparatory to shooting, and here as in rifle shooting, such holding of the breath contributes much to steadiness in aiming. To attempt to expel all the air in the lungs in one stiff puff would cause such a violent effort as to be certain to jerk the arms, and this jerking would be greatly exaggerated at the muzzle end of the ten-foot gun. Expel just enough air to send the arrow to the target, no more. One can't be too violent and at the same time be accurate. Try to learn the Cherokee's method of holding the gun—he knows better than we the art of handling this ancient weapon of his ancestors.

The matter of aiming depends upon the distance away from the target and the force of the blow. Since there are no sights, one has to sight along the shaft. In aiming at a target only a few feet distant, the end of the gun should completely cover the bull's-eye, shutting it out from view. For longer distances, the muzzle of the gun would of course be raised a little. In determining the elevation much depends on the force with which the arrow is to be propelled. In these matters, experience is the only safe guide.

The same precautions should govern blowgun shooting as hold sway in archery and rifle shooting. Every one should be behind the firing line. In camps and playgrounds where there are numbers of children around, an adult supervisor should always be present.

BLOWGUN CONTESTS

The contests with the blowgun resemble those with bow and arrow or any other shooting device. They involve shooting at a target for accuracy and shooting for distance.

TARGET CONTEST

If the archery target is used, the distances for experienced players are fifty and seventy-five feet, and for beginners and young players, twenty-five and fifty feet. If the small target of corrugated paper is used, the distances are fifteen to twenty-five feet.

Each contestant shoots four arrows each turn. Each shoots twenty-four arrows in all (six turns) from the near distance and an equal number from the far distance. Each arrow scores the number of the ring in which it sticks. The rings from the inside out score 9, 5, 4, 3, 1. An arrow on a line scores in the higher circle. If an arrow strikes the target and falls without sticking, it does not score points. The player with the highest score wins.

BLOWGUN SHOOTING FOR DISTANCE

This event should take place in an open field that is cleared of spectators and properly policed to prevent people from wandering into the possible line of arrows.

The players stand behind the line and shoot the arrows as far as possible. Each is given four shots and is credited with his best distance. The one shooting the farthest wins.

SHOOTING FOR HEIGHT

Clear the field of all spectators and contestants. Each contestant goes out on the field when his turn comes, there being no one else there at the time but the officials. The contestant holds his blowgun straight up and shoots the arrow as high as he can. The timers take the time with a stopwatch from the time the arrow is shot until it hits the ground. Each has three attempts and is credited with his best time. The one wins whose arrow stays in the air the longest.

NOVELTY SHOOTING

Suspend a toy balloon from the branch of a tree. The players take turns at a distance of twenty-five feet, shooting one arrow each turn, attempting to burst the balloon.

Instead of using the balloon, cut a bird out of cardboard and suspend it from the limb.

Set up a stuffed rabbit on the ground and establish a shooting line twenty-five feet distant. The contestants take turns attempting to shoot the rabbit.

PEA-SHOOTER CONTESTS

Boys like to use short blowguns as pea-shooters, using pebbles for ammunition. Many interesting informal contests may be enjoyed in this way.

Set up a tin can for a target. Each time it is hit, one point is scored.

The suspended balloon or cardboard bird used in the Novelty Shooting described above will make an excellent contest.

Tie a tin can to a string and hang it on a limb. Start the can swinging pendulum fashion thus providing a moving target.

CHAPTER XX

Darts—How to Make and Throw Them

Darts are as old as the history of civilization. In the grim struggle for life among the primitives the world around, darts have played an important rôle. And as is always the case, the children of these primitives in their play used imitations of the deadly weapons of their fighting fathers.

Darts fulfill no serious life purpose today, but their appeal to children is perennial nevertheless, and adults, once they are engaged in a contest, enjoy throwing them too. There is nothing odd about all this, for who does not enjoy throwing things? And among the things that may be thrown at a target with the hand, the dart appeals so strongly because it is so accurate—perfectly balanced and properly fletched with feathers, it flies true to its course. There is fascination always in sending an object precisely and unwaveringly to a bull's-eye, and when that object is one that is merely held in the hand and thrown, the feeling of satisfaction is much stronger than would be the case if the accuracy were obtained by the use of some mechanical contraption.

Dart throwing is an excellent activity for summer camps, for gymnasiums, for children's club rooms, and for playgrounds. It is frequently used as an intramural activity in colleges. In such organizations it is always wise to provide a quantity of commercial darts, which are very inexpensive and much more accurate than home-made ones. For informal use around the home and camp, however, children enjoy making their own.

The types of darts are many and varied, large and small, sharp-pointed and blunt, heavy and light, elaborate and simple. A few of the most suitable types for recreational use are discussed in the pages that follow, together with the contests that may be played with them.

AVOIDING ACCIDENTS

Danger exists only in the use of sharp-pointed darts, and even with these, a few simple rules will, if followed, eliminate all such possibilities. All players should be forced to remain behind the throwing line until all darts have been thrown. Then, and then only, are they permitted to go to the target and retrieve their darts. If possible, the target should be placed against a wall so that there will be no danger of stray darts flying past it. All spectators should be forced to watch from behind the throwing line. In camps for boys and girls, in club rooms, in gymnasiums, and on playgrounds, it is always advisable to establish a hard-and-fast rule that there is to be no dart throwing by children unless adult supervision is present.

II. HOW TO MAKE DARTS

A. CORNCOB DARTS

Whenever a crowd of boys are together with nothing definite to do, they begin picking up every old thing from the ground and throwing it. And on the farms of pioneers, the ever-present corncobs were handy things to throw. But somehow they were too light to throw far, and being long and narrow, they always turned broadside when thrown. Some inventive mind, however, hit upon the idea of sticking chicken feathers in the pithy center at one end, and thereby turned the lowly corncob into a dart that traveled far and accurately. From the pioneer days when Daniel Boone held sway down to the present moment, the boys who lived in the open country have found a favorite sport in throwing these corncob darts. True enough, these homely darts have no point and will not stick in a target, and are of no use under the bright and shining sun except as playthings, but as such they serve admirably indeed.

The short and stubby corncobs are the favorites—those which are as big around as the normal cob but which are only three or

aside from the modern dart, the corncob, matchstick, spool, and shingle darts are types which have been popular for centuries.

four inches long. Failing to find these, break up the long ones into sections about four inches long.

Into the pithy center at one end of the cob, stick four ordinary chicken feathers, so arranged that they fan out in four different directions, as shown in A, Figure 115. The length of the feathers depends on the size of the cob. After they are stuck in the cob, the feathers should extend out about the length of the cob itself. Try to find four feathers that are of about the same size and shape.

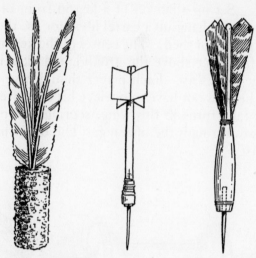

FIGURE 115. A CORNCOB DART, A MATCH-STICK DART, AND A MODERN DART

That is all there is to it—just stick the feathers in the end and the dart is ready to throw.

Informal as this activity may appear, it is nevertheless excellent for organized play on a playground or in a summer camp. A camp's most appropriate activities are those that use the things found in the woods and the open country. A bushel basket full of corncobs and a peck of chicken feathers picked up at a nearby farm will provide an interesting afternoon of dart making, and a headline event for the evening in the Pioneers' Corncob Dart-throwing Championship.

The sport in throwing these darts runs along two lines:

First, it's always interesting to see who can throw his dart the farthest (see Dart Throwing for Distance, page 338). And when each makes his own dart, the contest is doubly challenging—it tests not only one's throwing strength, but also the ability to fashion a good dart that will travel.

The other way to find sport with the corncobs is to throw them at a target. But since they have no point and cannot stick in a solid object, the target must consist of a hole through which the dart can pass. Set up a bucket or a keg in front of a wall, open end toward you, or hang up a barrel hoop, or use the small square window in a garage or shed. The center of the keg or hoop should be three to four feet above the ground. Mark a throwing line forty or fifty feet away. Each player should have three or four darts so that he does not have to retrieve his dart after each throw. The players take turns in throwing, scoring one point for each dart that passes through the opening. The one wins who scores ten points first.

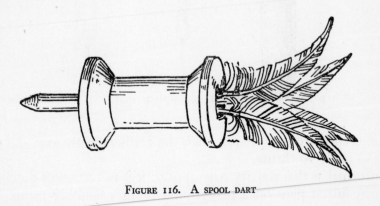

FIGURE 116. A SPOOL DART

B SPOOL DARTS

The principle of the spool darts is exactly the same as that of the darts made from corncobs. All there is to the making is the sticking of four chicken feathers into the hole at one end of the spool and then driving in some pegs of wood to hold the feathers in place. The feathers should be small and short. If desired, a pointed wooden peg may be driven in the end of the spool opposite the feathers, as shown in Figure 116.

This dart is handled just like the corncob variety and can be used in the same contests. As a rule a spool dart will not carry quite as far as a cob dart.

MATCH-STICK DARTS

Darts made from match sticks have been used by boys since time immemorial, but like so many other of the handmade implements of sport which brought joy in former years, they are being forgotten in favor of machine-made toys. This is unfortunate, for these little darts can be fashioned in five minutes and furnish as much sport for indoor use as any dart that the stores can supply.

Slit an ordinary match stick for a distance of about a half inch at one end, clip off the head of a pin and insert the blunt end into the slit, then wrap the end with thread to hold the pin in place. Now slit the other end in similar fashion for a distance of three-fourths of an inch. Cut two small pieces of paper one-half inch wide and one inch long, and fold each over into a V-shape. Slip these two pieces of paper into the slit, as shown in B, Figure 115, thus forming the wings that enable the dart to fly in a straight line. These little darts are often unusually accurate. Paint a bull's-eye target on a cardboard, and hang it on the wall for a target.

A SHINGLE DART

Here is a most fascinating kind of dart that can be fashioned in ten minutes from nothing more difficult to obtain than an ordinary shingle. It is not hurled with the hand but rather propelled by a string attached to a stick. The interesting thing about this dart is the great distances to which it can be sailed, shots of from two- to three-hundred feet not being at all unusual.

Split off a one-and-one-half inch strip from the side of the shingle. Leave this strip at its full width for a distance of two-

and-one-half inches at the thin end, and from there on, narrow it down to one-half inch as shown in A, Figure 117. Whittle the heavy end down to a point. Now place the dart on your knife blade and balance it until you find the center of gravity, and two inches toward the point from this center cut a notch as shown in B, Figure 117.

This completes the dart and now to make the stick with which to hurl it.

Cut a branch from a tree about two feet long and as big around

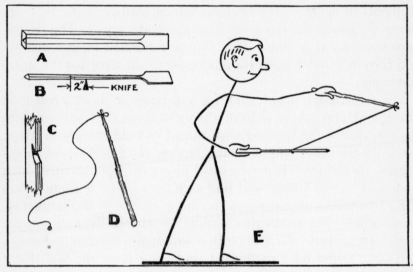

FIGURE 117. A SHINGLE DART

as your little finger. At the end of this tie two feet of strong twine. Tie a knot at the end of the string.

Now to send it sailing: Slide the string along the notch in the dart until the knot catches. Holding the end of the dart in the right hand and the stick in the left, pull back on the dart until the stick begins to bow. Then release the dart and watch it sail over the tree tops.

Instead of the branch of a tree, a much more effective bow can be made by tying together two or three stays or ribs from an old umbrella.   These have a great deal of whip, and will achieve greater distance than those made of wood.

It is remarkable how these shingle darts will cover the distance, and the greatest sport in their use is to see who can sail them the farthest.   From a throwing line, each contestant sails his dart in turn.   Each is given three attempts, and the one wins whose dart makes the greatest distance.

But do not neglect the target contests: One's first attempt at finding the bull's-eye may be discouraging but the knack will soon be discovered.   Make a target by covering a barrel hoop with newspaper—the paper helps to tell when the dart goes through the hoop.   Remember that a strong wind will take the darts off their course.   It is best to so place the target that the darts must be sent either directly into the wind, or directly away from it.

A MODERN DART

Darts of such excellence are on the market today at the cost of such a few cents that it is scarcely a profitable undertaking for one to try to make a handmade imitation, particularly since the fletching of the feathers is a rather difficult and tedious task.   The most popular darts in use today consist of a wooden plug with a sharpened metal point at one end, and four feathers glued in place at the other end to make it fly true.   This is the dart that is so widely used in the dart-throwing championship contests described later in this chapter, and in dart baseball.   There are also heavy metal darts on the market which are similarly used in these contests, particularly by adults.   For general recreational use and for all use by children, the wooden dart is preferable to the metal one, it being very serviceable, less expensive, and much safer.   Adults who take their dart throwing seriously, however, may prefer the metal type.

While the time consumed in getting together the materials and fashioning the darts hardly justifies the attempt to make them, yet some will prefer their own handmade products over the purchased ones.   Any solid, reasonably hard wood will answer the purpose for the plug—birch, maple, hickory, oak, ash, alder and yew are excellent. The plug is five-and-three-fourths inches long and shaped as shown in C, Figure 115. It is round, five-eighths inch thick at the widest point, and tapers down to one-fourth inch at the tip. The narrowed-down end to which the feathers are attached is three inches long, and the wide section which is gripped by the fingers is two-and-three-fourths inches long.

When the plug is whittled out, place it in a vice and drive a long slender nail into the big end. The nail should extend out one-and-one-half inches. Cut off the head of the nail and file down to a sharp point. It is well to drive this nail while the plug is still in the rough stage and before too much time has been invested in finishing it up, because the nail may split the plug and thus ruin it. After the nail is in place, put a quantity of liquid solder around the end next to the wood, allowing it to extend out from the wood about three-eighths of an inch. This will help to prevent the nail from being driven further into the wood and perhaps splitting it when the dart is thrown against a hard surface.

Now to the thatching, and this is the most delicate part of the procedure: Secure a couple of turkey feathers which curve in the same direction, that is, feathers from the the same side of the bird. Strip off the web from one side of each feather by holding the quill with the left hand, seizing the web between the thumb and forefinger of the right hand, and pulling toward the base of the feather. The web pulls off very easily. Now cut up the quill into sections three inches long, using a pair of sharp scissors. Dip the small end of the plug in glue and then place the four feathers equally distant from one another, as shown in C, Figure 115. If the four feathers were taken from the same quill, the web of each will curve slightly in the same direction—this is the natural curve of the feather. It is imperative that all feathers curve in the same direction, which will be the case provided the feathers were taken from the same quill or from quills from the same side of the bird. When each feather is put in position, run a pin through each end of the quill and into the wood to hold it in place temporarily. When all four feathers are thus pinned, wrap the ends with thread. When the glue is dry, remove the pins, and trim the feathers. The shape is shown in C, Figure 115—at the widest point each feather is three-fourths of an inch. A pair of sharp scissors is used for the trimming.

For descriptions of the contests in which darts of this type are used, see the section on Dart-throwing Contests at the end of this chapter.

RUBBER-BAND GUNS

The rubber-band gun is not a dart at all, but it has proved to be so popular among boys and girls that it is thrown into this

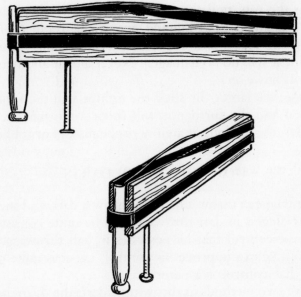

FIGURE 118. A RUBBER-BAND GUN

chapter for good measure. It is one of the most delightful of the shooting toys and curiously enough, appeals so strongly to adults that dad and uncle have been known to spend many an evening with it, too.

Figure 118 shows clearly how the gun is constructed. A small piece of wood, a clothes-pin, a nail, and a couple of rubber bands are all that are needed. From an old piece of board one inch thick, cut a strip nine inches long and two inches wide. Into this drive a nail at a point two inches from the end, as illustrated in Figure 118, allowing the nail to extend out two inches. Cut off one prong from the clothes-pin and fasten it on the end of the stick with a heavy rubber band as in the drawing. This completes the gun proper. To "load" it, slip a rubber band over the barrel end of the gun, stretch it over the top, and tuck the end down between the clothes-pin and board. The pressure of the clothes-pin will hold it there.

Hold the gun like a pistol, pretending that the nail is the trigger. Aim along the top, pull the trigger, and the clothes-pin releases the rubber band—it goes zipping across the room to its target with surprising speed and accuracy. And happily, if it should hit some one it will do no damage. Never aim at another person's face with it, however.

Of course, the larger the stick the tighter will the rubber band be stretched and the further it will shoot. To make a big gun on this order, use sections of an inner tube instead of rubber bands.

III. HOW TO THROW DARTS

Anyone who can throw a ball can throw a dart, and the chances are that his success in dart throwing will be quite consistent with the degree of control that he possesses in ball throwing. While one can do much to improve his control, yet it is quite generally conceded that control is a natural asset.

There are two methods in throwing a dart, the *overhand throw* and *the underhand*. The overhand throw is used by the great majority of people, but there are some very fine underhand artists. In the overhand throw, grasp the dart between the thumb and forefinger and throw it with the same motion used in throwing a ball, allowing the hand to follow through, and keeping the arm in line with the dart until it has hit the target. Do not take the eyes from the dart until it strikes.

In the underhand throw, place the dart in the flat of the palm with the end of the wood resting at the end of the middle finger. The dart lies parallel with the middle finger, the feathers extending up on to the wrist. The second and fourth fingers press against the sides of the dart to hold it steady. Swing the hand back, then toss the dart forward with much the same motion used in pitching a soft ball. Make a full arm swing, and allow the hand to follow through until the dart hits the board. This method will prove to be unnatural and unsatisfactory to most people, but some will find it much to their liking and will be very successful with it.

IV. DART-THROWING CONTESTS AND TOURNAMENTS

The dart-throwing contests for accuracy consist of throwing at a target of some sort. There are two types of targets in general use—the bull's-eye and the baseball board. Contests may also be held in throwing the darts for distance.

A. BULL'S-EYE CONTEST

The Target.—For outdoor use in such an institution as a summer camp or a playground, the dart-throwing board should be large enough so that the throwing line may be placed some distance from the target. Build a board six feet square of three-fourths-inch soft wood, being careful to select lumber that is clear and free from knots. The board should be nailed to uprights of two-by-four-inch material, made so that when the board is set in an upright position the bottom of the board will be two feet above the ground, thus placing the bull's-eye five feet from the ground. No supporting braces will usually be necessary in that the board may be leaned against a wall or against a tree. Paint ten concentric rings on the board, the center one being six inches in diameter and each succeeding ring three inches wide. This makes a target five feet over all, leaving a six-inch space on the sides. The circles should be painted black and white alternately and numbered from the center out as follows: 10, 9, 8, 7, 6, 5, 4, 3, 2, 1. This arrangement of ten circles is more satisfactory for dart throwing than is the usual archery-target arrangement of five circles.

This large five-foot target is ideal for indoor use also, if the space available is large enough to provide a throwing range of twenty to thirty feet. For smaller club rooms and for the home, a thirty-inch target may be used which is painted on a piece of wall-board thirty-six inches square. The center ring is three inches in diameter and each succeeding ring one-and-one-half inches wide.

Throwing Rules.—The throwing line should be twenty to thirty feet distant for the large outdoor target, and ten to twenty feet distant for the indoor target. Any number of players up to six may play at the same time. Each player has one dart, and each throws in turn until all have thrown, then all go to the board to retrieve the darts. Each player scores the number represented by the ring in which his dart sticks. A dart sticking on the line between two rings scores in the higher ring. The throwing continues until some one scores 100 points—this person is the winner.

Tournament Rules.—Dart-throwing tournaments to decide a championship are excellent events for summer camps, play-grounds, and clubs. Announcements should be made far enough ahead of time so as to give every one plenty of opportunity to practice and prepare.

In these events each contestant is allowed eighteen or thirty-six throws depending on the amount of time available. Each throw scores the number represented by the ring in which the dart sticks, and the contestant with the highest score wins. There are two methods which may be used in conducting a tournament of this sort: The players throw one after the other, each throwing his thirty-six darts when his turn comes, and the one making the highest score is declared the winner. In the second method the players are paired together, throwing alternately until their thirty-six darts have been thrown. The tournament thus continues until all have been eliminated except one—this man being the champion.

DART BASEBALL

This is one of the most interesting games that can be played with darts, and every camp, club, and playground that uses dart throwing will do well to construct a dart-baseball board. Figure

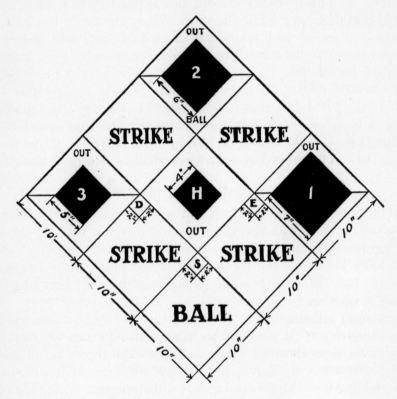

FIGURE 119. DART BASEBALL TARGET

119 shows the diagram of the target—it should be painted on a board six feet square. An economical arrangement is to paint the dart-baseball target on the back of the bull's-eye target described in the preceding section. The board may thus be turned so as to present whichever target the players prefer to use. For indoor use, the dimensions may be cut in half.

Referring to the diagram in Figure 119, "H" stands for a home run, "" refers to a single, "2" to a two-base hit, and "3" to a three-base hit. "E" represents an error, "D" a dead ball, and "S" a sacrifice hit.

The throwing line should be fifteen to twenty feet from the target. The players choose sides, one side acting as fielders and retrieving the darts, while the other side is "at bat." If a batter sticks his dart in the black square labeled "1" and thus makes a single, he leaves his dart there and advances it only when a succeeding player hits. If the succeeding player makes a two-base hit, the dart located on first base would be advanced thereby to third base. If a dart sticks in "E" or "D" the batter is entitled to first base and his dart is moved into the first-base square. If a dart fails to hit the board, or, having hit, it fails to stick, the batter is out. The procedure follows baseball as closely as possible.

DART THROWING FOR DISTANCE

This contest should take place in an open field and the leader in charge should take definite precautions to see that no one is within possible range of the darts and that none step beyond the throwing line while the throwing is taking place. It is also important that the grass be short enough so that the darts can be easily found.

Establish a throwing line behind which the contestants stand. Each contestant has one dart so marked that he can identify it. Each contestant throws his dart in turn and all throw before any go out to retrieve the darts. Each contestant is given three throws and the one who throws the farthest is the winner.

After all have made their first throw the judges place sticks in the ground to mark the points where the three farthest darts struck, making note of the name of the thrower in each case. After all have made their second throw, if any dart is lodged beyond these sticks, the stick nearest the throwing line is moved out to the new distance. The same process is repeated after the third round. The sticks mark the distance of the first, second, and third place winners.

INDEX